Prophet of Prohibition

Neal Dow and His Crusade

By Frank L. Byrne

Department of History
The Creighton University

GLOUCESTER, MASS.

PETER SMITH

1969

TO MY PARENTS

"His name will never be forgotten, nor his work undone," predicted a minister at the funeral of Neal Dow. During a lifetime which almost spanned the 19th century, this son of a Portland tanner had become the symbol of an international crusade to legislate the Demon Rum into oblivion. For his own state of Maine, he had written the first rigorous law prohibiting the manufacture and sale of liquor. In the 1850's, urged on by his exhortations, twelve states had imposed varying degrees of prohibition and from as far away as Great Britain numerous disciples had lauded Dow's doctrine. By his propaganda and his lessons in political strategy, he had made straight the way for the next generation's national prohibition. But, after the end of the Noble Experiment, few besides students of history continued to remember its seer.

In conformity with the second half of the prophecy at Dow's funeral, however, much of his work on American attitudes toward alcohol remains. In the mid-20th century, pollsters allege that nearly a third of Dow's countrymen still favor prohibition. Though all but one of the states have abandoned his policy, they enmesh the liquor business in a complicated web of regulations which leaders of powerful churches seek to tighten. Devoted bands of men and especially of women, who share Neal Dow's faith in the coercive power of government, dream of ultimately strangling the Demon Rum. Yet, while these modern prohibitionists rely on Neal Dow's premises and arguments in their controversy with the advocates of alcohol, neither they nor their opponents know much about his nature, methods and accomplishments. These facts comprise the gospel of the Prophet of Prohibition.

In telling the story of Neal Dow, I have had the generous assistance of many persons. None of them is responsible for any of my interpretations but, through their contributions, they made the book possible. Conventional expressions of gratitude are inadequate to express my obligation to them.

Mrs. William C. Eaton of Portland, Neal Dow's granddaughter, gave me access to the family papers in her keeping and patiently answered my many questions. In the best tradition of scholarship, this lady of old New England placed no restrictions upon my work. Her cooperation and kindly interest

PREFACE

were invaluable.

I am grateful for favors to the staffs of all the libraries mentioned in my bibliographical essay. In particular, I will long remember the hospitality and splendid research facilities of the Maine Historical Society and of the State Historical Society of Wisconsin.

John Allen Krout of Columbia University, the Reverend Robert Corradini, Larry Gara of Grove City College, Clifford S. Griffin of the University of Kansas, Ernest Isaacs, and Philip J. Staudenraus of the University of California, Davis, furnished helpful materials and suggestions. I am indebted to Bernard A. Weisberger of the University of Chicago, Maynard J. Brichford of the Wisconsin State Archives and Kenneth W. Duckett of the Ohio Archaeological and Historical Society for reading and ably criticizing the entire manuscript.

The University of Wisconsin assisted my work through a Kemper K. Knapp fellowship and, together with The Creighton University, has made possible the publication of this book. I also am grateful to my colleagues and especially to my long-suffering typists for their aid in the final preparation of the manuscript.

I reserve my ultimate, heartfelt thanks for William B. Hesseltine who aroused my interest in the Prophet of Prohibition. By his colorful criticism, he helped more than anyone else in my attempt to make Neal Dow live.

FRANK L. BYRNE

Omaha, Nebraska
October, 1960

vi

CONTENTS

Chapter I

THE TRAINING OF A CRUSADER

Early in the 1840's, Neal Dow opened the door of a Portland liquor shop, breathed distastefully the mingled fumes of rum and tobacco and stepped up to the bar. The self-righteous little man was one of the Maine city's leading foes of the Demon Rum. Yet that day he entered the Demon's lair as a suppliant. He had recently helped one of his wife's relatives, who was a periodic drunkard, to get a post office job. Fearing that his kinsman-by-marriage might relapse and lose the new position, Dow had decided to ask the keeper of the "respectable" liquor shop near the Portland Post Office not to serve the reformed man. He believed that the ex-drunkard still had sufficient pride to avoid "the lower dens."

With his reputation as an enemy of alcohol, Dow was undertaking a foredoomed mission. He received a hostile reply to his plea to the store's proprietor. The dealer argued that through license fees he had bought a legal right to sell liquor to Dow's relative. "I shall do so," concluded the bar-owner, "and I do not want you around here whining about it." In return, Dow indignantly poured forth his long-standing hatred of "rumsellers." "So you have a license to sell, and propose to support your family by impoverishing others," he cried. "With God's help I will change all this." Dow vowed to try to drive the liquor-seller and all his ilk from the community or out of their "infamous business."[1]

Neal Dow kept his vow. In the course of his long life, he wrote into Maine's statutes a prohibition against making or selling alcohol. He extended his crusade against an "infamous business" across the nation and throughout the English-speaking world. In his old age, Dow often retold the story of his fight for prohibitory laws. The son of an era which expected reformers to experience a conversion as dramatic as that of Saint Paul, he adjusted his recollections to suit the conventions of his contemporaries. He decided that his personal Road to Damascus had led to his quarrel in the Portland groggery. The old man depicted the incident as a moment of consecration. Yet, as Dow himself knew, he had much earlier dedicated himself to the fight against the Demon Rum. In fact, his very ancestors and birthplace had influenced him

1

toward becoming the Prophet of Prohibition.

Neal Dow's family tradition was one of unyielding self-righteousness. In the 17th century, his Puritan forbears had emigrated from England to settle in Massachusetts and then in New Hampshire. About 1675, Joseph Dow, Neal's first ancestor born in America, had sacrificed his position as a member of the dominant Congregational Church by joining the persecuted Quaker sect. Joseph Dow had fought hard for the right to hold his pacifist Quaker principles. In 1682 in a controversy over his refusal to take an oath, he had helped to win the removal of a royal governor. Despite continued harassment, his descendants had stubbornly maintained their faith. Neal Dow would apply their example to his own life. "He who swerves from what he believes to be his duty, through fear of the ridicule or opposition of his neighbors," he later declared, "can accomplish little or nothing."[2]

Industry and frugality were also traditional Dow virtues. From the first, Neal Dow's American ancestors had been successful farmers and minor capitalists. In 1790 at the age of 24, his father, Josiah Dow, had left New Hampshire to seek greater opportunity in the District of Maine. Then a part of Massachusetts, Maine had been the most undeveloped section of New England. Until the close of the devastating French and Indian Wars, the area had had few settlers. But a stream of Yankees like Josiah Dow had begun to flow in to exploit the vast evergreen forests which were Maine's chief resource. While most of the settlers had worked at producing and shipping lumber, Josiah Dow had taken advantage of a plentiful supply of the hemlock bark needed to tan leather. At Falmouth on the rocky seacoast, he had helped a relative to operate a tannery. Being both hardworking and shrewd, he had soon accumulated a small capital.

In 1796, Josiah Dow had married Dorcas Allen, the daughter of a prosperous local Quaker family, and had set up his own household in the adjoining town of Portland. His new home was on a peninsula which the Indians had aptly called the "Great Knee." The Fore River flowed around the kneecap and along the foreleg. Beyond the end of the stump was island-studded Casco Bay. The thigh and calf of the leg nearly encircled the shallow Back Cove. Men from Great Britain and Massachusetts had early attempted to settle on Portland's splendid harbor. Burned first during the French and Indian Wars and again during the Revolution, the settlement had struggled to survive. But by the end of the 18th century Portland had become a community of some 3500 people thriving through trade and shipbuilding. Josiah Dow had picked a likely place to make a small fortune.

At Portland, he had set up his own tannery. He had then bought additional land well outside the main cluster of buildings along the foreleg of the knee-shaped peninsula. On his tract, an open field on the road between the built-up area of Portland and the mainland, he had erected a two-story frame house. As plain in appearance as its Quaker owner, the building was a large, oblong box. The ridge of its steeply-pitched roof paralleled the road. The great chimney, around whose fireplaces the Dows' life would center during the cold winters, rose through the middle of the house. The prospering husband had provided a roomy, comfortable home for his future family. [3]

On March 20, 1804, Josiah's wife gave birth to Neal, their second child. The boy inherited the blood of a long-lived stock. Many of his ancestors on both sides of his family had lived to great ages. His older sister, Emma, and his younger sister, Harriet, who were both delicate in health, would not fully share in the family heritage. Neal, however, from the first had a strong constitution. Though he would later often complain of sharp headaches and an upset stomach, he never until old age suffered any grave illness. Besides a tendency toward longevity and a healthy body, he also acquired his parents' stature. Like his mother, Neal was slight in the chest and shoulders. And like robust, active Josiah Dow, he would be below average in height. To contemporaries, Neal Dow would usually appear small. [4]

The little boy very early gave indications of the bold spirit of his pioneer ancestors. When still in dresses, Neal saw a horse running away with a wagon along the rutted road in front of his father's house. He unhesitatingly stepped into the frightened animal's path and tried to stop the runaway. Fortunately for Neal, the horse swerved around him, smashed the wagon into a wayside elm and careened off down the road. By his boyish rashness, he had provided the neighborhood with a standing story for years to come. And, as the horse's owner remarked much later, he had foreshadowed subsequent brave but reckless deeds.

To the distress of his Quaker parents, their son was not only brave but belligerent. The spunky boy held his own in quarrels with his playmates. At the age of seven or eight, he had an epic battle with a strange opponent. Urged on by some adult loafers, he set out to fight a large monkey penned up near the waterfront. When the little boy ventured within reach, the biting, clawing monkey jumped up on him. Neal, who was armed with a stout stick, desperately struggled to beat down his adversary. At length he kicked and clubbed it into submission. Though he still wished to thrash the fallen animal, he gave in to the bystanders' calls to desist. The bloody, dirty boy felt like quite a hero. He discovered, however, that his peaceable parents took a different view of the fight. But, though his body and brain ached with their blows and preachments, he retained his fighting spirit. While he accompanied his parents to the Friends' meetings, he was no pacifist. Again and again, he would fight in undignified physical and verbal brawls. [5]

Neal nevertheless learned to practice some of the Quaker virtues. When a visiting seamstress was sewing his first trousers, he demanded two pockets. His mother frugally decreed in favor of one. Neal cried and complained. "Lucy," directed Dorcas Dow, whose small body housed a strong will, "thou mayest sew up the pocket thou hast made." The boy found that pleas for luxuries fell on deaf ears. On another occasion, he bought a wooden whistle instead of whittling one for himself. His canny father warned, "I am afraid that thou wilt come out of the little end of the horn if thou spendest thy money so foolishly." Neal brashly replied, "I'd rather come out of the little end than

3

stick in the middle. " Though the answer cost him the whistle, he continued to make hasty, hot-tempered statements. He did, however, develop traits of thrift and industry helpful throughout his career. [6]

Neal Dow also received a thorough indoctrination in the Friends' abstemious views. True, he saw his father indulge in the minor vice of tobacco-chewing. He knew, however, that Josiah Dow considered the "nasty stuff" to be a preventive for cancer. After a boyish trial of smoking, Neal developed a lifelong disgust for the weed. At a very early age, Neal also learned that Quakers opposed drunkenness and permitted the use of distilled spirits only as a medicine. He never forgot hearing his father sadly remark at the dinner-table, "At last poor Friend_____ has drunk up his land!" His attention caught, the boy listened to Josiah Dow's account of the conveyance of a piece of property to pay an errant Quaker's liquor bill. Neal soon learned to "abhor the very idea of liquor drinking . . . . " The abstemious, frugal boy viewed with disapproval many of the pleasures of the adult world.

Going beyond his personal conduct, Neal early developed a feeling of responsibility for that of his neighbors. He watched his mother give charity to drunkards' dependents who begged at her door. He went with her on visits to investigate conditions in the homes of the needy. Under her instruction he began to believe in a relationship between drinking and poverty. Neal became conscious of the economic and social gulf separating the Dows from poverty-racked sinners. He also learned that indifference to the welfare of these inferiors was "a sin and a shame. " Imbued with the self-righteousness of his Quaker ancestors, he grew up with a desire to bring others into conformity with his principles. [7]

Neal found that many of his fellow New Englanders felt a similar obligation to regulate their neighbors' acts. They had inherited a tradition based on the Calvinist theology of the section's Puritan founders. According to Calvinism, the Congregational clergy and church members had been the Lord's elect or chosen ones. It had been the right and duty of the elect to rule society in God's name for His greater glory. Under the Puritan theocracy, the elect had used the power of government to compel the non-elect to support the church, attend religious meetings, avoid swearing and shun drunkenness. At the beginning of the 19th century, though Calvinism was undergoing much modification, the connection between church and state continued. And in all phases of New England life the concept of the trusteeship of the godly remained strong. [8]

In the Portland of Neal Dow's youth, a well-defined group still set the standards of the community. Merchants, lawyers and the clergymen of the established Congregational Church took precedence over those who, like his father, engaged in "mechanic employments. " Before the Revolution, the "quality" had indicated its superiority through distinctive dress and official formality. As a boy, Neal watched with awe the elaborate ritual still used to open court. The judge, preceded by the sheriff carrying a drawn sword and escorted by four tipstaves, made an impressive progress to the courthouse. He punished offenders against the Massachusetts code with the stocks and pillory, the whipping-post and the gallows. While all but the latter fell into disuse in Neal's child-hood, he took a boyish interest in the decaying instruments of the old regime. Under the teachings of his father and his town, he became a firm believer in the obligation of government to use stern punishment to enforce righteousness.

Neal's own family was beginning to take a place among Portland's leaders. Unlike the mercantile aristocracy, the Dows had no direct share in the town's principal business. The merchants made their fortunes principally through trading the lumber and wood products of the undeveloped backcountry for West Indian rum, sugar and molasses. Local distilleries located near the docks converted much of the latter into profitable New England rum. But the dis-ruption of trade preceding and during the War of 1812 bankrupted many mer-chants. Throughout New England, on the other hand, industries like the Dow's tannery controlled local markets and became relatively more important. Neal's father began to change from an artisan into a manufacturing employer. He was a firm supporter of the locally-dominant Federalist party. In 1812, in-dicating his improving status, Josiah Dow became a selectman and thereafter held minor political posts. [9]

Young Neal Dow saw his father participate with the traditional trustees for the morality of New England in a movement to enforce social order. The clergy of the established Congregational Church had begun to worry about the challenge of Unitarianism, Deism and other heresies to orthodox Calvinist theology. Moreover, the region's ecclesiastical rulers faced increasing op-position to their tax-supported status from the Baptists and other dissident sects. At the same time, with a Jeffersonian Republican administration in Washington, the Federalist politicians who ruled New England felt concern over the rise of Republicanism in their area. Clergymen and officeholders, the partners in the old theocracy, viewed both religious and political heresy as part of one great wave of sin that threatened to sweep away the traditional social order of New England. In 1812 through a series of sermons at New Haven, Connecticut, the Reverend Lyman Beecher became the voice of those harking back to the glories of the Puritan theocracy. Specifically, the per-suasive pulpit orator called upon godly officials and citizens to organize and use the law to stop the spread of sinful abuses. [10]

On April 24, 1812, at the Portland Friends' Meetinghouse, Neal's father and 68 other community leaders joined the reform movement by forming the Cumberland Society for Suppressing Vice and Immorality. Because of the original number of members, those hostile to the county society quickly dubbed it the "Sixty-Nine." The Reverend Ichabod Nichols, pastor of the First Parish Congregational Meetinghouse, was one of the Sixty-Nine. The recently-or-dained minister was leaning toward the Unitarian heresy. Another young preacher, the Reverend Edward Payson of the Second Parish Meetinghouse, also joined the society. Payson, who was an unhealthy, consumptive zealot, burned like his sermons with the fierce fire of Calvinist orthodoxy. By re-fusing to recognize Nichols as a true Christian minister, he had started a widening split in Portland Congregationalism. But both men were ardent Federalists and opponents of social innovation. With the War of 1812, which their party bitterly opposed, flaring on the horizon, they joined prominent Federalist laymen in warning that only reformation could avert divine wrath from the world.

Josiah Dow and his fellow Sixty-Niners intended to suppress profanity, breaches of the Sabbath and especially drunkenness. The latter offense, they believed, was on the increase. With rum usually plentiful and cheap, drinking was a part of almost every occasion. In his boyhood, Neal Dow saw drinking and drunkenness at parades, town-meetings and militia musters. At one of the latter, to the little boy's "intense horror and disgust," a drunkard collapsed on him and held him down. Most people regarded spirits as an essential strengthener for hard work and a fortifier against heat and cold. Workmen stopped twice a day to drink rations of their employers' rum. Like the other Sixty-Niners, however, Josiah Dow was beginning to believe that rum-drinking among the town's poorer people was leading to pauperism and endangering the social order. To persuade men to become temperate and moral, the reformers distributed copies of the Reverend Lyman Beecher's sermons. But they also announced from the first that they expected the aid of the law.

The Sixty-Nine, by attempting to enforce a law against retailing liquor by the glass, sought to cut off the supply of the town's poorer working men. In the spring of 1815, the Reverend Payson delivered an impassioned sermon which drove the authorities to prosecute several retailers. The reform group, whose ranks included both moderate drinkers and wholesalers of liquor, did not go on to attack the wealthy importers and distillers of rum. An "Association of Retailers and Mechanicks" organized to defeat the Sixty-Nine's effort to impose discriminatory prohibition of liquor-selling. One opponent asked if the Sixty-Niners would think an association of laborers justified in forbidding wealthy men to tempt themselves to excessive drinking by keeping glittering decanters of spirits and wine. Members of Portland's Jeffersonian Republican minority charged a plot to bolster up Federalism and state-supported religion. The community had split on social, political and religious lines.

From his parents and playmates, Neal Dow heard something of the angry controversy over the Sixty-Nine. In his presence, the elder Dows often discussed the reform campaign. On the streets, Neal heard urchins screaming "Sixty-Nine" and saw them daubing the number on walls and fences. In June, 1816, the Quaker learned with excitement of unsuccessful attempts to set fire to both the meetinghouse which he attended and that of the Reverend Edward Payson. The Sixty-Nine, as well as similar reform societies throughout New England, had aroused opposition fatal to their very existence. In the period following the War of 1812, the established churches and their Federalist allies also went down in defeat. But Neal, who had already learned to despise spirits, had received from the early reformers a lesson in the use of legal methods to scourge liquor-sellers and force righteousness upon moral and social inferiors. [11]

To prepare him for the day when he would help to set Portland's standards, the growing boy received the best available schooling. He joined the sons of the "most substantial families" in attending "the private school of the time" and in later going to the Portland Academy. When he was thirteen, his parents decided that he would benefit from mingling with people outside his own home. In the fall of 1817, Neal and his younger sister, Harriet, sailed down the coast to attend the Friends' Academy at New Bedford. There, he boarded in a Friend's household. He met many wealthy Quakers, who were among the leading men of the Massachusetts seaport, and visited the nearby families of his schoolmates. He began to learn manners suitable to his family's rising social station.

Though the undersized boy tried to equal his schoolmates in sports, he took greater pleasure in his studies to which he applied himself with his accustomed industry. By practicing elocution and composition, he laid the groundwork for his later skill as an orator and writer. He dutifully memorized Latin and Greek but was much more fond of history. In the library-room of the Academy's two-story frame building, he also spent hours poring over "choice books of voyages and travels." Throughout his life, he would be acutely conscious of his role in the histories of his own and other countries. But a Quaker committee had carefully excluded all books "ill-adapted to the nature of the institution." Neal encountered no author or instructor likely to cause him to question the traditional New England values of his upbringing.

Neal particularly appreciated the Academy's course in "natural philosophy" or physics. He considered the school's "philosophical apparatus" to be extensive and well-constructed. By experimenting with the simple scientific instruments, he established a liking for all branches of mechanics. In later life, the tanner's son would frequently apply the theories learned at New Bedford to his business. He would help to construct the first steam-engine built in Maine and install in the Dow tannery the first stationary engine made in Portland. He would be an enthusiastic supporter of the industrialization so characteristic of 19th century America.

In 1820, after returning to the Portland Academy for a final term, Neal Dow finished his formal education. He wished, like the sons of other leading families, either to go on to college or to read law. He found, however, that his parents regarded advanced schooling as a "device of the adversary" to be obtained only "at great peril to the immortal soul." Perforce, Neal quit school and went to work in his father's tannery. He sought to continue his education through reading. He burrowed through the libraries of his family and friends. In company with a friend who was studying medicine, he read enough medical books to convince himself that he knew as much as many physicians. But in all his education he experienced no effective challenge to his boyhood view of society. He regarded learning as a means of assuring his respectable position within the existing social order. He was sure that "the intelligent, the virtuous and the learned," like himself, should rule and reform "the ignorant, the depraved and vicious."[12]

As preparation for financial leadership, Neal received from his shrewd father practical training in business management and investment. As his first lesson in the latter, Josiah Dow bought him a third interest in the township of Linneus in northeastern Maine. In 1821, Neal and an older cousin set out by stagecoach to survey the wilderness tract. At Oldtown, they bought a boat and hired a pair of watermen to help pole the flat-bottomed craft up the Penobscot River. They promised one of the two that they would include liquor among their stores. But the rum-hating employers bought only a quart of spirits for the lengthy excursion. They blandly explained to their thirsty assistant that they had not realized "how much an able-bodied drinker could consume." At seventeen years of age, Neal had first deprived another man of liquor. He later claimed that his employee had admitted feeling better without the tipple. As for Neal, he had enjoyed the feeling of woodland adventure and the prospect of future profits. [13]

Soon after his surveying trip, Neal became eighteen and subject to a legal requirement to attend periodic militia musters. Maine men of Dow's social position generally either obtained commissions or paid small fines for missing drill. Temperate Neal Dow, who regarded the musters as "most disgraceful exhibitions of drunkenness," was averse to seeking rank in such "Falstaffian commands." Neither did the thrifty youth choose to pay fines. He found that a law exempting volunteer firemen from musters offered an economical loophole. In 1822, he joined many other "enterprising and influential young men," as he called them, in the ranks of the Portland Fire Department. For the moment, at least, he had decided to carry a bucket instead of a musket. [14]

Neal had deliberately decided not to claim the exemption from militia duty granted to Quakers. As in his belligerent boyhood, he did not share the Friends' conscientious opposition to fighting. Indeed, while he grew up an ardent Federalist, he disapproved of that declining party's extreme opposition to the War of 1812. At about the time he joined the fire department, the Friends' Quarterly Meeting which he had attended since childhood learned of his advocacy of the use of "'carnal weapons'" and sent a committee to deal with him. Neal, refusing to recant, quickly received his dismissal from the Society of Friends. In breaking with the strict minority sect, Neal had the company of many 19th century Friends among his own relatives and throughout New England. While the ex-Quaker began to attend Congregational services, he never became enough interested in creeds to join another church. Neither did he forget many of the lessons of his Quaker boyhood. [15]

By the age of eighteen, Neal Dow had learned from his parents and town to be industrious, thrifty and above all, abstemious. He shunned spirits like poison. Moreover, as one of Portland's future rulers, he had learned of his right and responsibility to strike the fatal cup from the lips of the unrighteous. Long before his quarrel with the Portland liquor-seller, he had seen from his father's example that he could and should help to use the law to ban rum-retailing. But he had not yet pledged to fight all strong drink. In his young manhood, the trained crusader would consider joining an organized anti-alcohol army.

Chapter II

TAKING THE PLEDGE

As he reached maturity, Neal Dow despite his Quaker attributes differed very little in his attitudes from many other members of Portland's upper and middle classes. True, he was serious and temperate. But the influential Congregationalists of the Reverend Edward Payson's church, who had already voted to suspend spirit-drinking members, took an equally Puritanical view of life. Both the ex-Quaker and his Congregationalist friends enjoyed such "moral" amusements as hunting, chess and flute-playing. At parties, they served and drank wine. Not even those like Dow who regarded spirits as the devil's distillation saw any evil in the use of the milder, naturally fermented drinks. Only gradually would Dow distinguish himself from his fellows to take the lead in a fight against all forms of alcohol. [1]

The young man already was acquiring the look of a leader. By hard work at the tannery and exercise afterward, he was strengthening his slight frame. Though only about five and a half feet tall, he had the appearance of power and physical vigor. His face, moreover, revealed strength of spirit. Beneath his high forehead, deepset blue eyes peered defiantly at a sinful world. His cheekbones boldly stretched his skin into triangular creases with his nose as their apex and his wide mouth as their base. As if daring the unrighteous to disregard his views, he pressed his thin lips together and tensed his firm jaw. Curly brown hair, while adding an incongruous touch of frivolity, bound together Dow's features in a handsome frame. After noon each day, when he left the tannery and donned the garb of a gentleman, he looked like one of his town's future first citizens. [2]

When Neal Dow came of age, in imitation of the travellers of whom he had read, he took what he later humorously recalled as his "Grand Tour." Unlike the aristocrats of richer towns, he did not go to Europe. Instead, he jounced by carriage and stagecoach across northern New England to the growing resort of Saratoga Springs, New York. He then took passage on a boat over the newly-opened Erie Canal. At Utica, he fell in with a Swiss gentleman of "rank and fortune" named Vischer. Under the guidance of his new friend, who was an amateur civil engineer, the serious-minded Dow studied the details of the

9

canal's construction and became an admirer of its promoter, Governor DeWitt Clinton. The self-righteous youth approvingly noted that the New York governor had believed in the canal project despite the derision of many and had ultimately triumphed. Dow would later have similar faith in his own schemes. Reaching the canal's end, Dow and Vischer looped back through Canada and then went as far south as Philadelphia. When the Portland traveller returned home, he felt ready to take his place among his town's mature men. 3

Soon afterward, in April, 1826, he became a partner in his father's tannery. As a member of the "fairly profitable" firm of Josiah Dow and Son he had an income sufficient to meet his current needs and to permit him to begin investing in bank stock. A year later, he joined the Maine Charitable Mechanic Association. The Portland employers who composed the Association were interested in elevating the status of artisans and manufacturers and in increasing the usefulness of their journeymen and apprentices. The bookish Dow warmly supported the Association's Apprentices' Library. He preferred, as he later indicated, to see young employees surrounded by books rather than by the bottles of local groggeries. He often rode "Governor Clinton," the fine new horse which he had named after his New York hero, into the "'village'" to discuss the library's affairs with other employers and to use its books. In a worshipful recollection of Dow's encouragement of the library, one former shop-clerk pictured him as "a tanner and a gentleman, a mechanic and a man of literary attainments." Among men rising into the growing middle-class, the young businessman was winning respect. 4

Dow also found opportunities for leadership and popularity in the Portland Fire Department. After a serious fire in 1826, he drafted a bill to divide the loosely organized bucket brigade into companies able to man fire engines. Before the legislators of the young State of Maine, who were then meeting at Portland, the young fireman successfully advocated his measure. On April 3, 1827, he and other men of his own neighborhood formed the Deluge Company. Having taken a leading part in reorganizing the department, he received as his immediate reward the company's clerkship. Dow would write in his clear hand the records of many such groups and would learn to wield a secretary's unobtrusive control. The adventurous little man enjoyed pulling the ornate Deluge Engine in races with other companies to reach fires. Energetic and enthusiastic, he began to convert his fellow volunteers into friends and supporters. 5

The new participant in Portland's public life became quite conscious of his need for speaking ability. To acquire it, he practiced oratory in a local debating club and soon became its secretary. In forensic ability, he could not rival two fellow members, William Pitt Fessenden and Francis O. J. Smith. Both men were law students but, while the former was cold, conscientious and conservative, the latter was a warmhearted, unscrupulous opportunist. As allies and enemies, Dow would repeatedly meet these leading young Portlanders. Though for years he himself was nervous at the start of a speech, he gradually gained in confidence and oratorical skill. He began to speak out at town-meetings and political rallies. He was developing into a methodical, businesslike speaker.

In his first major political speech, Dow took a position founded upon his economic and social interests. The tanner believed in a protective tariff to aid manufacturers like himself. He also continued to favor government by the educated and wealthy. He resented the efforts of the Democratic Republicans, who were backing General Andrew Jackson of Tennessee for the presidency, to revive old prejudices against the defunct Federalist party and thereby gain a hold over the "masses." In 1828 at a Portland rally for Jackson's opponent, protectionist President John Quincy Adams, Dow recited in an unmelodious baritone voice a speech supporting the Massachusetts National Republican. Sure that only "ignorant and depraved" Portlanders backed Jackson, he made no secret of his contempt for the idol of the rum-tippling lower classes. Just before he finished his carefully-memorized declamation, a Jacksonian heckler interrupted him with a question. Dow, being much disconcerted, resolved not to rely again upon a "committed" oration.

In time, the fledgling speaker developed a strategy to deal with both hecklers and more formal opponents. Through it, he expressed his belligerent nature. He first armed himself with repartee. Testing his verbal weapons in local political meetings, he learned that by violent personal attacks he could command public attention. He concluded that he could best defeat an abstract principle through concrete assault upon the principle's proponents. He realized that by his strategy he showed a "seeming disregard for personal feelings." Dow claimed, however, to feel no more antagonism toward the men he assailed than a soldier entertained "for the embattled foe upon whom he must fire with deadliest aim." He found his victims often unable and unwilling to salve their wounds with such an explanation. In future debates, Dow would make a staggering number of personal enemies. [6]

Dow took up boxing to protect himself and to develop further his muscular body. In 1828, he often walked along the Portland peninsula to the eastern end of town to exercise in a new gymnasium. He became quite friendly with its sponsor and his cousin, 34-year-old John Neal. An author and a lawyer, Neal had just returned from a stay of several years in British literary circles. Dow resembled his relative in several ways. The two men's faces and small bodies showed family similarities. Both were ex-Quakers. But Dow had a less mercurial temperament than John Neal. The latter's sudden bursts of generous enthusiasm and violent temper caused many Portlanders to stigmatize him as "eccentric." From John Neal, who had had considerable experience in impromptu fights, Dow took sparring lessons and fancied himself "fairly expert for an amateur." Often, both on the offensive and defensive, he would apply his training in the use of physical force. [7]

While exercising under John Neal's direction, Dow had the first of many quarrels with his cousin. He wrote a letter in a disguised hand, signed it "Auguste" and sent it to a literary weekly being edited by John Neal. In it, he berated an unnamed rich man for making only a small contribution to a local

11

charity. Thrifty Neal Dow anonymously branded wealthier Portlanders as proverbial for their niggardliness. Such men, he stormed, "ought to be driven out of our society by the scorn and contempt of every virtuous man." As John Neal learned after printing the letter, Dow had not stated that he had later seen the same rich man contribute substantially to the charity. Dow thus embroiled his cousin in a quarrel with the object of the attack. John Neal, who soon discovered the author of the letter, was for a short time very angry with "the mischief-making, meddlesome Neal Dow."[8]

In his call for benevolence on the part of the wealthy, Dow had repeated a common demand of his age and section. More and more New England Congregational and Presbyterian ministers were preaching that those saved by God would give proof of their salvation through benevolence. Calvinist theologians, such as the Reverend Edward Payson, further taught that the truest benevolence lay in eliminating the moral defects of one's fellow-man and bringing him into conformity with God's will. Clergymen losing state support and Federalist leaders shorn of national power maintained that their continued rule as trustees of the Almighty was an essential part of the divine plan. Dow did not rest his belief in benevolence and trusteeship upon the same doctrinal base. But he had learned in his Quaker youth to feel obligated to assist and reform his neighbors. Like his father and the early Sixty-Niners, he was ready to unite to control society.

During Dow's young manhood, a group of organizations sprang up to act upon the doctrines of benevolence and trusteeship. The Reverend Lyman Beecher, a reform leader of the era of the War of 1812, later exulted that "at the very time when the civil law had become impotent for the support of religion and the prevention of immoralities, God began to pour out his Spirit upon the churches . . . ." Beecher referred to the organizing, mainly by Congregationalists and Presbyterians, of many national reform societies with local auxiliaries. Wealthy laymen financed and administered the groups. Unlike the reform movement of the period of the Sixty-Nine, the new societies disassociated themselves at least temporarily from law enforcement and proposed to persuade men to be righteous. Moreover, each of the national societies had a particular purpose ranging from the education of ministers to the colonization of free Negroes in Africa. All, however, retained their founders' original objective of bringing the country into conformity with their Puritan ideals.[9]

Neal Dow, as a rising member of his community's ruling group, became a backer of the benevolent societies. While too thrifty to contribute heavily, he became a frequent subscriber of small sums to societies to provide the poor with Bibles, tracts and the necessities of life, to educate and evangelize the West and to improve the morals of his town's many seamen. In his boyhood, he had acquired the traditional Quaker opposition to slavery and thus took special interest in aiding the Negro. He was one of a minority of three Portlanders willing to admit a mulatto to John Neal's gymnasium. He would become an enthusiastic supporter of the American Colonization Society's program of freeing Negroes and creating a home for them in Africa. And, with his abhorrence of rum and other distilled spirits, he was particularly ripe for a new organized drive against drunkenness. [10]

Dow first enlisted in the crusade against the Demon Rum under the banner of the American Society for the Promotion of Temperance, commonly called the American Temperance Society. In 1825, the Reverend Lyman Beecher, who had helped start the earlier moral reform movement, called for an organized drive against drunkenness. On February 13, 1826, at Boston, a small meeting responded by forming the American Temperance Society. The Reverend Justin Edwards, an ardent orthodox Congregationalist, was the prime mover of the new group. He was member of the Publishing Committee of the American Tract Society and several of his associates at the meeting were also prominent in other benevolent societies. Edwards proposed to persuade the temperate to remain so, wait for the intemperate to die and thus free the world of drunkenness. Becoming the new society's secretary, he set out to raise money and spread his temperance gospel.

In October, 1827, at Portland's First Parish Congregational Meetinghouse, Neal Dow heard Edwards expound the American Temperance Society's principles. Following the reasoning of Beecher's widely-reprinted sermons, Edwards proposed to redefine the word "temperance." No longer would it denote moderation. In the name of "temperance," Edwards called upon Portlanders to abstain entirely from drinking "ardent spirits." In Beecher's published sermons, Dow also read hints that the temperance leaders were also against wine and the milder fermented drinks. Moreover, Beecher indicated that he had not lost hope of eventually supplementing persuasion with legal suppression of liquor-selling. For at least the moment, however, the temperance men were content to limit their demand to voluntary abstinence from distilled spirits. Dow, who had early learned to hate rum, enthusiastically pledged his loyalty to the temperance cause. [11]

A few months later he struck his first major blow against alcohol. In the spring of 1828, he attended a meeting to plan the celebration of his own Deluge Engine Company's first anniversary. One of the firemen moved that, in accordance with prevailing custom, the company should furnish liquor. Dow jumped to his feet to argue against the proposition. He did not convert most of the other members to his temperance views. But he had previously won their personal regard through his enthusiastic work for the company. The firemen, who included some leading young men, voted to sustain their clerk's scruples. While continuing for several years to serve wine, the Deluge Company held Portland's first spirit-free public festival. His part in accomplishing this brought Dow invitations to address temperance meetings. He deepened his interest in the cause. [12]

He found many of his fellow citizens no more willing than most of the firemen to adopt total abstinence as a personal rule. Following Edwards' visit, a number of leading men organized the Portland Association for the Promotion of Temperance and pledged merely to "discountenance" the use of spirits. With its very loose pledge, the Association attracted a wide range of support.

Among its members during its short life was the Reverend Ichabod Nichols, a Unitarian and former member of the repressive Sixty-Nine. The young lawyers, John Neal and William Pitt Fessenden, practiced their oratory at the Association's meetings. Like Dow, Neal and Fessenden were wealthy enough to enjoy imported wine in their homes. Even some liquor-wholesalers anxious to suppress drunkenness among the poor participated. A local editor expressed disgust at hearing attacks on rum and its results by men "who are daily engaged in dealing out to whoever hath means wherewith to buy, the very poison and curse thus loudly denounced." Like the Sixty-Nine, many of the new temperance men mainly wished to reform their poorer neighbors. 13

Tannery-owner Dow found interest in the new anti-rum movement strongest among other master mechanics. Unlike the West India merchants who dominated the town's economy, the mechanics had no direct interest in the profitable business of importing molasses and distilling rum. Instead, like Dow, many of them began to believe that their employees' purchases of spirits were actually contrary to their interests. From his observations while assisting the needy, Dow decided that drinking by workingmen injured their health, decreased their efficiency and impoverished their families. He readily agreed with Lyman Beecher and Justin Edwards that the Demon Rum was responsible for much of the cost of maintaining jails and almshouses. As Dow later remarked, he and the other masters considered money spent for spirits "more unwisely used than if thrown into the sea." He himself was learning and would use most frequently the economic arguments for temperance.

Dow and the master mechanics especially resented the direct cost to themselves of their workingmen's drinking. At eleven and four o'clock on each working-day, the town bell tolled. Throughout Portland, employees dropped their tools and paused to refresh themselves with their masters' liquor. Merchants, who often paid their own obligations partly in rum and other goods, could simply draw spirits from their stores to supply their laborers and seamen. They also profited through selling the required casks of rum to the mechanics. But rum-hating Dow and other master mechanics faced the bitter choice of spending money for liquor or finding it difficult to hire help. They decided that only united action could resolve the dilemma.

Through his membership in the Maine Charitable Mechanic Association, Neal Dow participated in the employers' attempt to curb the workingmen's drinking. In the winter of 1828-29, he served as junior member of committees to consider eliminating the rum ration and asking the legislature to outlaw debts for liquor. Not for many years would the opponents of rum achieve the latter objective. But on January 13, 1829, Dow and the other members of the first committee submitted a report condemning the free distribution of spirits. They warned that the practice was not only destructive to their workmen's "reputation, morals, and health" but was "by actual calculation . . . a serious loss to the employer . . . ." The masters voted fifty to one to furnish no more rum. Liquor-sellers and drinkers assailed the decision. Dow felt that the resulting controversy caused several doubtful members of the Association to commit themselves definitely to temperance.

Certain that the prosperity of the community was interchangeable with that of the master mechanics, Dow then sought legal help for their effort to eliminate the traditional "'grog time. '" In the spring of 1829, he proposed that the Mechanic Association request the selectmen to ask the forthcoming town-meeting if it would discontinue the daily "'Eleven O'Clock Bell. '" Receiving the masters' approval, he became their agent to present his suggestion to the selectmen. He won the town officials' promise to consider the matter -- but nothing else. In his failure to silence the bell, the young temperance agitator might have found a warning that his ideas would take root with difficulty in Portland's rum-soaked soil. Dow would learn to look to higher governmental bodies for aid in reforming his unwilling townsmen. [14]

On July 4, 1829, as the Mechanic Association's orator of the day, he gave full expression to his belief in the trusteeship of himself and other employers over the morals of the community's workingmen. He attributed the mechanics' previous relegation to "the second rank in society" to their failure to obtain "an extensive education" and to their practice of "the frequent and regular, though what is falsely called the temperate use of ardent spirits . . . ." He proclaimed the duty of masters to correct their inferiors. Dow praised the Associations's previous establishment of the Apprentices' Library and elimination of the rum ration. Such measures, he concluded, could not fail to "strengthen the hands of our government" and "add infinitely to the permanency of our free Institutions. " By the speech, which became his first published temperance tract, Dow made himself one of the conspicuous leaders of the local anti-rum movement. [15]

Since the start of the temperance agitation Dow and his co-believers had directed their fire almost solely at spirits, the favorite tipple of New England's poorer citizens. Distinguishing between distilled and fermented drinks, they had not attacked the rich man's wine or the farmer's cider. Indeed, after Dow's Independence Day address, the Mechanic Association washed down a banquet with liberal draughts of wine. But in the writings of one of his first temperance teachers, Lyman Beecher, Dow had read that wine bred an appetite for stronger drink and thus led to intemperance. Moreover, like a few more zealous advocates of abstinence, he began to doubt the consistency and effectiveness of drinking expensive wine and at the same time urging the poor to give up their cheap New England rum. He pondered if it were not his duty as one of his community's moral leaders to set a better example for his inferiors.

In 1829 at the age of 25, Dow resolved his doubt about the propriety of serving wine. Planning a party with his two sisters, he felt that they ought to break with their social circle's custom in the matter. But he and his older sister, Emma, feared that omitting wine might offend their friends. Dow had not yet made the temperance cause so important in his life as to overshadow completely the opinions of contemporaries. His younger sister, Harriet, a sickly girl with a strong Quaker conscience, demanded that they do what they thought right. At her insistence, the Dows became the first of their set to give a wineless party. Neal Dow later believed that its influence led "all religious or seriously inclined" Portlanders eventually to do likewise. He himself drank no more wine and within a few years opposed its use even as medicine. He had committed himself against alcohol in all its alluring guises. 16

Neal Dow had become one of his town's most extreme advocates of temperance. He had gone beyond the stand of those community leaders mainly interested in eliminating drunkenness among workingmen. He had decided that for their own good and for the sake of example to others both rich and poor must join him in pledging to abstain from all intoxicating drinks. As yet, however, the prominent Portlander had devoted no more time to temperance than to several other interests. He had not dedicated himself to a single cause. Only after establishing his own household and business would he determine the nature of his life's mission.

Chapter III

A MAN'S MISSION

As he glided homeward in his sleigh on a snowy night in the winter of 1827-1828, Neal Dow might well have considered the pattern of his future life. He had just met and fallen in love with his future wife. Only a few hours earlier, when he had set out to take his sisters, Emma and Harriet, to a party in the village of Portland, he had had no premonition of the evening's importance. At his sisters' request, he had stopped at the home of one of their friends, nineteen-year-old Maria Cornelia Maynard, to take her with them to the party. Because of a lame ankle, he had excused himself from getting down to help their guest into the sleigh. Swiftly, the sleigh-full of young people had swayed over the snow-covered ruts leading from their outlying neighborhood into town. On the way and at the party, Dow had become acquainted with Cornelia. From acquaintance, he had advanced rapidly to affection.

Indeed, Dow found much to like about Cornelia Maynard. In her, he saw a handsome girl, small like himself, with a soft, rounded face and short brown curls. The aggressive young man admired his new friend's quiet, retiring nature. Moreover, their contrasting personalities stemmed from similar backgrounds. Cornelia, who was the daughter of an impoverished Massachusetts merchant, also traced her ancestry back to early New England. Like Dow, she had gone to private schools. She was a devout member of the Congregational Church. Best of all from Dow's viewpoint, he found that Cornelia shared his interest in reforming and relieving the poor. She would be a fit helpmate for a moral leader.

When the evening was over, Dow bundled Cornelia and his sisters into the sleigh and drove homeward into the darkness west of the village. At his new friend's house, he forgot the lameness which had earlier excused him from helping her. Despite Cornelia's girlish remonstrances, he insisted on handing her down from the sleigh and escorting her to the door. His sisters knowingly observed their brother's conduct. As he climbed into the sleigh, Harriet commented, "Neal, I am glad to see thy lame ankle appears to be much improved!" Dow did not permit sisterly derision to blight his romance. Within a year, he proposed marriage to Cornelia and received her consent. Because of the emo-

17

tions kindled on that night in the winter of 1827-28, he had begun the lengthy process of establishing his own household and deciding the course of his adult career. [1]

With the meticulous care which was one of his hallmarks, Dow prepared for his married life. First, he bought part of the field across the road from his father's house. In the nearly thirty years since Josiah Dow had built the family homestead, other prosperous Portlanders had erected houses nearby but the neighborhood was still rural. In fact, because of a large marsh near the Dows' land, townsfolk called the area the "Swamp Ward." In 1829, Neal Dow had a plain but substantial brick house built on his property. The mansion was two stories high with an attic for servants' quarters. Breaking with Quaker simplicity, Dow had its parlor decorated with fine hardwood and marble. He even installed a bathing room with running water and a small hot air furnace. The mechanically-minded Dow always wished to have the latest technical improvements. He spent over $5,000 on his house and property. On January 20, 1830, he married Cornelia before a Congregational minister and moved into their new home. That summer, riding in their own chaise, he took his bride on a wedding tour among their New England relatives. [2]

From 1831 to 1850, at intervals of about two years, Neal and Cornelia Dow had nine children. Four of them, all boys, died in infancy. Two sons, Frederick Neal and Frank, and three daughters, Louisa, Emma and Cornelia, survived. Dow was an affectionate husband and father. "I long to see you and embrace you and kiss the little ones," he wrote his wife five years after their wedding. " -- do it for me and tell them father sent the kiss." But he was also a demanding parent. Like his own father and mother, he emphasized the virtues of hard work. He was anxious that his children study and thereby prepare themselves to advance in the world. At every opportunity, he indoctrinated them in his temperance views. On summer evenings, when he often took his family for drives in the country, he pointed out ramshackle houses and remarked, "Rum there" or "Rum did that." He was teaching his assumption that riches rewarded righteousness. [3]

As proof of his belief, Dow might have pointed to his own financial success. In the 1830's, he was developing a source of income less demanding of his time than the family tannery. He began using his surplus funds to make loans secured by mortgages on real estate or merchandise. The young capitalist was stern with delinquent debtors. He told one that "it is a hard thing to satisfy a man who owes if at the same time he is called upon to pay. . . ." Besides making private loans, Dow invested in the growth of the Portland area by buying stock in a canal, a cotton-mill and several banks. He became and remained for over forty years a director of the small Manufacturers and Traders Bank. By the end of 1836, through his conservative methods, he had built up an annual income from interest and dividends of over $1800. [4]

Dow frequently joined in investments with two Portlanders much like himself. One was Eben Steele, a tableware retailer. Dow regarded Steele, whom he had known since boyhood, as his closest friend. The two businessmen shared a common shrewdness. Some contemporaries thought that Steele was exacting and unfeeling. Dow, however, admired his associate's private charities. A pious Congregationalist, Dow's friend helped to support a succession of ministerial students. At Steele's suggestion, Dow and he also gave their profits on one transaction to Dow's cousin Abraham Dow, the husband of Steele's sister.

In William W. Thomas, Dow found another friend and partner. Thomas, who was Dow's own age, was the son of a prominent merchant and banker. In the early 1830's, he was retailing drygoods. Already, however, Thomas was amassing what would become one of the largest holdings of Portland real estate. He was a Congregationalist and, like Dow, supported the benevolent societies associated with that church. Dow, Steele and Thomas were all politically opposed to the Jacksonian Democratic party. All three were temperance men. All were members of the younger group of Portland's righteous rulers. [5]

Together with Steele and Thomas, Dow speculated in Maine timberland. In the early 1830's, when Dow realized over $6,000 on his father's investment for him in the township of Linneus, he yielded to the temptation to make more profits through buying increasingly valuable acreage in northeastern Maine. Unlike more reckless speculators, Dow set out to examine a large tract before purchasing it. On May 14, 1835, he reached Bangor and promptly decided that the lumbering town was "entirely given over to Mammon." The guardian of Portland's morality regretted that Bangor had too few "who fear God and love righteousness . . . to give anything like a tone to the manners or morals of the people." He fastidiously complained that some of the speculators who crowded the town entered his hotel parlor "all reeking with the nauseating fumes of tobacco, enough to make a body sick." Dow was glad to exchange Bangor's odors of tobacco and rum for the pine-scented air of his prospective purchase.

In July, 1835, after Dow's exploration, he, Steele and Thomas bought a bond or option on half a township near the Passadumkeag River. By loaning money to other speculators in the tract, they acquired full ownership of almost a fourth of the township. In 1836 and 1837, Dow and his friends secured mortgages on 1500 additional acres of "wild land" and later foreclosed. After the financial Panic of 1837, they lost hope of profits. But, because the partners had invested prudently and had an ample combined credit, Dow did not share the ruin of many of his fellow-speculators. He eventually sold out at only a slight loss. He had received one more justification for cautious business policies. Thereafter Dow did not indulge in "mere speculations." [6]

In the long run, the Portland businessman found his most profitable opportunities in the real estate of his own town. The seaport on the peninsula was growing rapidly. In 1832, after its population had passed 13,000, it became a city. Dow's home on the gradual rise called Bramhall's Hill was still west of the heart of town. But the business and residential districts were spreading westward along Congress Street, the name given the road which ran past Dow's house to the mainland, and eastward up Munjoy Hill at the peninsula's tip. Through foreclosure and purchase, Dow began to acquire land and buildings scattered from his own neighborhood to the western edge of Portland's populated center. By investing in the probable path of the city's development, he laid the foundation for his fortune. [7]

The prospering young businessman looked and lived like a man of wealth. He had abandoned the Quakers' plain dress. Beneath his coat, he wore a velvet and lace vest and on his head a "Satin Beaver" hat. He carried a gold watch worth nearly $200 -- more than six months' wages for many a workingman. In his thirties, Dow was a dapper, well-dressed little man. Though he never dissipated, he and his family enjoyed lives of comparative luxury. He could afford to send his wife for vacations in the country and take her on a trip to the White Mountains. During the Panic of 1837 and the subsequent hard times, Dow paid out large sums for a parlor organ and an elaborate bookcase for his growing library. He would always have ample means to maintain himself and his household in better than middle-class style. And, to him, an important part of his way of life was the leisure available for community leadership. [8]

In the 1830's, Dow began to take increasingly prominent positions in Portland's public life. In winter, he concentrated upon his duties as secretary of the Atheneum, a private library, and as president of the local lyceum or lecture-sponsoring group. In summer, he enjoyed his role as president and coxswain of the Nautilus Boat Club. At all seasons, the clerk of the Deluge Engine Company studiously sought to master the details of fire-fighting. In 1831, by vote of the company, Dow became its First Director or Captain. Politically, being still opposed to the Democratic party of President Andrew Jackson, he backed the locally dominant National Republicans and their successors, the Whigs. For his efforts, he received such lesser appointments as membership on the board of Overseers of the Poor. And in 1839, by the votes of Whig aldermen, he became Chief Engineer of the city's 700 firemen. He was beginning to exercise leadership in several groups composed largely of young men. [9]

Dow also began to associate himself with the most influential of Portland's churches. While still single, the ex-Quaker had had a seat at the Unitarian First Parish Meetinghouse. After marrying Cornelia, a devout Congregational church member, he joined her in regular attendance at the Second Parish Congregational Meetinghouse. As the Congregationalists organized churches closer to his home, he successively bought pews at the High Street and State Street Churches. While not a church member, he criticized sermons in a proprietary manner. He remarked of one minister's effort, ". . . there was only one short 'phrase' in it which I disliked, and I doubt not he would, upon reflection, dislike it too." When away from home, Dow avoided travelling on the Sabbath and seasoned letters to his wife with religious sentiments. He contributed to Congregational charities. Though little interested in creeds or denominations, Dow had the general outlook of the denomination that had traditionally set his city's standards. [10]

The prominent Portlander shared with the Congregationalists a feeling of trusteeship for the community's morals. He often tried to lead attacks on social evils. Dow temporarily included Masonry among his targets. In 1826 in central New York, an Anti-Masonic crusade had started as a democratic outburst against the allegedly dangerous and aristocratic secret order. Politicians opposed to President Andrew Jackson had soon taken control of the movement. New England Anti-Masonry, which was strong among orthodox Congregationalists, also had overtones of opposition to Unitarianism and Universalism. In the 1832 presidential campaign, partly because he disliked the reputation as a duelist of National Republican candidate Henry Clay, Dow backed William Wirt, nominee of the Anti-Masonic party. He soon decided that in Maine the Anti-Masons could not beat Jackson. Just before the election in a vain attempt to prevent the re-election of the hated Democratic president, he joined other Anti-Masons in appealing to their co-believers to vote for Clay. Over two years later, however, when Anti-Masonry was fading, Dow still termed himself "a determined opponent of the Masonic Institution."[11]

From the intrigues of the Masons, Dow and other New England Congregationalists turned their attention to the sin of slavery. Dow did not join the small faction calling for the immediate abolition of the Southern institution. Many Northern men of property objected that the intemperate abolitionists were angering the South and interfering with trade. Like other leading Portlanders, Dow preferred to help the Negro through the more moderate American Colonization Society. He became a warm backer of the Society's program for shipping free Negroes to Africa. As late as the spring of 1836, he begged philanthropist Gerrit Smith not to abandon the Colonization Society and go over to the abolitionists. Dow warned that the wealthy New Yorker, whom he did not know, was unjustified in taking an action so injurious to "a cause which I regard as extremely important . . . ."

In later years, when Dow liked to think of himself as a pioneer abolitionist, he often recalled that he had helped to protect the abolitionist Maine Anti-Slavery Society from a Portland mob. On the night of October 17, 1836, together with what a local editor called "a large number of respectable citizens, not abolitionists," he answered the request of the mayor to put down a threatened riot against an anti-slavery meeting at the Quaker Meetinghouse. While John Neal, another well-known backer of the Colonization Society, guarded the door, Dow led thirty or forty members of his Deluge Engine Company inside. The belligerent little man had his firemen throw out one rowdy and later helped to escort the speakers to safety. He and other conservative social leaders had preserved law and order. Not until years later, however, would Dow openly identify himself with the unpopular abolitionists. [12]

Instead, associating again with many of his area's leading men, he began to take an increasingly important part in the temperance movement against drink and drunkenness. In the early 1830's, he aided in organizing city and county temperance societies. Finding most Portlanders unwilling to join him in abandoning wine, he helped to set for the new societies a standard of total abstinence at least from spirits. Both men and women signed the pledge of the Portland Young Men's Temperance Society. To affect workingmen unwilling to take the pledge, the members of the Maine Charitable Mechanic Association continued their policy of furnishing no liquor to employees. Going further, a nearby cotton mill in which Dow held stock compelled the Irish laborers who built it and the operatives who worked in it to promise to drink no rum at any time. At the end of 1833, Secretary Neal Dow of the city temperance group boasted that 1300 Portlanders, a tenth of the city's population, had pledged themselves to shun spirits.

And yet, as they made plain in their reports, Dow and other Portland temperance men felt that they were lagging behind their fellows in other parts of the state. In proportion to its small population, rural Maine was seething with as much anti-alcohol fervor as the larger New England states. Led by their ministers, country folk were attacking rum and refusing to license its sale. In contrast, Portland temperance men contemplated their seven distilleries manufacturing the bulk of Maine's rum and annually shipping a half million gallons throughout the state. They ruefully estimated that their city had one seller of liquor to supply every 150 men, women and children. Though they believed that spirit-drinking was decreasing, they confessed that they had not yet converted a majority of Portland's people. 13

To win over the uncommitted, Dow learned to add a new urgency to his writing and speaking. He used his post as Overseer of the Poor to collect accounts of the atrocities of alcohol. With these, he illustrated his temperance arguments. In a report covering 1834, Dow told of investigating the case of a pauper family shivering and starving in a room with broken windows in the dead of the bitter Portland winter. He blamed the drinking of the mother, a pipe-smoking "squalid wretch," for her children's misery. He claimed, in fact, that he did not "remember a single instance of suffering in the families of sober and industrious people." In another report, he alleged that of the $5000 spent annually to aid Portland's paupers, "I had almost said $4999 ought to be charged to rum account, but certainly all but $200." As in his first agitation in the Maine Charitable Mechanic Association, Dow was attempting to appeal to the interests of both humanitarians and taxpayers. 14

Dow took every opportunity, formal or informal, to spread temperance. One day, as the little director was leaving his bank, he saw a crowd gathered around a country boy and an old nag. Dow learned that the adolescent, who had been drinking, had permitted a horse-trader to harness his horse for a test. The city man had driven off, leaving the broken-down horse in exchange. Watched by the mayor and other leading citizens, Neal Dow immediately took charge. He had the boy leave the nag at the trader's stable and then found the dishonest dealer in a wagon pulled by the boy's horse. Seizing the animal by the bridle, he had one of his tannery employees unharness it. By the trader's furious swearing, he knew that he had made another personal enemy.

22

When he returned the horse to its owner, the grateful boy asked what payment Dow wished. "Well, my good fellow," the reformer patronizingly inquired, "you had been drinking, had you not?" Receiving an affirmative answer, he asked, "Promise me that you will never drink again, will you?" The country-man gave his word. Dow was becoming a well-known, everyday agitator against alcohol. [15]

Dow turned his growing persuasive talents against the use of wine. Like advanced temperance men throughout the country, he believed that failure to demand abstinence from all intoxicating drinks was preventing their triumph. The agitators complained that, by sipping imported wine, wealthy temper-ance men were endangering their own sobriety and setting a bad example for the spirit-tippling poor. Dow and the other advocates of total abstinence called themselves "teetotalers." Through their opposition to wine, they called in question both the social habits of the rich and the Communion practices of the Christian churches. They antagonized numerous original temperance men, both lay and clerical, and drew them into a controversy known as the "wine question."

Dow helped to bring the wine question to Portland. Since the beginning of the 1830's a small Portland Temperance Society had opposed wine. In Febru-ary and March, 1835, and in the same months of 1836, the teetotaling group held public debates to popularize its view. On the latter occasion, Dow par-ticipated. His cousin, John Neal, spoke in opposition to the teetotalers. While an enthusiastic advocate of abstinence from spirits, Neal had continued to ob-serve the social custom of serving wine to guests. In favoring moderate wine-drinking, Dow's cousin spoke for an important segment of Portland's upper-class. But in what an editor called his "truly philantropic style," Dow helped several ministers to counter Neal's Scriptural and medical argu-ments. The teetotalers had the sympathy of a majority of the audience at the meetings. They soon became the only active local temperance group. [16]

Throughout the nation, the anti-wine men were similarly altering or aban-doning the earlier societies for abstinence from spirits. In August, 1836, at Saratoga Springs, New York, a National Temperance Convention set up an organization for the scattered teetotalers. The Reverend Justin Edwards, the chief promoter of the American Temperance Society, helped to persuade the delegates to replace the original national group with an American Temper-ance Union pledged against the use of all forms of alcohol. For a second time, the reformers had narrowed the definition of "temperance." The Union, like the old Society, worked closely with the other reform societies associ-ated with the Congregational and Presbyterian churches. Many of the same ministers and wealthy businessmen continued to exercise control. But, es-pecially in auxiliary societies, a large number of influential men refused to give up their wine. The crusade was purging its ranks. [17]

In a local controversy over wine, Dow helped to disrupt Maine's original state temperance organization. He acted not as a leader but as a supporter of Corresponding Secretary Thomas Adams of the Maine Temperance Society.

Adams, a Congregational minister twelve years Dow's senior, had led several unsuccessful attempts to induce the state society to strengthen its pledge of abstinence only from spirits. On February 1, 1837, at the group's annual meeting in Augusta, tall, imperious President William King again opposed Adams. A former state governor and a charter member of the society, the wealthy King argued that wine was essential to "the intercourse of gentlemen." Finding that the majority agreed with King, several of the teetotalers bitterly charged that their opponents were not "the real friends of temperance." On February 2, Dow joined about twenty other anti-wine delegates in forming the teetotaling Maine Temperance Union as an auxiliary of the American Temperance Union. The old state society turned over its newspaper, which Adams edited, to the Maine Union and became inactive. Dow had acquired a small voice in determining the policies of the living half of the state's central temperance body.

To Dow's satisfaction, the new Union immediately decided to discuss at its next meeting the question of petitioning for prohibition of the sale of liquor as a drink. [18] From the Sixty-Niners and later from Lyman Beecher, he had early learned to favor such use of local laws to reform a community's drinking habits. He later gave particular credit to General James Appleton for inspiring him to a broader vision of statewide prohibition. A grim, heavy-set man, Appleton was twelve years older than Dow. In the early 1830's, Dow had heard of Appleton's petition to the Massachusetts General Court for a law against retail liquor-selling. After 1833, when Appleton had moved to Portland, Dow spent hours in Appleton's jewelry shop discussing temperance. He began to see that a state law might gain the end of Portland's anti-alcohol minority. As a result, the younger reformer paired statewide prohibition with his earlier objective of persuading his fellow-citizens to become teetotalers.

Immediately after the organization of the anti-wine Maine Temperance Union, Dow aided Appleton in an attempt to realize their goal of prohibition. On February 3, 1837, while acting as a Whig representative from Portland, Appleton had the Maine legislature's lower house place him at the head of a joint committee on the liquor-license laws. Dow and other temperance men sent Appleton petitions for the abolition of licensing and the substitution of prohibition. Upon Appleton's subsequent recommendations to the legislature, Dow based his own later arguments for prohibition. In a report on February 24, his middle-aged friend contended that even poorly enforced prohibition would make liquor-sellers disreputable, decrease the temptation to patronize them and thereby reduce intemperance. Appleton unsuccessfully urged the lawmakers to forbid anyone but doctors or druggists to sell "Strong Liquor" in quantities less than 28 gallons. Dow later regarded the date of the Appleton Report as the birthday of the Maine movement for anti-alcohol legislation. He was not the infant's father but he would soon become its unchallenged guardian. [19]

Through his speeches later in 1837, Dow revealed that he was ready to assume greater importance in the crusade against the Demon Rum. Since his abortive oration during the 1828 presidential campaign, he had become a competent public speaker. On April 23, he delivered a long, logically-organized address at Portland's Mariners' Church. He ably suited his materials to the congregation of tars. Dow stressed to the sailors that rum provided neither strength nor protection against the effects of weather. In the contemporary fashion, the temperance orator lavishly illustrated his arguments with extensive anecdotes. These, too, he drew from his audience's experience. He painted verbal pictures of sea disasters and a clash with a pirate to show the seaman's need for alertness and sobriety. Dow concluded by urging the mariners not to turn from their cheap grog to "those fashionable slops, upon which gentlemen get drunk. " He thus continued the war against wine-bibbers.

In stressing the need to become a teetotaler, Dow used with new ease his early tactic of the personal attack. He told how an unnamed kinsman, who was a prominent Portlander "would crack a bottle of Champaign, and drink to the success of the Temperance cause in foaming glasses. " He charged that his relative's example had probably drawn many young men into drunkenness. Dow failed to notice that his cousin John Neal, to whom the anecdote might have applied, had entered the church. After the speech, wine-drinking Neal charged Dow with having made a personal reference. The embarrassed teetotaler, who had close business and personal ties with John Neal, quickly dissembled. "You!" Dow cried, "a thought of you never entered my head . . . ." Dow thereby gave Neal the option of accepting the daring denial, as he did, or of identifying himself with the described temperance traitor. The reform speaker was a bold verbal fighter.

By the content of his speeches, Dow demonstrated his complete dedication to the temperance crusade. Having begun the 1830's with a general interest in the cause, he had developed a specific creed and had consecrated himself to spreading it. He expressed his principles in fanatical terms. In preference to drinking wine or "Strong Beer," he suggested that his Mariners' Church audience remain true to rum. The latter, he argued, was cheaper and would "make shorter work of him who uses strong drink. " Dow viewed the drinker's speedy demise as a blessing for "the sooner he goes down to a drunkard's grave, and ceases to poison society by his example the better. " To prevent new drinkers from replacing dead drunkards, Dow hoped for legislation to cut off the supply of liquor. "It cannot be necessary I am sure, " he confidently asserted on September 24, 1837, "to go into a formal argument to show that the retailing of ardent spirits ought to be prohibited. " As the twin articles of his creed, Dow had selected teetotalism and prohibition. [20]

Dow soon found that the principles which satisfied him antagonized many of his fellow-citizens. Like his cousin John Neal, many important men and early temperance advocates refused to become teetotalers. On February 16, 1837, in an address to the public, the Executive Committee of the old Maine Temperance Society had predicted that teetotalism would lead to questioning the authenticity of Biblical references to wine. The Portland CHRISTIAN MIRROR, a Congregationalist weekly strongly friendly to temperance, also spoke sorrowfully of the teetotalers' disagreement with Saint Paul's endorsement of the beverage.

PROPHET OF PROHIBITION

William A. Drew, an officer of the old state society and editor of Maine's Universalist journal, went further in opposing the new Maine Temperance Union. Drew charged that Congregationalists dominated the teetotaling Union and urged his co-religionists to shun it. Amid the dissension between partial abstainers and teetotalers, many temperance men lost interest in fighting the Demon Rum.[21]

Dow's second principle of prohibition proved to be as obnoxious as teetotalism to some Portlanders. In a fruitless petition to the 1838 legislature, 1200 Portland women admitted that the persuasive methods which had spread temperance through the rural areas were almost ineffective with their seaport's many mariners and fishermen. They pleaded "that Law shall establist a corrected sentiment there, where individual influence is powerless." On September 30, 1839, the Portland electorate demonstrated that Dow and his co-believers were still in the minority. In response to a request from the Maine Charitable Mechanic Association, the city's aldermen held a referendum on the question of ending liquor-licensing. By 599 to 561, the voters favored licensing. Dow had received another reason to look to the state for legal help in drying up his rum-loving community.

In 1838 and 1839, Dow and other members of the Maine Temperance Union again backed General James Appleton's unsuccessful attempts to win a legislative ban on retail liquor-selling. But, as Dow admitted, many temperance men within and without the Union argued against the move and became lukewarm in support of the cause. They feared that the extremists intended to make prohibitionism as well as teetotalism a new requirement for loyalty to "temperance." On February 5, 1840, at Augusta, the majority of the delegates to the Maine Union's annual meeting disregarded Appleton's objections and voted to recede from their demand for immediate prohibition. Speakers called instead for a return to persuasion. The drives for teetotalism and prohibition had led to disruption and defeat.[22]

In the weakened condition of his cause, Neal Dow faced not only a challenge but an opportunity for leadership. The withdrawal of earlier temperance chiefs and the repudiation of the middle-aged Appleton left the way open for a new man and new measures. By the end of the 1830's, Dow was ready to be that man. He had become wealthy enough to devote considerable time to temperance and dedicated enough to make the cause his life's mission. To overcome the weakness of his own city's anti-alcohol men, he had learned to seek the aid of a state prohibitory law. He had the persuasive ability to win statewide support for his creed of teetotalism and prohibitionism. He would fill the depleted ranks of the temperance army with new recruits and make himself their commander.

Chapter IV

RECRUITING AND SKIRMISHING

In the early 1840's, as Neal Dow sought ways to revitalize the Maine temperance movement, he found the columns of his newspapers increasingly filled with stories about the sensational meetings of the "Washingtonians." He learned that during April, 1840, six Baltimore drinking men had taken the teetotalers' pledge and had organized a new temperance society. Admiring the character but not the drinking habits of George Washington, the converts to teetotalism called themselves "Washingtonians." Each member of the society assumed the responsibility of bringing other tipplers to the group's meetings. They conducted their gatherings in the manner of the "experience meetings" common in the evangelical churches. The "reformed drunkards" told emotion-packed stories of their previous degradation under the sway of the Demon Rum and of their joyous return to sober respectability. The Baltimore society soon sent missionaries to convert thousands in other cities. Dow and other earlier temperance men, reading accounts of the temperance revival, began to see that the drunkards whom they had often consigned to an early grave might instead become much-needed reinforcements for the anti-alcohol army. [1]

With his growing interest in prohibition, Dow had for several years given only secondary attention to persuading the intemperate to adopt total abstinence. He had even sneeringly alluded to persuasion as "the grog sellers' favorite weapon 'moral suasion.'" But, in February and March, 1840, Dow had witnessed with surprise the success of the Reverend Joseph C. Lovejoy, an agent of the Maine Temperance Union, in converting to teetotalism many of Portland's occasional drinkers, some drunkards and even a few liquor-sellers. In support of Lovejoy, Dow began to tramp from house to house circulating the temperance pledge. He too met with considerable success. On February 23, 1841, he reported to the Portland Temperance Society the luminous possibility of rescuing the victims of alcohol's atrocities. He encouraged the Society to vote to drive from its city within the next year the grim spectre of intemperance. Dow was preparing the way for Washingtonianism. [2]

Because part of the appeal of the new movement lay in its allegedly spontaneous character, Dow did not openly take the lead in introducing Washingtonianism to Portland. Instead, he used a behind-the-scenes technique developed by his associate, the Reverend Thomas Adams, in starting a Washingtonian society at Augusta. Dow began by seeking out some "working-men, friendly to temperance." Then, with his usual careful planning, he had them invite many of their acquaintances to a meeting. On the evening of May 14, 1841, fifty men gathered in the room which Dow occupied in his dual roles as Chief Engineer of the fire department and secretary to the school committee. In Dow's opinion, about half of them were "'hard cases.'" To avoid antagonizing them with the threat of prohibition, he and the other old-line temperance men present limited the discussion strictly to "so-called 'moral suasion.'" Dow tried to convince the workingmen that their drinking habits injured their health and impoverished their families. To his delight, he persuaded twenty-five of them to sign his previously-prepared total abstinence pledge. He had launched the revival.

Dow's recruits continued the meetings and pledged themselves to the original Washingtonian principle of soliciting their friends to attend. On the following evening, a crowd of men in Dow's large room adopted a constitution for the Portland Washingtonian Temperance Society. By permitting anyone who had ever been in the habit of using intoxicating drinks to join, they left the door open for Dow and other members of the old temperance societies. As president, they chose a sea-captain and, as vice-president, a joiner. The latter, John T. Walton, had not even touched liquor for several years. A 43-year-old bachelor, he had dark hair, peculiarly long ears and a face as rugged and grim as the Maine seacoast. Dow found Walton, who was a forceful speaker and a former Whig legislator, to be one of his most useful and loyal followers. Through his influence over Walton, the earlier temperance man would exercise power in the new society. [3]

Dow worked hard to spread the Washingtonian temperance revival. He spoke at as many as ten meetings a week. Arguing that moderate drinkers should set a better example to drunkards, he persuaded members of his fire department to join a Young Men's Total Abstinence Society. Dow's wife and those of other temperance men joined the Martha Washingtons, a women's auxiliary devoted to assisting and spreading teetotalism among the poor. For a gala Washingtonian parade at Portland on Independence Day, 1841, Cornelia and five other temperance women furnished an expensive silk banner portraying the contrasting results of drunkenness and abstinence. The old Portland Temperance Society and individual teetotalers financed the sending of Washingtonian missionaries to neighboring towns. In Maine, as in the rest of the nation, the Washingtonian tide rose quickly and swept along great numbers of people.

Through the Washingtonian revival, Dow and the other early teetotalers replaced those temperance men lost to the cause during the controversy over the "wine question." The rapid increase of the Washingtonians, all of whom took the teetotalers' pledge, for the first time made total abstinence the generally accepted standard of the temperance movement. Some of the new teetotalers were ex-drunkards whose former lives, in the words of a Portland editor, were "adverse to all the principles in which they were now rejoicing." Even men who had earlier sold rum, like Dow's uncle Jedediah Dow, hailed the Washingtonians as "this band of brothers" and took the pledge. But, equally important, Washingtonianism revived the interest of lukewarm temperance men and lured back some who had abandoned their efforts. Dow's cousin John Neal, for example, gave his considerable oratorical talents to Washingtonianism. In their first year, the Portland Washingtonians alone pledged over 1400 men. Dow had helped to create an army of water-drinkers. [4]

The little temperance agitator was eager to convert the new teetotalers to his second principle of prohibition. Throwing aside his moderate approach to the reformed men, Dow resumed his abuse of "rumsellers." He defined the "rumseller" as "a man capable of dancing to the jingle of his own coins, while surrounded by the tears and lamentations of those whose husbands and fathers, brothers and friends, have been sacrificed to his cupidity. . . ." He found many of the ex-drinkers willing to agree that they had been the liquor-sellers' helpless victims and ready to join his assault on the "Drunkard makers." Violent Neal Dow encouraged the reformed men's existing penchant for invective.

By their strong words, Dow and his Washingtonian cohorts once again antagonized less extreme temperance men. In the summer of 1841, the Reverend Asa Cummings, editor of the Portland CHRISTIAN MIRROR, protested against the vulgarity and abusiveness of a Washingtonian speaker. While a veteran temperance man, the Congregational minister advocated putting the advancement of religion before any worldly reform. In a newspaper letter, Dow immediately struck back. Without naming Cummings, he implied that the critic of the Washingtonian wished to exercise sectarian control over the temperance movement. Thereafter Dow would consistently subordinate denominationalism to the welfare of his cause.

He considered his refusal to soften attacks on liquor-sellers and moderate temperance men to be a necessary part of his war on the Demon Rum. In newspaper articles, he pointed out that the Demon's chief defense was the good reputation of many temperate drinkers and liquor-sellers. He believed that Washingtonian persuasion and criticism would convert or silence the first group. As for the second, he relied on his continual association of the word "rumseller" with crime and poverty to drive all "respectable" men from the business. Then, with the enemy reduced to a few hopeless drunkards and unscrupulous dealers, Dow planned "by a few shells to explode his magazines." The prohibitionist continually relied on legal "shells" to blast temptation and win a permanent temperance triumph. [5]

In his prohibitionism, Dow ran counter to the ideas of some Washingtonians. Unlike the reformed drinkers of Portland, whom he had controlled from the beginning, Washingtonians in other parts of the state and nation frequently were hostile toward the old church-associated temperance men and toward their reliance upon the power of the state. Having themselves sometimes gone to jail for drunkenness, numerous ex-drinkers opposed legal measures against either the liquor-seller or the drunkard. Such Washingtonians advocated the exclusive use of moral suasion. On September 22, 1841, a Maine Washingtonian Convention at Augusta even favored admitting liquor-sellers to membership in hope of converting them. The reformed men of the state capital also began publishing their own weekly WASHINGTONIAN in ruinous competition with the MAINE TEMPERANCE GAZETTE, the newspaper of the Maine Temperance Union. As teetotalism had done earlier, Dow's second principle of prohibition was provoking dissension in the temperance ranks.

By helping the GAZETTE to escape its competitor, Dow aided the Reverend Thomas Adams, its editor and his old ally, and increased his own importance in the state's temperance movement. On October 18, 1841, with the endorsement of the leaders of the Maine Temperance Union's Western District, he asked the Congregationalist editor to move the GAZETTE from Augusta to Portland. The Portland Washingtonians compliantly seconded Dow's invitation. Adams accepted and changed the name of the weekly to the MAINE TEMPERANCE GAZETTE AND WASHINGTONIAN HERALD. With easy access to the state society's newspaper, Dow chortled, ". . . we shall be able to write the Rumsellers down--to 'choke them off.'" In December, through appointment to a vacancy on the Union's Western District Executive Committee, he received recognition of his expanding influence. Dow was in a strategic position to overcome the opposition to prohibition. [6]

Early in 1842, Dow began to clash openly with the anti-prohibitionist teetotalers. He and the Reverend Thomas Adams took the lead in arguing against a request by some moral suasionist Washingtonians that the legislature repeal the state's license-laws. Dow, together with other early temperance men, had once favored repeal. But many New England small towns, where temperance sentiment was strong, had discovered that they could refuse to grant licenses and then enforce the penalties against unlicensed retailing. Through such tactics combined with persuasion, large areas of rural Maine had already eliminated most liquor-selling. By the end of 1841, Dow had helped to induce the Portland authorities also to refuse to issue licenses and was ready to experiment with limited, local prohibition. He and Editor Adams therefore helped persuade the legislators to reject a repeal bill. While Dow continued to face opposition among the state's Washingtonians, he had saved a legal weapon useful to his Portland followers. [7]

Dow soon put the theory of local prohibition to the test. In April, 1842, he promised that "the sun of 1843 shall not rise upon the head of a Rumseller in this city, who is known to be such, unless he sells in quantities not less than 28 gallons. . . ." To stop the liquor-sellers from luring back his Washingtonians, he sought to have them prosecuted for operating without licenses. In June, however, County Attorney Augustine Haines refused to act except upon complaints from the mayor and aldermen. Like numerous other lawyers, the Democratic officeholder was averse to Dow's prohibitionism. By a subsequent newspaper controversy with Haines, Dow also added the prosecutor to his growing list of personal enemies. [8]

RECRUITING AND SKIRMISHING

To intimidate the reluctant city fathers into making the complaints required by Haines, Dow immediately marshalled the strength of the old temperance men and the new Washingtonians. Through the summer and fall of 1842 in almost weekly meetings at City Hall, he, Washingtonian John T. Walton and prohibitionist James Appleton agitated first for law enforcement and later for a referendum on the subject. On November 3, the mayor and aldermen finally called for an election on the question of whether "unlicensed and unlawful" liquor-selling should "be countenanced and sustained in this city or not?" Only three years before, Dow had lost his first Portland referendum on the license question. Yet on November 11, despite the efforts of Portland's hundred liquor-sellers, his side piled up a 926 to 486 vote victory. His Washingtonian recruiting drive had made the difference. 9

Belatedly alarmed by the success of Dow and the Washingtonians, the temperance leader's opponents prepared to hit back. They particularly resented his use of his position as Chief Engineer of the Portland Fire Department to spread temperance. Dow had succeeded in banishing alcohol from the festivities of all but one "genteel" fire company. While he was attending one of the latter organization's dinners, the toastmaster drank to "Brandy and water--water for the fire, and brandy for firemen." Dow immediately raised his glass of cold water and replied, "Brandy and water--water extinguishes fire, and brandy extinguishes firemen." By such ceaseless efforts, Dow drove his enemies to counterattack.

On January 25, 1843, 528 of Dow's foes petitioned the Democrat-controlled Board of Aldermen to remove the Whig Chief Engineer. Randolph A. L. Codman, a leading lawyer and Whig politician, represented the petitioners. He liked his own glass too well to approve of Dow's prohibitionism. Until Codman's early death in 1853, Dow would find him a most persistent enemy. To repel the assaults of Codman, who was a brilliant orator, the embattled fire chief retained Francis O. J. Smith. In the old Portland Debating Society, Dow had heard some of Smith's first forensic flights. Since then, Smith had become a lawyer, Democratic congressman and reckless speculator. Dow disagreed with his attorney on temperance and almost every other issue. But he could rely upon Smith, who belonged to the same party as most of the aldermen, to make a vigorous and effective defense.

At a series of hearings on the petition, Dow faced charges of incompetence and despotism. Several firemen called as witnesses testified, however, to his efficiency and ability to handle men. In answer to an allegation that Dow had deliberately permitted a liquor-store to burn down, his lawyer proved that at the same fire the chief had saved two other "rumsellers'" establishments. By skillfully drawing attention to the source of the charges against Dow, F. O. J. Smith also undermined the petitioners' whole case. To the amusement of the audience, Smith read the name of the liquor-seller who had originally signed and circulated each section of the pasted-together petition. Dow's lawyer then added, "And here follow the names of all his customers."

Dow scored a complete victory. On March 13, 1843, the petitioners' lawyer, Randolph A. L. Codman, announced that public prejudices militated against a "correct decision" and withdrew from the field. Eleven days later, the aldermen unanimously acquitted Dow. The predominantly-Democratic Board soon after reappointed the Whig fire chief. In the municipal election a few days later, Dow and his friends prevented the anti-prohibitionists from electing pro-license officials to reverse the result. He was winning his first temperance bouts in the political arena. [10]

But, shortly after Dow's victories, he encountered a split in the ranks of the Portland Washingtonians and a set-back to his plans for local prohibition. The publishers of the Reverend Thomas Adams' weekly began overruling the prohibitionist editor and refusing to print some of Dow's violent articles. Early in May, 1843, while Adams had his newspaper printed elsewhere, his former publishers began to issue an independent journal. The new organ expressed the views of those Washingtonians who favored applying only moral suasion to both the seller and drinker of liquor. A month later, by postponing the prosecution of some sixty indictments for illegal liquor-selling, County Attorney Augustine Haines threw another block in the path of Dow's drive for prohibition. Dow was meeting opposition both inside and outside his crusade.

On July 13, 1843, at City Hall, Dow, James Appleton and other prohibitionists held a meeting to attack the obstructors. The auditorium on the second floor of the handsomely-colonnaded building was Portland's most popular public meeting-place. Of the varied groups which had gathered there, however, few were more rowdy than that evening's crowd. Dow and a dozen friends, having heard rumors that their foes intended to seize control, had come armed. Despite the prospect of trouble, Dow rose to insinuate that the Democratic county attorney was to blame for the delay in prosecuting liquor-sellers. He demanded an investigation. Editor Eliphalet Case of the Democratic EASTERN ARGUS then verbally attacked Dow. Case was a former minister and a professed temperance man. When Dow rose to reply, friends of Case and moral suasionist Washingtonians in the crowd raised an uproar. Dow's followers shouted back and chaos reigned.

Amid the clamor, Dow sat uncowed and unconciliatory. Leaning far back in a chair on the platform, he folded his arms and glared at his opponents. At one point in the evening, he yelled, "You lie" at one of the publishers of the moral suasionist Washingtonian newspaper. After this provocative insult, according to Eliphalet Case, the hotheaded little prohibitionist shoved the Washingtonian printer and threatened to draw a knife. Finally, at the importuning of his followers, Dow gave in and adjourned the drawn battle.

The prohibitionist leader used the interference with his meeting to discredit moral suasion and promote his cause among the Washingtonians. Following his usual tactic, he made a personal attack upon the opposition leader, Eliphalet Case. Dow accused the Democratic editor of conspiracy with the "enemies of Temperance." In reply, Case attacked Dow for calling those who disagreed with him "rum sympathizers" and "friends of rummies." According to Case, Dow was driving out of the local temperance organizations all "who could not believe in his right to tyrannize over them. " In early August, 1843, Dow's Portland opponents organized a moral suasion temperance society. To indicate their dislike for Dow's prohibitionist coercion, they called themselves Peace Washingtonians. As in earlier controversies, Dow and the extremists were in the process of drumming more moderate men out of the true temperance ranks. [11]

Dow, on the other hand, became a target for the abuse of those opposed to his extreme prohibitionism. On February 13, 1844, while he was walking on one of Portland's business streets, a man seized him from behind and threw him down on his back. As Dow kicked away his assailant, a passer-by hurried to the rescue and the attacker fled. Jumping up, Dow ran after the fleeing man, pulled him down and held him till help came. Dow found that the captive, who was a seaman and a stranger, was carrying an unusually long whip belonging to a Portland liquor-seller. He believed that some "rumsellers" had paid the man to humiliate him with a flogging. Dow blamed his foe, County Attorney Augustine Haines, for twice failing to win the hireling's conviction for assault. Shortly afterward, John B. Gough, a nationally-famous Washingtonian orator, toasted "N. D. , knocked down, not dead. " To his co-believers, the plucky Dow had become a minor martyr. [12]

Dow decided to protect himself and other prohibitionists against further attacks. He sometimes went armed and at night cautiously kept to the middle of his city's dimly-lit streets. On one evening in the mid-1840's, he suspected that anti-prohibitionists might mob a witness against an unlicensed Portland liquor-seller. He thrust a brace of pistols into his coat-pockets and called upon two of his firemen to help him to escort the witness safely away from the courthouse. Returning home, the prohibitionist threw his coat across the bannister of the front stairway. Thus jarred, one of the pistols in the coat-pockets fired. To Dow's horror, the bullet sped past the head of one of his daughters, smashed the hall-lamp and scattered broken glass on the girl. The chastened father gave up carrying weapons for protection against his enemies. [13]

Though disarmed, Dow continued to use verbal violence against both liquor-sellers and moral suasionists. In speeches from late 1843 through 1844, he systematically associated the two groups and thereby tried to ruin the Portland Peace Washingtonians. He took as his favorite target the Portland moral suasionists' newspaper. On February 7 and 8, 1844, he, John T. Walton and other delegates to the Maine Temperance Union's annual meeting at Augusta spent considerable time in also abusing the state capital's Washingtonians. Because the Augustans had persuaded their city's liquor-sellers not to permit drunkenness in their shops, the prohibitionists accused the moral suasionists of negotiating with "murderers and devils. " The hostile editor of the state's Universalist weekly charged that the prohibitionists fell upon anyone opposing their ideas "like a pack of blood hounds snuffing for his jugular vein.. . ." Nevertheless, Dow found the moral suasionists within the Union still strong enough to table a resolution in favor of prohibition. Nor was he able through an appearance before a legislative committee to persuade the state's lawmakers to impose heavier penalties for the "infamous crime" of illegal liquor-selling. Dow had not quite vanquished his foes. [14]

Yet within a year, though Dow's efforts to suppress local liquor-sellers continued to be futile, he won the campaign he had led against the moral suasionist Washingtonians. By early 1845, the newspaper of the languishing Peace Washingtonians ceased publication. On January 29, 1845, at the Maine Temperance Union's yearly meeting at Augusta, Dow saw proof that the prohibitionists had taken firm control of the remaining Washingtonians within the state anti-alcohol organization. The Union voted to revert to its pre-1840 demand for a statewide ban on liquor-selling and placed Dow at the head of a committee to present its request to the legislature. The membership on the committee of John T. Walton, whose passage to Augusta Dow had helped to pay, symbolized the blending of the Washingtonians into Maine prohibitionism. Through the revival, Dow had become the acknowledged leader of a strengthened cold water army. [15]

And Dow had earned his exalted rank. Since the low ebb of the Maine temperance cause in the late 1830's, he had done as much as any single man to revive the flagging crusade. Persistent effort, even when other prohibitionists were apathetic, had been and would be one of the reasons for Dow's chieftainship. He had devoted long hours and miles of travel to starting and spreading Washingtonianism in the Pine Tree State. Using his fully-developed mastery of the personal attack, he had done much to crush dissent among the Washingtonians and to convert many of them to prohibition. He had failed, it was true, in his attempt to use the license-laws to suppress Portland's liquor-sellers. But, with an enlarged, enthusiastic force, he was ready to seek from the legislature a more effective weapon.

Chapter V

THE EVE OF SUCCESS

"In our State, we think ourselves upon the eve of complete success," Neal Dow informed a Massachusetts temperance editor in 1845. "The time is not far distant," he further prophesied, "when we shall have a law entirely prohibiting the traffic in intoxicating liquors, as a drink. . . ."[1] For the concept of statewide prohibition, which he had originally acquired from General James Appleton, Dow had built a numerous following. And, to intimidate politicians whom prohibitionist petitions did not impress, he was learning how to show his strength at the polls. Within both himself and his movement, he would complete the fusion of reform with practical politics.

Dow was intensely partisan. Contemptuous of the Democrats, he had electioneered often for the Whigs. He had received from them the post of Chief Engineer and several lesser positions. After a Whig landslide victory in the 1840 state and national elections, he had asked John Neal, his cousin and a Whig politician, to urge his appointment to the governor's military staff. Though Dow had never even served in the militia, he had received a colonel's commission. From January through March, 1841, Colonel Dow had then published in Portland's Whig journal a series of letters on the need for improving the fortifications of the larger cities. He had asked John Neal to recommend him to superintend the building of proposed defences at Portland. Dow's cousin, linking together the commission, the letters and the desire for the superintendency, later commented, "Was there ever a better-contrived manoeuvre?" While Congress had failed to give Portland any new fortifications, Dow had demonstrated through his scheme that he knew how to manipulate political machinery.[2]

Yet, as Dow later recalled, he did not consider himself to be "a party man in the politician's understanding of the term. . . ." In the 1840's, he made his home a rendezvous for men who professed scorn for mere office-seekers and put their favorite reforms above party loyalty. Some, like Dow, emphasized temperance. Others, like General Samuel Fessenden, a Portland leader of the abolitionist Liberty party, directed most of their energies against slavery. While not joining the antislavery political party, Dow too was active in aiding fugitives from slavery and otherwise opposing the Southern institution. He later recalled that a Portland Negro gratefully said of him, "His face is white, but, God bless him, his heart is black." Like most of his fellow-prohibitionists, Dow had also become an abolitionist. He and his reform-minded associates were, in his own opinion, "better fighters in the ranks of minorities . . . than popular favorites and available candidates for place and honor." He would often kick over party traces to advance his plans for reforming society.

"But," Dow later admitted, ". . . I appreciated the importance of organization, and as far as consistent sought to give effect to my political views in co-operating with parties." After 1843, he sought to win prohibition in his native city through manipulation of the political organizations. While retaining his connection with the locally-powerful Whigs, he frequently bolted their candidates. At almost every municipal election, Dow and his temperance men made independent nominations and contracted expedient alliances with abolitionists, anti-foreigners and elements of the Democracy. He thereby kept the city government in the hands of men pledged to grant no liquor licenses. As the prohibitionist leader well knew, however, many Portlanders maintained their thirst for spirits and wine. The city fathers also catered to such drinking voters. Dow concluded that the politic local officials were willing to give the foe of liquor-selling anything he asked, "always excepting the enforcement of the penalties. . . ." Despite his political successes, Dow found that in rum-tippling Portland local prohibition was impotent. [3]

To stamp out unlicensed liquor-selling in his city and throughout Maine, Dow intended to use his numerous following to win statewide prohibition. As early as November, 1843, when circulating petitions for more punishment for unlicensed liquor-sellers, he had warned of the political consequences of opposing his program. He had threatened that if legislators voted against his request "their political fate would be sealed." Unheeded by the lawmakers, he subsequently led a delegation from the Maine Temperance Union before a committee of the 1845 legislature. On January 30, 1845, Colonel Dow, as editors were beginning to call him, demanded an end to all retail liquor-licensing and a ban on sales of liquor in quantities less than twenty-eight gallons. He furnished the legislators with the text of an "Act for the Suppression of Drinking Houses and Tippling Shops." On February 26, the House of Representatives without debate voted down what opponents called "the 'Ram Rod' bill." The Colonel had not yet impressed the politicians with the strength of his army. [4]

Dow laid a large share of the blame for the summary rejection of his bill upon Representative Phineas Barnes of Portland. Barnes was a former college instructor, a lawyer and the editor of the PORTLAND ADVERTISER, the state's leading Whig organ. In the early Portland temperance movement, Dow had worked with Barnes and had twice backed his successful campaigns for a seat in the Maine House of Representatives. The Whig legislator was willing to tighten the provisions of the license law but he felt that Dow's bill was more restrictive than "the practical condition of society and the genius of our institutions would permit." As punishment for Barnes' opposition, Dow personally promised to nip in the bud the thirty-four-year-old politician's career. On September 6, 1845, at a Whig mass meeting in the Portland City Hall, Dow and other Temperance Whigs unsuccessfully attempted to block Representative Barnes' renomination. [5]

The foiled Dow then led his followers in a bolt. In the election on September 9, they supported only one of the Whig candidates for Portland's three seats in the Maine House of Representatives. Against Barnes and William Pitt Fessenden, the other Whigs, they ran a Whig and a Democrat as independent Temperance candidates. Although Dow's Temperance faction won only 15 per cent of the vote, a provision of the state constitution requiring representatives to receive a majority of the ballots cast permitted the bolters to force Barnes and Fessenden into repeated run-off elections. When in a minority, the prohibitionist chief frequently made such attempts to throw the balance of power against his enemies.

Dow wrote an anonymous handbill to back his prohibitionist bolt. Because Barnes and Fessenden had opposed his bill in the last legislature, he self-righteously warned that "every voter will declare by his vote, whether he is upon the side of temperance, virtue, and religion, or not." On the night of Saturday, September 27, distributors scattered on doorsteps Dow's contribution to the Sabbath reading of Portland householders. By the "Saturday Night Circular," as his enemies called it, Dow excited as much hostility as support. On October 8 in the fourth trial, enough Democrats deserted their own candidates to elect Barnes and Fessenden. But Dow had demonstrated to future legislators the danger of thwarting his will. [6]

During the winter of 1845-46, Dow sought support in the strongly pro-temperance rural areas for a law to help him to enforce prohibition upon Portland's many sellers and drinkers of liquor. He suggested the holding of temperance conventions throughout the state and attended many of them. As he had in the previous winter, he toured western Maine in his own sleigh. He took with him to share the oratorical burden, craggy John T. Walton, his Washingtonian lieutenant, and George H. Shirley. The son of Portland's former Federalist printer, Shirley had replaced the Reverend Thomas Adams as editor of the town's temperance weekly. The new editor, who was only twenty-nine years old, was of medium height. He was socially untutored and generally provincial in his ways. Dow, however, found him especially useful for such clerical tasks as arranging lecture schedules and conducting correspondence. The cold water commander was building a loyal staff to aid him in the political battle for prohibition.

From February 9 to 20, 1846, Dow and his aides conducted nineteen meetings in churches, schools and town halls. Occasionally, the prohibitionist chief faced small audiences but sometimes sleighs flying temperance banners brought in hundreds of country folk. He made a particular point of denouncing local liquor-sellers, who were often prominent men, and of comparing

37

their fine homes with those of drinkers in his audiences. Always he proposed political activity to gain a law to stamp out the "rumsellers." He believed that he was helping to convince his listeners that "'talking temperance' and working for temperance will do little good, unless they vote for temperance also. . . ."[7]

Through piles of petitions, Dow gave visible proof of the mounting prohibitionist sentiment. He had over two reams of forms for petitions printed. After addressing meetings, he sought the signatures of the audiences. His wife, Cornelia, helped persuade 3800 Portland "females" to sign their own appeal for prohibition. Dow begged for someone in every school district to circulate his petitions. In June, 1846, when the Maine legislature first began to meet in the summer, the prohibitionists stacked petitions bearing 40,000 signatures on their representatives' desks. Dow and his fellow-officers of the Maine Temperance Union also summoned its members to a meeting at Augusta. Once again controlled by the Portland prohibitionists, the Union designated three men from Dow's city to present to the legislature the petitioners' views. Besides Dow, the committee included his mentor in statewide prohibition, sixty-year-old James Appleton, and Washingtonian John T. Walton.[8]

On the afternoon of June 25, 1846, Colonel Neal Dow entered Representatives' Hall to deliver the prohibitionists' principal speech before the legislative committee on the license laws. With characteristic concern to obtain a maximum effect, he had previously had suspended behind the speaker's chair a petition fifty-nine feet long. In support of it, he painted a grim picture of local incidents of intemperance, which he claimed to have observed personally, and demanded a law against liquor-selling to prevent them. By his fluent, orderly exposition, Dow won the admiration of an abolitionist newspaper correspondent. The writer, noting that Dow was "a man of one idea," averred that he seized that idea "with a grasp so firm that the rumseller cannot escape the painful compression which his crimes merit." The Colonel had become a convincing, locally-noted temperance orator.[9]

Bombarding the legislature with both words and petitions, he finally forced the lawmakers to concede the principle of prohibition. By delaying the elections of Barnes and Fessenden, he had helped to convince politicians of the temperance men's strength. Fessenden himself had decided that he "would gladly aid in abating" the nuisance of "tippling-shops." The Democrat-controlled legislature passed with many amendments a bill prepared by General James Appleton. The lawmakers banned the sale of spirits and wine in small quantities. They thereby struck at tippling-shops, not wholesalers. As in Dow's bill of 1845, the legislators allowed towns to license bonded agents to retail liquor for "medical and mechanical purposes." But, by providing only small fines for violators, they ignored Dow's perennial requests for fearsome fines and jail sentences. On August 7, 1846, Governor Hugh J. Anderson, a pro-temperance Democrat, signed the bill. Dow had won a limited legislative victory.[10]

He hastened to spread the glad tidings of the Prohibitory Law of 1846. As

Corresponding Secretary of the Maine Temperance Union, he issued a printed circular letter which included a copy of the act. He sent one of his circulars to the Reverend John Marsh, the Secretary of the American Temperance Union, for publication in the JOURNAL of the nation's leading anti-alcohol group. Although other states had restricted liquor-selling and had permitted towns to enact prohibition, Dow could boast that Maine's new law was the first instance in which a "civilized and Christian State" had wholly outlawed the sale of liquor as a drink. He had earlier informed Marsh that Maine's motto was "Dirigo" or "I direct." The prohibitionist leader hoped that his state's law would indeed give direction to "the governments of all our sister States, and of every Christion Nation. "

On September 7, 1846, in a letter written from Portland, Dow promised Marsh that "there shall not be a grogshop in this city in ninety days after this date. "[11] A month later, when the prohibitory law took effect, he tried to set the promised example of enforcement. As Dow filled the calendar of the municipal court with liquor law prosecutions, the harassed dealers experimented with various means of evasion. One sold tickets of admission to his backroom. There thirsty Portlanders put the tickets in empty glasses mounted on a wheel. Unseen hands spun the glasses behind a partition and returned them filled with forbidden rum and whiskey. Yet, despite their ingenuity, many persistent violators eventually paid fines for which they blamed Dow. Anti-prohibitionists dumped bottles in his yard, dead cats in his carriage and "objectionable packages" on his doorstep. On January 11, 1847, someone smashed Dow's window with a bottle of asafetida which "dispersed its fragrance through the whole house. " In the eyes of friend and foe, Dow was becoming the either hailed or hated symbol of prohibition. [12]

In the Whig-controlled Board of Aldermen, which had failed to enforce the old license laws, Dow met a grave obstacle to his efforts to apply the Prohibitory Law of 1846. The city fathers feared that effective prohibition would drive away Portland's important inland trade. The new law permitted them to issue only five licenses to sell liquor for medicinal and "mechanical" purposes but they granted a total of seven permits. Dow and the prohibitionists complained that the bonded licensees, who included several former illicit dealers, were selling liquor as a beverage. On January 13 and 14, 1847, the aldermen conducted a hearing on the prohibitionists' charges against one license-holder. When Dow introduced witnesses to illegal sales, the dealer's lawyer branded them "pimps and spies. " From one of them, a hotel porter, he drew an admission that Dow himself had paid the cost of her alcoholic evidence. On January 18, the aldermen threw out Dow's case against the liquor-seller.

Belligerent Neal Dow quickly struck back at the officials. On January 25, 1847, he appeared before them to present the prohibitionists charges against Joshua Dunn, another of the licensed dealers. What editor George H. Shirley called "bloated rummies and rumsellers, steaming with the fumes of the grogshop" packed the room. Dow subjected the hostile audience to a temperance speech studded with thinly-veiled references to prominent Portlanders whom he alleged drink had ruined. To the aldermen's surprise, he then announced that he did not intend to present his evidence against Dunn. Dow had "no supernatural proof . . . ," he sarcastically admitted to the assemblage, "and it is not worthwhile to occupy your time with any other." As the brash little prohibitionist left, only a man's loud exclamation of "you are a [damned] liar" broke the stunned silence. After the aldermen had discharged Dunn, the cheering crowd dispersed with cries of "Go to [hell] Neal Dow! Hurrah! ha! ha! ha!" Dow and his followers later in 1847 elected aldermen obedient to at least the letter of the Prohibitory Law of 1846 and, that summer, beat off a weak drive to have the legislature repeal it. But Dow admitted that he needed better enforcement procedures and stiffer penalties to daunt the Portland "rumsellers."13

In the fall of 1847, Dow made the most spectacular of his early fights to win a legislature likely to enact a severe prohibitory law. He found an occasion in the attempt of Phineas Barnes, who had stayed out of office for a year, to regain one of Portland's three seats in the Maine House of Representatives. On September 11, 1847, Dow's enemy secured the nomination of the Whig mass caucus. In the election two days later, however, only one of the Whig candidates secured the majority required for election. A small scattering vote limited to pluralities the totals for Barnes and the third Whig. With the endorsement of the Portland Washingtonian Temperance Society, Dow entered the race. On September 27 in the run-off election to fill the remaining two vacancies, his supporters voted for him and for one of the Democratic candidates. While the prohibitionist-backed Democrat won, Dow, Barnes and the Democratic nominee for the last vacancy prevented each other from getting the needed majority. On the third and fourth trials at election, as Democrats allied with Dow switched their votes to him, the prohibitionist leader succeeded in getting a plurality over the hated Barnes. He was almost within reach of his first high office.

In a desperate attempt to detach some of Barnes' Whig supporters, Dow directed to the city's religious element an appeal similar to his 1845 "Saturday Night Circular." Temperance editor George H. Shirley, who had kept almost silent during the campaign's earlier maneuvers, published Dow's message as an unsigned editorial. The prohibitionist chief demonstrated with the clarity of cold water the fusion in his own mind between politics, reform and religion. He besought Portland's temperance men to ask their Creator "What Would'st Thou Have Me To Do?" lest on election day they unwittingly "be found contending against God." He branded Barnes and the remaining Democratic nominee as "Rum candidates" who regarded a strict prohibitory law as "'against the Bible and sound morals!!!'" Dow never doubted either his own righteousness or his opponents' lack of it.

But, as in the case of his intemperate "Saturday Night Circular," Dow aroused more opposition than support. Editor Barnes angrily charged in his PORTLAND ADVERTISER that the unsigned attack on him had all the "marks" of "Mr. N. D." --"first, a childish weakness of logic--next, a strange and irreverent mixture of religious appeal and personal calumny" and last, "an excessive self-importance. " Tacitly admitting his authorship of the pro-Dow editorial, Dow replied with a denial that he had attacked Barnes' reputation for personal temperance. Despite Dow's interpretation of his words, outraged friends of Barnes and enemies of prohibition crossed party lines to rally behind the Whig candidate. In five more trials at election, Dow fell behind his enemy. The prohibitionist candidate held only a hard-core following of from five to six hundred voters. On December 22, 1847, when Barnes received a majority, the scrappy little prohibitionist perforce acknowledged defeat. [14]

Following his repudiation at the polls, Dow temporarily retired from the fight for prohibition. For over a year, he concentrated on his investments in railroads and other businesses and wrote only a few temperance articles. Having thought himself to be upon the eve of success, he had come to the bitter realization that he could at the moment neither enforce the Prohibitory Law of 1846 nor elect a legislature willing to enact a harsher law. Dow, as a Maine temperance editor later explained, resolved upon inactivity as the only way "to arouse the community to a sense of their duty. . . ." The editor, who had opposed Dow's new policy, claimed, "The experiment was a bold and a fearful one. " Temperance men then and later shuddered that liquor-selling increased and "drunkenness set in like a flood of burning lava. "[15] The prohibitionist chief appeared to be further than ever from the "complete success" which he had predicted in 1845. He could not yet be sure that the darkness following his political defeat was the night before his day of victory.

Chapter VI

THE NAPOLEON OF TEMPERANCE

"Where is NEAL DOW? Can nothing be done? Is there no remedy?" According to a temperance writer, Portlanders of the late 1840's, who believed that a wave of drunkenness was sweeping over their city, asked such questions. And, indeed, interest in suppressing intemperance was rising among many of Dow's fellow-citizens. On February 22, 1849, nearly 800 of them, including most Portland clergymen, petitioned the city authorities to enforce the Prohibitory Law of 1846 against 300 liquor-sellers. The city fathers agreed to try and also asked the legislature to enact a more stringent law. [1] By temporarily stopping his own attempts at enforcement, Dow had encouraged other opponents of liquor-selling to take the field. As the century's first half expired, he was ready to resume his command of the aroused prohibitionists. Armed with a powerful new weapon, Colonel Dow would lead his army in his most successful offensive.

He first proposed to equip his followers with a device to overcome the liquor-sellers' last legal bastions. While he had deprived the dealers of their right to sell spirits as a drink, he had not yet been able to stop them from stocking and even displaying large quantities of liquor. And, from his futile attempts to enforce the Prohibitory Law of 1846, he had learned the difficulty of finding credible witnesses to specific sales of strong drink. In 1848, however, the Massachusetts legislature had considered and rejected a bill providing for the seizure of liquor to be used as evidence against its owner. At that time and again on June 12, 1849, at a meeting attended by Dow, his county's Washingtonian Convention had hailed the principle of the Bay State bill. Dow decided that seizure would solve his enforcement problems. On August 15, 1849, at Dow's request, the Democrat-controlled legislature passed a bill permitting justices of the peace to issue warrants to search buildings and seize liquor kept for illegal sale. Because the bill passed within three days of the lawmakers' adjournment, Governor John Dana was able under the Maine Constitution to withhold his decision on it until the next legislative session. Dow's weapon hung in helpless suspense. [2]

While dependent upon Dana for the fate of his bill, Dow was in a strong position to counterattack against a possible veto. The disrupted condition of his state's political parties offered him the best opportunity of his long lifetime to throw the balance of power. In the 1848 presidential campaign, when the Whigs and Democrats had failed to endorse the Wilmot Proviso against the extension of slavery into the territory conquered in the Mexican War, elements of both major parties had bolted. Dow and other Whigs with antislavery leanings had joined Democrats and members of the abolitionist Liberty party in organizing the Free Soil party. While the Free Soilers met defeat in Maine and the nation, factions within the state's long-dominant Democracy continued to take sides on the question of slavery in the territories. In accordance with the policy of their party's national leadership, Governor Dana and other members of the office-holding clique called the "Wildcat" or "Hunker" Democrats opposed the Proviso. Another group within the party coalesced behind the controversial measure and called itself the "Antislavery Democrats." In 1848, overcoming the Wildcats, the Antislavery Democrats elected their leader, Hannibal Hamlin, to the United States Senate. In the following year, they controlled the nomination of Governor Dana's successor. Should Dana eventually veto Dow's bill, the prohibitionist leader could seek a bargain with the dissident members of the governor's own party. [3]

Dow could easily work with the Antislavery or Hamlin Democrats. He had first met their leader in the 1830's when Hamlin, a swarthy, convivial youth, had studied law at the Portland office of abolitionist Samuel Fessenden. Like Dow, Hamlin had early learned to dislike slavery and had split with his party's Wildcat rulers on the issue. Having been elected to complete an unexpired term, the new senator faced an early reckoning with the vengeful Wildcats. In February and early March, 1850, while in Washington to attend a National Temperance Convention, Dow talked with Hamlin and found the Antislavery Democrat "particularly polite." Congress was then debating a solution to the problem of slavery in the territories. By the settlement, which became known as the Compromise of 1850, leading Democrats and Whigs hoped to quell both the Free Soil agitation and Southern threats of disunion. Dow and Hamlin agreed in opposing any extension of slavery to appease the Southern "chivalry." Despite his partisan differences with Hamlin, Dow had an ideological basis for an alliance. [4]

The prohibitionist chief soon learned his practical need for the new tie. On May 7, 1850, outgoing Governor John Dana committed the Wildcat faction against prohibition by vetoing Dow's bill as an "ill digested outrage upon almost every right of our citizens." On May 16, the Democrats in the House of Representatives, of whom the majority were Hamlin men, declined to override the veto. Needing the help of the Antislavery Democrats, Dow helped them to get the legislative majority required to re-elect Hannibal Hamlin to the national Senate. In the crucial ballot on June 25, 1850, at the behest of Hamlin's lieutenant, Dow and other prominent Free Soilers persuaded several of their party's legislators to vote for the leader of the Antislavery Democrats. Two months later, in the same House of Representatives which had

43

sustained the Dana veto, enough Hamlin Democrats voted with the Free Soilers and Temperance Whigs to pass an even stricter Dow prohibitory bill. By a tie vote, Wildcat senators blocked the measure. But Dow was close to revolutionizing Maine for his crusade. 5

To complete his control over the legislature, Dow conducted a final offensive. During the summer of 1850, by winning the presidency of the Maine Temperance Union, he had achieved formal recognition of his leadership of the state's anti-alcohol army. In the September election, the Temperance President and his followers attacked anti-prohibitionist lawmakers and often were able to throw the balance in favor of the anti-prohibitionists' opponents. As a means of organizing the necessary shifts across party lines, Dow found particularly useful a fraternal order called the Brotherhood of Temperance Watchmen. Members of the local Temperance Watchman Clubs, which for two years had been spreading through western Maine, pledged themselves to work for the enactment and enforcement of prohibition. After the votes of Watchmen and unorganized prohibitionists had purged some of the foes of his bill, Dow was confident that the next legislative session would grant him his long-awaited victory. 6

Neal Dow was anxious to be in a position to enforce--and to advertise--his anticipated prohibitory law. He regarded the mayoralty of Portland as well-suited to his purposes. In the forty-six years of his life, his native city had quadrupled in size to reach a population of 21,000. From its central location on the peninsula, the little town of Dow's youth had spread out in both directions. Looking out his eastern windows, Dow could see, instead of open fields, some of the city's finest houses. Trade with the West Indies continued to help support the city's prosperity but distilling of rum was giving way to sugar-refining. Railroads, in which Dow had an interest, controlled the trade of the backcountry. While no longer the state capital, Portland was in every other respect the metropolis of Maine. Once ensconced in its City Hall, Dow could choke off much of the state's liquor-trade and convert Portland into a model for the world's prohibitionists. 7

As the candidate of the locally-dominant Whig party, Dow ran for the Portland mayoralty. Though some of the Whig leaders were unwilling to give to a frequent bolter the post with its $1000 annual salary, the prohibitionist Whigs had controlled the nominating meetings. But on April 8, 1851, when Dow went to vote, he discovered that his party foes were distributing special Whig ballots headed by the name of another temperance man. The veteran bolter was tasting his own medicine. Because of the split among the Whigs, he received a plurality but not the required majority over Democratic candidate George F. Shepley. In preparation for a second trial at election, the Whig PORTLAND ADVERTISER urged all members of its party to vote for Dow as the regular nominee. On April 21, Dow received the support of most Whigs and of some prohibitionist Democrats. Only a few anti-Dow Whigs went over to the opposition. By 1332 votes to the Democracy's 986, he won his first major political office. While Dow admitted that having the endorsement of the city's major party had helped, he regarded his victory as an approval of his "zeal" and "methods" in fighting the Demon Rum. [8]

Having obtained what he viewed as a mandate for enforced prohibition, Dow settled himself in the quiet study at the rear of his big brick house to write another bill to stop liquor-selling. By titling his new proposal, like his original bill of 1845, "An Act for the Suppression of Drinking Houses and Tippling Shops," he expressed its limited purpose. He forbade both wholesalers and retailers to manufacture liquor or to sell it as a beverage. To minimize opposition, however, he left several leaks in his dike. As under the Prohibitory Law of 1846, he permitted towns to appoint bonded agents to sell liquor for "medicinal and mechanical purposes." Moreover, in compliance with a decision of the United States Supreme Court, he exempted foreign liquor in the "original packages" from the law's operation. Anyone respectable enough to convince a bonded agent of his righteous intentions or wealthy enough to keep a cellar of imported liquor might continue to drink at home.

As Mayor Dow stated in his inaugural address, he favored a prohibitory law "sufficiently stringent in its provisions and summary in its processes to effect its objects." To adapt the bill to his first requirement, Dow increased the fines over those provided by the 1846 law and introduced a jail sentence of from three to six months for persistent liquor-sellers. By summary enforcement procedures, he attempted to satisfy his second requirement. He permitted any justice of the peace to try most violators of his proposed law. To discourage those convicted from appealing to the district courts, he required them to post appeal bonds with four sureties and to pay double fines if finally convicted. In general, Dow smoothed the path of the prosecution, multiplied difficulties for the defense and limited the discretion of often hostile judges. In so doing, he acted upon his early faith in the efficacy of stern, sure punishment.

As in his 1849 and 1850 bills, Dow's greatest innovation was the provision for search and seizure. He permitted any three voters, who suspected someone in their town of keeping liquor for illegal sale, to obtain a warrant to search any building used wholly or partly for business purposes. Eliminating the unlimited search permitted by his 1849 bill, he required evidence of an actual illegal sale from persons seeking a warrant to enter a dwelling. He threw upon the owner of seized liquor the burden of proving that it was legally imported or the property of a bonded agency. Dow punished those unable to give such proof with a small fine and destruction of their liquor. He thought that the search and seizure provision would make it easy for prohibitionist officials to transfer the Demon Rum from seller to sewer.

With his bill written, Dow pressed for its speedy enactment. On May 26, 1851, at Augusta, he appeared for the sixth time before a legislative committee to advocate prohibition. The reform leader, with his fashionably long brown curls, his blue jacket and his fancy vest, cut a dapper figure. As he had after the passage of the Prohibitory Law of 1846, he made a bold pledge of enforcement. He promised, while his deepset blue eyes sparkled with fervor, "If you will enact this bill, the sun shall not rise on Portland, January, 1852, and find there a single open grog-shop. " Dow could count on the support of all eight Free Soil legislators and on some temperance men in the dominant Democracy and in the Whig minority. Besides, because of his aid to the Anti-slavery Democrats and his ability to control the balance in close districts, he could command the votes of other lawmakers. On May 29, eighty-one of his friends and allies in the lower house overrode forty opponents to order the engrossment of Dow's bill. The prohibitionist chief was on his way to overwhelming victory.

On the following day, under suspension of the rules, the Senate debated the engrossment of the prohibitory bill. Senator Shepard Cary, an Aroostook lumberman and a prominent Wildcat Democrat, spoke for the opposition. In bombastic style, he protested against a Democratic legislature's becoming "the registrar of the inquisitorial edicts of the temperance fanatics of Portland. . . . " That city's "popinjay Mayor, " Cary warned, intended "to overturn the democracy of the state and put himself at the top of the heap. . . . " Nine Democratic senators backed the old Wildcat. But, disregarding Cary's prophecy, fourteen other Democrats joined three Whigs and a lone Free Soiler to order the bill's engrossment. On May 30, a smiling Dow watched both houses obediently vote the formal enactment of his measure. Letter for letter and word for word, he had attained his wish.

Dow personally carried his bill from the Senate Chamber to its last hurdle, Democratic Governor John Hubbard. A bushy-browed man with an upthrust shock of hair, Hubbard was a practicing physician. In 1849, with the backing of the Antislavery Democrats, he had won the governorship. Several Democratic legislators had already advised Hubbard, who was not a teetotaler, that he could safely veto the prohibitory bill. But the governor faced an uncertain political future. In 1852, after the Compromise of 1850 had finished calming the agitation against the extension of slavery, Hubbard's Wildcat opponents expected to retake control of the party and state. To gain the third term customarily awarded to Maine's Democratic governors, Hubbard might need the support of Neal Dow's well-organized prohibitionist army. On June 2, 1851, the tippling governor signed the prohibitionist's bill. While Dow knew that the reluctant support of some politicians had helped to give him his weapon, he was sure that the new law was "the will of the people. "[9]

Although the prohibitory law went into effect at once, Dow took the politic course of delaying the enforcement of the seizure provision in Portland. He wished, as he later recalled, to avoid friction with the holders of large stocks of liquor. On June 5, 1851, he proclaimed that he would allow dealers who sold no more strong drink a "reasonable time" to ship away their goods. Most of the wealthy wholesale merchants took advantage of Dow's period of grace. The last of the city's once numerous distilleries also closed. On June 21, Dow learned that one wholesaler, who had refused to ship away his stock, had sold some rum. The little mayor personally supervised the confiscation of the defiant dealer's spirits and later had them poured into the sewer. By this first seizure under the new law, he frightened the keepers of the hotels and "genteel saloons" into signing an agreement to sell no more liquor. Despite the muttering of some merchants about the effect of prohibition on the city's trade, Dow believed that he had successfully introduced his policy.

The prohibitionist mayor admitted, however, that he found some retailers to be remarkably persistent. Obtaining liquor from out-of-state wholesalers, they adopted new ways of doing business. Some began keeping their main supply of liquor off their premises. To conceal the small quantities of liquor needed for immediate sale, they learned to contrive increasingly clever hiding-places within their buildings. As Dow by publicity and legal action drove out of business some of the more "respectable" liquor-sellers, new types of drinking-places sprang up to fill the gap. A number of workingmen began selling liquor in their living quarters. Many of them were among the Irish attracted to the city by the railroad construction which Dow himself had enthusiastically supported. Young bloods also rented private rooms to house drinking clubs. Both groups were taking advantage of the provision of Dow's law requiring evidence of a specific illegal sale before the issuance of a warrant to search a dwelling. Dow had driven the Demon only a short distance underground.

To dig out the concealed violators, Mayor Dow relied, not on his novel search and seizure weapon, but on the traditional method of getting witnesses to actual sales. In the Brotherhood of Temperance Watchmen, which had helped him in past elections, he had a corps of volunteer agents. In addition, the prohibitionist mayor hired professional informers. By paying the costs of the "war" from the liquor-sellers fines, he avoided drawing on the city treasury and finally accumulated a balance of several hundred dollars. When some sellers pledged to stop, he ceased further prosecution for their past offenses. In September, 1851, however, he had a three-time offender sent to jail. By the end of the year, he had convicted seventy persons under his prohibitory law. Dow was putting to the test his belief in legal pains and penalties. [10]

In three quarterly reports to the City Council on his enforcement of the prohibitory law, Dow claimed to have almost wiped out the Portland liquor-traffic. He admitted that a "few secret grog-shops" owned mainly by "foreigners" remained but argued that their small-scale operations were much less tempting than "open" sale. For the first time, he hinted that he might need "some additional provisions" for the "entire extinguishment of the traffic." The mayor alleged, however, that the reduction already made in liquor-selling had greatly decreased crime, drunkenness and pauperism. As proof, he cited reports from his police and almshouse master. "The watch house," he dramatically proclaimed in September 1851, "is now used to keep seized liquors instead of drunkards. . . ." All in all, the prohibitory law's author portrayed his creation as a thorough, almost automatic success. [11]

Dow used varied means to bring his account of his law's triumph to the attention of the nation. He wrote personal letters. On August 4, 1851, he sent a copy of his law to a man outside Maine and exhorted him "to reenact it in your State--you can do it if you try." In August, Dow also acquired a newspaper outlet for his propaganda. His supporters, the 5000 members of the prohibitionist Brotherhood of Temperance Watchmen, began to sponsor the MAINE TEMPERANCE WATCHMAN. Dow was friendly with the editor of the new Portland weekly, "Elder" Benjamin D. Peck. An ex-minister, the politically-ambitious Peck had been a power in the tiny Free Soil party and had become head of the Temperance Watchmen's Central Committee. He showed by his fat figure and by his taste for personal abuse that he limited his own practice of "temperance" strictly to abstinence from alcohol. Peck reprinted and sold bulk orders of Dow's reports on the new statute's remarkable results. Moreover, Dow's City Council distributed all three of his reports at public expense. Within a few weeks, Dow and his friends had scattered their documents across the northeastern United States. [12]

By his publicity, Dow quickly won the backing of prominent American temperance agitators. One of the more influential of these was the Reverend John Marsh, the Corresponding Secretary of the American Temperance Union. In his fifteen years as editor of his organization's monthly JOURNAL, Marsh had endorsed successive panaceas for intemperance. He readily embraced Dow's new remedy. In the summer of 1851, when Marsh visited Portland, Augusta and Bangor, Dow convinced the elderly Congregationalist that prohibition was effective throughout Maine. Marsh and his Executive Committee called a National Temperance Convention to popularize Dow's law. In a letter to the delegates, who met on August 20 and 21, 1851, at Saratoga Springs, New York, Dow described the ease and completeness of his victory over the Demon Rum. Marsh pushed through resolutions urging the nation's temperance men to use both propaganda and the ballot box to gain for their own states the "Maine Liquor Law." Dow had acquired for his law the specific endorsement of the anti-alcohol movement's national leaders. [13]

Through the efforts of Marsh and other publicists, Dow soon saw the "Maine Law" and himself become nationally famous. In addition to the American Temperance Union, the American Tract Society, the American Home Missionary Society and the rest of the complex of organizations closely associated with the Congregational and Presbyterian Churches threw their forces behind Dow's law. Before May, 1852, Marsh's society alone trumpeted the merits of the Maine Law in 235,000 copies of its adult and juvenile periodicals, in 10,000 pamphlets and in 80,000 pages of tracts. Marsh stressed the novel search and seizure provision of the Maine Law. In describing its results, he stripped every subtle qualification from Dow's glowing reports of Portland conditions and claimed for the Maine Law total success. Dubbing the law's author the "Napoleon of Temperance," Marsh cried that Dow had "brought into the battle-field every officer of State, . . . turned its whole artillery against the rum-fortifications, and in less than six months, . . . swept every distillery and brew-house, hotel-bar, splendid saloon and vile groggery clean from the State." Napoleon of Temperance! The little Portlander was gaining more than fame. He was receiving adulation.

Convinced by the widespread reports of the Maine Law's efficacy, most of the country's many temperance men joined Dow's crusade. As the fall of 1851 froze into winter in the New England and Middle Atlantic states, the evangelical clergy and temperance laymen met to vote their approval of the Maine Law. One ecstatic Massachusetts minister proclaimed "It is in harmony with the LAW OF GOD. . . . Its leading principles were taught by Jesus Christ." The clergyman argued, "If God be for it, who can be against it?" A Rhode Island Son of Temperance burst forth:

> Come all ye friends of temperance, and listen to my strain,
> I'll tell you how Old Alchy fares down in the state of Maine.
> There's one Neal Dow, a Portland man, with great and noble soul,
> He framed a law, without a flaw, to banish alcohol. [14]

As the author of the much-praised Maine Law, Dow became within a few months one of his country's leading temperance men. On February 18, 1852, at New York, a short-lived National Temperance Society of the United States held a banquet in his honor. Among the notables present at the dinner was Horace Mann, promoter of public education, who regarded Dow as "the moral Columbus." Dow listened to the eminent educator tell the audience that the Maine Law ranked with "the discovery of the magnetic needle, the invention of printing, or any other of the great strides in the progress of civilization." General Sam Houston of Texas, who had become the temperance society's President partly to forward his ambition to become President of the United States, then presented to Dow a very large gold medal. Concealing his pride, Dow acknowledged the valuable gift as a tribute to his cause rather than to himself. He had received the first of many gold and silver laurels. [15]

While the Napoleon of Temperance gained honor in distant places, he was adding to his detractors in his native city. John Neal became one of his more vocal critics. Dow had several times previously found his cousin, who had been an early temperance advocate, among those opposing his extreme measures. But Neal, after joining a Congregational church in 1851, had publicly supported his denomination's pro-Maine Law policy. Then, on January 12, 1852, the Portland Municipal Court convicted of liquor-selling Margaret Landrigan, "Alias 'Kitty Kentuck.'" Despite the Irish boardinghouse keeper's long record of similar offenses, Neal believed that she was innocent. Lawyer Neal and three of his friends signed the heavy bonds required under the Maine Law to permit an appeal. An anonymous writer in the MAINE TEMPERANCE WATCHMAN insinuated that the Landrigan bondsmen had a personal interest in "Kitty." Neal angrily attributed the article to his venom-penned cousin. In a later published defense, Dow did not disavow responsibility. [16]

By writing another article entitled "History of a Neighborhood, A True Tale," Dow further infuriated John Neal and also other leading Portlanders. In this signed short story published in a New York temperance magazine, he told of the horrible results of intemperance in each of the households along a fine avenue in a city within sight of the White Mountains. John Neal recognized that Dow, again using real life illustrations, had clearly described the families of Neal and other residents of Portland's fashionable State Street. To expose Dow to his victims, Neal had the article reprinted in Portland. In a long controversy with his cousin, Dow later denied that his "True Tale" was a true account of any specific street. Moreover, he sneered that the able, influential man described in the story could not possibly be John Neal. His cousin shot back that Dow had torn up "the dead bodies of a whole generation, like a ghoul . . ." and had then said, "How could you ever suppose I meant you? Did you ever elope with your own mother?" Despite his bold denials, Dow had made his bitterest enemy. 17

The mayor also aroused less passionate but more powerful enmity among the Portland merchants. When he had suppressed wholesaling of liquor, he had received protests from wealthy Portlanders who feared that his action might injure their important trade with the backcountry. Then, on January 14, 1852, though his Maine Law contained no specific authorization for the policy, he had his police begin making regular searches and seizures on every boat and train entering Portland. As Dow later explained, he hoped to stop smuggling to illegal liquor-dealers in both his own city and its hinterland. On March 2, 1852, an "association of independent men" began publishing the Portland MAINE EXPOSITOR in opposition to Dow's enforcement policies. Both the EXPOSITOR and the Democratic EASTERN ARGUS alleged that the Whig mayor was hurting the business of the city-financed Atlantic and St. Lawrence Railroad. Though Dow denied it, his opponents also charged that he had permitted policemen searching for hidden liquor to bore repeatedly into boxes of valuable merchandise. Near the end of his term, Mayor Dow was under heavy fire. 18

The city's political parties prepared to fight out the 1852 municipal election on the issue of Dow and his methods. On March 20, the Democrats held a public mass-meeting, instead of their customary party caucus, at Portland's City Hall. Charles Q. Clapp, a leading Democrat and one of the city's richest men, harangued the rally against the mayor. The Democratic leaders secured the nomination by acclamation of the venerable Albion K. Parris, a former congressman, judge and five-term state governor. Seeking the support of moderate men of all parties, the EASTERN ARGUS claimed that Parris favored the Maine Law but would avoid Dow's "unwarrantable mode of executing it." Dow accepted his enemies' personal challenge. He and his Temperance Watchmen again took control of the Whig party machinery and secured his renomination. In two wards, however, the anti-Dow Whigs ran bolting tickets. Dow had begun to melt party lines. Indeed, as one of his Whig supporters admitted the prohibitionist chief had become the leader of a "Neal Dow party." 19

As in previous campaigns, Dow and his faction bid for the support of Portland's church members. Although Judge Parris had been an early temperance man and was a lifelong Congregationalist, Elder Peck of the TEMPERANCE WATCHMAN pontificated, "It cannot be denied that voting for Mr. Dow is voting for morality, virtue and religion, while voting against him is voting against all these interests." But Editor Asa Cummings of the Portland CHRISTIAN MIRROR undermined the Dowites' religious appeal. Since the days of

Washingtonianism, Dow had publicly deplored Cummings' lack of enthusiasm for extreme temperance agitation. An early foe of intemperance, Cummings had expressed resentment at receiving such moral criticism from a man who was not a church member. He believed that Dow was arrogantly attempting "virtually to dictate to ministers and churches. . . ." In the last issue of his weekly before the 1852 election, Cummings commented, "A change in the administration of the law in a town or city, will not necessarily draw after it a neglect to execute the law." The knife-wielding reformer had received in his turn a subtle thrust into his vitals. [20]

On April 6, 1852, despite a severe snowstorm, a record-breaking crowd of voters cast its ballots. While Dow got 1496 votes, a slight increase over the previous year, Albion K. Parris piled up a crushing 1900 ballots. The rueful Whig editor explained that the bulk of the city's Democratic minority had united with "church members and 'world's people, temperance men and rummies" to protect Portland's commerce and "to vote down Neal Dow." Elder Peck particularly blamed the aging "Father" Cummings' "Five Lines" for the defeat. To temperance men outside Maine, however, Dow explained that "the rum sellers of Boston" had spent $17,000 to defeat him. Although the Dowite Board of Aldermen had controlled admission to the voting lists, his followers spread through the country allegations that the Democrats had imported "great numbers" of Irish railroad laborers to create their majority. Dow and his local supporters thereby hid his unpopularity with many Portlanders from his increasing number of more distant converts.

On April 10, 1852, Dow invited his associates in the repudiated city administration to an oyster supper. [21] As his baritone voice blended with theirs in the strains of "Auld Lang Syne," he had little cause for sorrow or vain regrets. Though defeated, he still had the ardent support of forty-four per cent of Portland's voters. In the 1852 mayoralty election, he had finally shattered the ranks of the old parties and had made enforced prohibition the decisive factor. Through his alliance with the Antislavery wing of the dominant Democracy, he had an opportunity to perform a similar feat in state politics. Elsewhere in the country, his effective propaganda had made the Maine Law a rising issue. With Whiggery weak and Democracy divided, the Napoleon of Temperance strode forward to national conquest.

Chapter VII

OUT OF THE EAST UNTO THE WEST

"As the lightning shineth out of the East unto the West," paraphrased Secretary John Marsh of the American Temperance Union, "so, under its power, a great moral reform spreads."[1] For the stimulation of the widespread Maine Law movement, to which Marsh referred, Neal Dow had the chief responsibility. In the early 1850's from the East to the West, the law's author proselytized for the universal enactment of prohibition. While widening his arid domain, he helped to bring about great changes in American political parties and made himself a national leader.

Because of his family and business situations, Dow was better able than many men to seek prominence for himself and his law. He had married a wife who completely shared his temperance views. Though he had never been separated from Cornelia and their six children for more than a few weeks, he had accustomed her to his frequent absences on speaking trips. Dow could leave his home affairs in his wife's capable hands. To assure ample support for himself and his family, he still relied heavily upon shrewd management by his octogenarian father. After the death of Neal Dow's mother in 1851, Josiah Dow and his invalid daughter, Harriet, had continued to live in the old homestead opposite his son's house. Though lame as a result of a serious fall, the old man hobbled out to direct the tannery's operations and ably watched over the family's investments. While Neal Dow sometimes thought of relieving his father of business cares, the prohibitionist chieftain invariably gave priority to the advancement of his cause.[2]

In his attitude toward the importance of his Maine Law propaganda, Dow was a thoroughgoing fanatic. He thought more about prohibition than about his own family. On September 4, 1852, only a few weeks after the death of his two-year-old son, Russell, Dow sadly admitted to his wife that he found it difficult to realize that the infant had "passed rapidly away from beneath our ardent gaze, or even that he has existed at all." He frankly accounted for "the dreamy feeling which I have when I think of our angel boy" by admitting that "my heart, as well as my thoughts, have been, perhaps, too much occupied . . ." with his objectives for the Maine Law. "I have felt willing to sacrifice to them my life, . . . and my thoughts have not had time to linger long around the loved ones of my own household. " While the temperance leader sighed for "the delights of domestic tranquility, " eventually even his reform-minded wife feared that he would forget his home and her. Dow spent considerable time in writing letters to allay her anxiety. But he maintained his single-minded dedication to his Maine Law crusade. [3]

From 1852 into 1855, Dow repeatedly left home on long temperance speaking tours. He travelled from Maine northward to Canada, westward to Illinois and southward to Maryland and Virginia. Riding on the new railroads wherever possible, he was often able to reduce his expenses by using free passes. He devoted particular attention to areas inhabited by New Englanders and their descendants. Among them, the earlier temperance movement had been strongest. Before large crowds in halls, churches and the open air, Dow spoke for from one to two hours at a time. Sometimes, as when he was going before the New York legislature, the orator felt "like a man to be hung, and would gladly have crept out of any place with the fence down. . . . " Generally, however, he quickly regained his "usual self-possession--and a little more. " As a New York editor noted, the little man's baritone voice was frequently not very strong. But Dow almost always impressed his listeners with his straightforward manner and intensity of purpose. Across half the nation, he won a sympathetic hearing for his principles. [4]

As his basic program, Dow always urged other states to re-enact the Maine Law. He found, as he delightedly told his wife, that the name of his brainchild had become the generally-accepted synonym for prohibition. To those who contended that the Maine Law infringed upon man's natural rights, he replied that men had no "rights which are incompatible with the general welfare. " The former Federalist would always take an extremely broad view of governmental authority. Having thrown the balance of power to win the original Maine Law, he urged his audiences to copy his political tactics. Dow informed the New York prohibitionists that "our uniform experience in Maine" showed the wisdom of adopting wherever possible the nominees of regular parties. "By pursuing such a course . . . , " Dow thought, "you cannot fail of a complete triumph. . . . " The Maine Law leader was making of prohibition a nationwide political question. [5]

In his own state's 1852 gubernatorial election, Dow declared the Maine Law to be the ruling issue. On June 29, the formerly-dominant Wildcat Democrats bolted the renomination of Governor John Hubbard by the Democratic legislative caucus. Anticipating a Democratic victory in the presidential election, the Wildcats wished to regain control of the disposal of patronage from Hubbard and the Antislavery Democrats. The Wildcats, in an attempt to rally anti-prohibitionists against the governor, attacked Hubbard for signing the Maine Law. Dow therefore argued that "common considerations of gratitude" should impel prohibitionists to rescue the governor. In August, he stumped the Penobscot Valley to urge Temperance Whigs and Free Soilers to abandon their own regular candidates in favor of Hubbard. On September 13, Dow and his followers helped to give their statute's signer a large plurality but not the constitutionally-required majority. In the legislature, which picked the winner, continued Democratic factionalism gave the governorship to Whig candidate William G. Crosby. While Dow had failed to elect his candidate, he and his law had contributed to the shattering of the Maine Democracy. [6]

Dow had little reason to hope that his old political comrades, the Whigs, would derive permanent profit from their Maine gubernatorial victory. In the 1852 presidential election, feeling himself to be under "peculiar obligations" to those Temperance Whigs who had earlier backed Hubbard, he had supported Whig candidate Winfield Scott. Indeed, with his customary strong dislike for Democrats, he had proposed that the Whigs brand Democratic nominee Franklin Pierce "a drunkard and nothing less." But, as Dow later admitted, he had given his secret sympathy to the hopeless cause of the Free Soilers. He was increasingly opposed to the South and to slavery. When Pierce had routed Scott, Dow lamented to Gerrit Smith, a noted New York abolitionist, that "the Whig party affected to ignore the North--and split upon it, as a noble ship upon a sunken rock. . . ." Dow anticipated a political realignment along sectional and antislavery lines. He predicted that Northern voters would assert their "right to be considered, in the management of the affairs of this great nation. . . ." As the new Northern party emerged, the prohibitionist chief would seek to make his Maine Law a basic article of its creed. [7]

In the winter of 1852-53, as legislatures met across the nation, Dow might well have felt encouraged at the politicians' growing acceptance of his law. In Maine, his legislative friends plugged loopholes in his statute and amended provisions declared unconstitutional in other states. Vermont's Whig-controlled legislature joined the lawmakers of Rhode Island and Massachusetts, who had enacted the Maine Law earlier in 1852, in putting their state within Dow's prohibitory paradise. Western states with a large infusion of New England settlers also joined the movement. In Michigan, a coalition of Whigs and Free Soilers enacted a Maine Law subject to a referendum. A similar alliance in Indiana provided for local option on retail liquor-selling. Even the British province of New Brunswick passed a partial prohibitory law. By his year of propaganda, Dow had won many converts. On May 12, 1853, when he addressed the American Temperance Union's annual meeting at New York, he was in a triumphant mood. He proudly proclaimed that "the suppression of grog shops" had become "the great political question of the day." [8]

During the 1853 elections, the Maine Law's author helped to increase further the importance of prohibition. Throughout the North, both Free Soilers bereft of an issue by the Compromise of 1850 and Whigs seeking a new program to recoup their 1852 losses rallied around the Maine Law. By his speeches and writings, Dow sought to win votes for candidates pledged to his statute. Through the summer and fall of 1853, he stumped Maine, Pennsylvania and the Old Northwest. In his own state, where the anti-prohibitionist Wildcats had regained control of the Democratic party's machinery, he campaigned against the

Democracy's nominee. A bolt by the Antislavery and Maine Law Democrats, similar to that of the Wildcats in 1852, threw the election into the legislature and resulted in the choice of a Whig governor pledged to prohibition. In the other states in which he campaigned, Dow also helped to increase the political strength of his cause. The lawmakers elected in Ohio severely limited liquor-selling and several other state legislatures almost enacted prohibition. Dow was constantly receiving new reasons for confidence in the Maine Law's future. [9]

As prohibition won successive political victories, Neal Dow fought hard to hold its gains against counterattacks. In his own city of Portland, he had many personal enemies who spitefully spread across the country reports that his law was a failure. John Neal, with his writing ability, was one of Dow's more dangerous critics. In August, 1853, as part of a running attack on the Maine Law, Dow's cousin charged that there was "more intemperance and more drinking" in Portland and "probably" throughout Maine than "at any other time for twenty years." Prior to the 1853 Portland mayoralty election, in which Dow had received a few votes, the local prohibitionists had made similar allegations of an increase of drunkenness since the end of Dow's term as mayor. On his speaking tours, however, Dow discovered that John Neal's charges were achieving a wider circulation. To prevent an ill-effect upon his movement, the Maine Law leader himself entered the fray.

In an answering series of letters, Dow twisted John Neal's claim that concealed drinking was common at Portland into proof that his law had ended "open" grogshops. While he carefully avoided making a public personal attack on Neal, he privately noted with satisfaction that his sympathizers believed his cousin to be crazy and were spreading reports to that effect. To complete the discrediting of Neal's charges, the Dowites prepared a certificate of denial. They shrewdly enlarged Neal's statement that prohibition had increased intemperance into a claim that there was "more liquor sold and drank." Claiming a desire to protect Portland's "fair reputation," the prohibitionists induced even some of the anti-Dow Whig leaders to join the 354 signers of the denial of Neal's alleged slur on the city. The American Temperance Union widely distributed the certificate. Dow believed, as he told his wife, that through the controversy he had won additional support for himself and his Maine Law. [10]

Besides dealing with enemy attacks, Dow faced the problem of preventing the friends flocking to his banner from entangling the Maine Law cause with other reforms. Any direct association of prohibition with such controversial programs as women's rights and the abolition of slavery might antagonize some possible supporters of his law. From September 6 to 8, 1853, while presiding over a World's Temperance Convention at New York, Dow therefore compromised other principles to protect prohibition. Although he had previously expressed himself in favor of women participating in temperance meetings, he discovered that many of his supporters among the Congregational and Presbyterian clergy violently objected to the attempts of a "female" to speak. After first ruling in her favor, Dow acquiesced in maneuvers which gagged feminists. To his wife, he boasted that by "a strong hand and a strong will," he had quelled "the bloomers and women's men." The Maine Free Soiler also made no protest against the barring from the convention of two Negro temperance men. By his conduct, Dow demonstrated his agreement with the Convention's decision to concentrate on prohibition and thus not "jeopard important elections in different parts of the land."[11]

Within a few months, however, Dow found a way popular at least in the North to ally prohibitionism with his antislavery views. Early in 1854, by endorsing a bill to organize Nebraska Territory and let its people decide whether it would be free or slave, the Democratic national administration reopened the question of slavery in the territories. In late March and early April, while campaigning for Maine Law candidates in the Connecticut legislative election, Dow exploited the indignation of many Northerners against any new opportunity for the spread of slavery. A hasty alliance of Maine Law men, Whigs and Free Soilers, with overtones of anti-foreignism, swept to victory and speedily enacted a stringent prohibitory law. To Maine's Senator Hannibal Hamlin, his Antislavery Democratic ally, Dow exulted that "the 'mummies' have got a 'Waterloo'--in which 'Nebraska' has an interest! Rum and that iniquity have gone to the wall. . . ." Having cooperated for years with the Free Soilers, Dow readily consented to team his Maine Law movement with the renewed antislavery enthusiasm. But, he later emphasized, "I was determined, so far as I could influence events, that this should be done without imperiling Prohibition."[12]

Dow, having added opposition to the extension of slavery to his Maine Law faction's creed, soon also included anti-foreignism. In his state, as in much of the rest of the nation, hostility was rising against immigrants generally and especially against Catholics. There was a mushrooming of nativist lodges whose members, because of their denials of knowledge of the secret societies' activities, won the name of "Know-Nothings." In April, 1854, when Dow made a determined but unsuccessful effort to regain the Portland mayoralty, the first rumors spread of Know-Nothing activity in the city's politics. While politicians of all parties sought to gain the support of the new force, Dow was in a particularly good position to work with the nativists. Politically, he had usually fought the Democracy, the party to which most of the Irish were loyal. As a prohibitionist, he had for two years blamed the Irish "foreigners" for the bulk of the violations of the Maine Law. By the time of the 1854 gubernatorial election, his Maine Law men had succeeded in taking control of the state's Know-Nothing movement. Whether or not Dow himself actually joined the secret order, as his enemies charged, he, Editor Benjamin D. Peck and Peck's temperance newspaper openly avowed Know-Nothing principles. Dow was anti-alcohol, antislavery and anti-foreign.[13]

On the basis of his three principles, Dow helped to bring about a fusion of the old political parties' broken components. On July 6, 1854, at Portland, he induced a State Temperance Convention to endorse Anson P. Morrill, gubernatorial candidate of the Antislavery and Maine Law Democrats. The Free

Soilers and Know-Nothings later also raised the Morrill banner. In legislative and congressional districts, Dow helped to arrange an even more perfect fusion of Morrill-Democrats, bolting Whigs and Free Soilers. He and Elder Peck stumped western Maine for the fusion candidates. In the election on September 11, Morrill received the votes of the factions that had endorsed him and in addition drew off about half of the normal Whig strength. The Antislavery and Maine Law Democrat thus gained a commanding plurality over the candidates of the Regular Democrats, the Whigs and the Anti-Maine Law Democrats. While Morrill lacked the majority required for election, the fusion-controlled legislature promptly settled the contest in his favor. For the first time since the great Whig landslide of 1840, Dow had backed a gubernatorial winner. [14]

As Maine went, so went at least the northern part of the nation. Coalitions of Whigs, Free Soilers, Anti-Nebraska Democrats and Know-Nothings, many of whom Dow had earlier proselytized for prohibition, swept most Northern state elections. The victorious allies increasingly began to call themselves "Republicans." They were usually favorable to the Maine Law and hostile to the foreign-born and to the extension of slavery. On February 22, 1855, for example, the Maine Republican State Convention bid for the support of antislavery men and nativists and recognized the "Maine Temperance Law" as "a vital element" in its party's "organization and life." After years of fighting the Democrats and bolting the Whigs, Dow and his prohibitionists had helped to bring about the formation of a strong party committed to their creed.

In the winter of 1854-55, following the Republican political revolution, Dow saw his Maine Law become the general rule across the northern United States. In New England, only New Hampshire had not yet prohibited liquor-selling. The Middle Atlantic states of New York and Delaware passed Maine Laws, New Jersey and Maryland almost did the same and Pennsylvania followed Ohio's earlier example in partially restricting liquor-selling. In the West, Indiana, Iowa and Michigan enacted or re-enacted Maine Laws, Illinois provided for a referendum on the subject and only two vetoes by Wisconsin's governor kept the Badger State out of Dow's empire. New England-born settlers on the country's far frontiers were agitating for prohibition and even some Southerners began to petition for the Maine Law. As Dow read telegrams announcing the accession of several Canadian provinces to his cause, he might well have anticipated his universal triumph. True, he still faced considerable opposition in the cities. There, wealthy businessmen, fearful that prohibition would hurt trade, united with such foreign-born groups as the Irish of Portland, Boston and New York to discourage the enforcement of Dow's law. Having spread prohibition "out of the East unto the West," Dow prepared to mop up these last puddles of the Demon Rum. [15]

For the needed mops, Dow looked to the lawmakers. As always, he was sure that with more legal penalties he could end liquor-selling. Early in 1854 at Montreal, Canada, he had vowed to stop the dealers' "infernal practices, if it takes all the hemp in Kentucky." After the victory of his faction in the 1854

Maine election, he admitted that "perhaps the time has not come" to class "rumselling" with "the gravest crimes" but he demanded that the lawmakers make the offense at least a felony. On January 25, 1855, the prohibitionist chief submitted an "'Intensified Maine Law'" to his state's legislators. Containing thirty-four sections of fine print, Dow's bill was longer than the original Maine Law. The Republican-controlled legislature pulled from the measure some of what one member called its "scorpion stings." But Dow received favorable responses to his requests for imprisonment for first offenders, heavy fines for most violations and permission to seize liquor in transit. Surveying the new prohibitionist victories in Maine and throughout the North, the Reverend John Marsh of the American Temperance Union predicted that Dow's much-revised statute was soon "to become the law of all the States of the Union; and, under diverse forms, of the civilized world."[16]

The author of the Maine Law shared in the prestige of his handiwork. Though proud of his growing fame, Dow sought to preserve an outward air of modesty. He instructed his family not to follow his supporters' example in using the title "Honorable" in his mailing address. He referred to personal compliments as tributes to his cause. But, to his family, he described in lavish detail how admirers wearied his hand with shaking, women named babies for him and orators decked him with verbal laurels. In January, 1854, however, when repeating a New York minister's evaluation of Dow's reputation as even more desirable than that of Washington, the subject of the compliment humorously commented to his daughter, "There, wasn't that 'laying it on thick'. . . ." Dow liked better such tangible testimonials as silver pitchers and a massive silver tea-service. These gifts, usually presented in gratitude for speaking tours, pleased the acquisitive Dow because of their intrinsic worth but even more because of the prestige they symbolized. To his family, he gloated over the anticipated discomfiture at his success of such hostile Portlanders as the Reverend Asa Cummings of the CHRISTIAN MIRROR. To please his friends and gall his foes, Dow had his valuable trophies exhibited at a Portland jeweler's shop. Before the voters who had rejected him in 1852, the Prophet of Prohibition flaunted proof that elsewhere he was not without honor.[17]

To restore completely the stature lost in the 1852 defeat, Dow wished to regain the Portland mayoralty. He had failed in two previous attempts but in 1855 he had a large and united following. Dow secured the secret endorsement of the Know-Nothings and the nomination by acclamation of Portland's first Republican caucus. Moreover, he had a new device for reducing the number of hostile Irish-born voters. On March 17, 1855, less than a month before the Portland mayoralty contest, Republican Governor Anson P. Morrill signed a Naturalization Law requiring foreign-born voters to register their naturalization papers with their municipal authorities at least three months prior to any election. If stringently enforced, the Know-Nothing-sponsored act would have at least prevented the addition to the voting lists of any more naturalized voters. At the end of March, Dow confidently went to Boston to deliver temperance lectures and relied on his followers to make the necessary preparations to carry the election.

Despite their sources of strength, Dow and the Republicans still faced heavy odds. Besides the Irish laborers and men directly interested in liquor-selling, many of the city's businessmen opposed Dow as a threat to commerce. Democrats like Charles Q. Clapp, West India merchant and owner of extensive real estate, united with Whigs like railroad promoter John A. Poor and John B. Brown, owner of the Portland Sugar House, to back James T. McCobb for the mayoralty. The Anti-Dow nominee was a Democrat friendly to the Maine Law. To prevent the Republicans from restricting the Irish vote, an alderman who had moved to Boston several months earlier retook his seat and thus gave the Anti-Dowites a majority on the body charged with correcting the voting lists. On April 2 and 3, 1855, however, Dow's three supporters on the Board of Aldermen used dilatory tactics to balk the Anti-Dowites' attempts to ignore the Naturalization Law by permitting newly-naturalized men to vote. While the prohibitionists finally allowed the addition of several hundred names to the list, they prevented some applicants from voting. In the bitterly-contested election, both Dow's friends and enemies had used desperate tactics.

On the morning of election day, April 3, 1855, Dow returned to cast his vote and savor his victory. After the counting of the 3745 ballots, he found that he had won by a majority of only forty-seven votes over the forces of what Elder Peck called "Rum, Hunkerism, Catholicism and Corruption." On election night, he heard his followers marching to his house behind a band to cheer their leader. Addressing the crowd, Dow hailed his triumph as a success for the Maine Law movement. In an appeal to his Know-Nothing friends, he also called for "measures to restrain the right of suffrage, now exercised by our foreign population. . . . " The prohibitionist chief spoke over the groaning of Anti-Dowites and the noise of street fights. But, while he had become the mayor of a sorely-divided city, he could rejoice at being in a position to enforce his Intensified Maine Law. And, as his sympathizers made haste to tell the country, he had wiped away the stain of his earlier defeat and had proven his political strength. The author of the rapidly-spreading Maine Law had reached a new height of importance and potential power. [18]

Dow did not intend to remain mayor of Portland for long. On April 9, 1855, in his inaugural address, he announced that he would probably not seek re-election. With the new Republican party scarcely a year away from its first national convention, higher offices beckoned. In mid-1855, a writer employed by a pro-Maine Law society to write an official biography of Dow predicted that the prohibitionist leader could command a strong vote throughout the North as a candidate for the vice-presidency of the United States. "With NEAL DOW as the presiding officer of the Senate," opined the Maine Law propagandist, "the scenes of drunkenness which disgraced the last Congress could scarcely be repeated. "[19] Mayor Dow had a year in which to demonstrate and dramatize his executive ability. By his conduct in enforcing his Intensified Maine Law, he would help to decide his own future and that of his crusade.

Chapter VIII

SUBLIME FANATIC

"Mighty reformer! Oft the trump of Fame,
Blown by thyself, has sent abroad thy name!
Sublime Fanatic! who to aid thy cause,
Slights trifles such as Constitutions, Laws!
O Pimp Majestic! whose sharp gimlet eye,
All jugs conceal'd and demijohns can spy!
Astute Smell-fungus! Striving as a goal,
To poke thy nose in every dirty hole!
Pimp, Spy, Fanatic! arrogant at heart!
Language would fail to draw thee as thou art!"

Shortly after Mayor Neal Dow's re-election, while his admirers predicted for him a glorious future, an anonymous Portland poet poured forth this scorching denunciation of the Maine Law chieftain. The writer heaped similar coals of fire upon the heads of Dow's prohibitionist and Know-Nothing associates in the city government. Dow and his ardent supporters had aroused such hatred in the hearts of nearly half of Portland's voters. By his personal attacks, his upsetting of elections and his interference with the wholesale liquor-trade, the prohibitionist leader had alienated many of his city's politicians and wealthy merchants. Moreover, in the 1855 mayoralty campaign, Dowite slurs against "Irish Cattle" and the attempt to bar from the polls "ignorant Irish Catholics" had heightened the antagonism of the city's foreign-born. Through his policies as mayor, Dow could easily bring down the crushing avalanche of opposition. [1]

Dow made no attempt to appease his foes. Instead, he vigorously enforced the Intensified Maine Law. Each morning, the little man went to his office in the City Government House, took his seat upon a dais and directed the hunt for "rumsellers." He sent his police to root out bottles of liquor from behind the walls and under the floors of hotels and semi-concealed liquor-shops. The mayor could rely upon Judge Henry Carter of the new Police Court established at Dow's request to show no sympathy for either Irish or native-born "rumsellers. " He had enjoyed the support of Carter's PORTLAND ADVERTISER in the mayoralty election. Indeed, opponents regarded the judgeship as the Whig editor's reward for becoming a Republican. With Carter's help, Dow was able to intimidate even a drunkard into giving information against a liquor-seller. The mayor and his many supporters soon drove the infuriated "rum-sellers" into the city's dark corners. Thus far, Dow had successfully demonstrated the effectiveness of his law. [2]

But, by disregarding some of his own statute's many technicalities, Dow exposed himself to a counterattack. In both the original and the Intensified Maine Laws, Dow had authorized municipalities to operate agencies to sell liquor for medicinal and industrial uses. On May 3, 1855, he became chairman of a committee to set up such an agency in a store in the City Hall. Before the Board of Aldermen had appointed an agent and without a prior appropriation, Dow ordered over $1600 worth of liquor for the agency. On May 31, when the liquor for the agency arrived, the bill bore Dow's name, whereas his law required that it be directed by name to an agent. Thus, when the aldermen appointed an agent, he would have to transfer title to the liquor to that official. So strict was the Intensified Maine Law's prohibition of anyone but an agent from dealing in liquor that such a transfer might well constitute an illegal sale. The man who had often interpreted the law to suit his prohibitory purpose was in a weak position if his enemies should twist his act to serve their ends.

On the evening of May 31, Dow met with the aldermen and elected a city agent subject to approval of the agent's bond. Alderman Joseph Ring, an Anti-Dowite, commented that the mayor had bought the newly-arrived liquor on his "own hook." Thinking that Ring was joking, Dow agreed. When the hostile alderman asked Dow if he thought he had made a good speculation, the sarcastic mayor quipped, "I don't know but I shall. " Ring, as he later admitted, did not think that Dow had actually made the purchase for private profit but he saw a chance to give the mayor a dose of the Intensified Maine Law. If charged with keeping liquor for illegal sale, the law's author would be liable to seizure of the stock which he had ordered. While Dow would face a $20 fine and a thirty day jail sentence if convicted, a more serious danger would be the possibility that either spectators at the seizure or some official might pour out the liquor. Should this happen, a provision of Dow's law would block either him or the city from recovering the value of the destroyed property. Even if the courts finally held that the city had owned the liquor, Dow's political enemies could blame his mismanagement for the loss of $1600 of the taxpayers' money. The mayor had unwittingly exposed himself to economic or political danger. [3]

By repeating his conversation with Dow to the publishers of the Democratic EASTERN ARGUS and the Whig STATE OF MAINE, Alderman Ring set in motion a movement to seize the liquor in the City Agency. On Saturday, June 2, 1855, both of these Anti-Dow newspapers reported the incident and the ARGUS also reprinted its story as a handbill. Calling on the city marshal to seize and pour out the mayor's liquor, ARGUS editor John M. Adams cried, "Let the lashwhich Neal Dow has prepared for other's backs, be applied to his own, when he deserves it." That afternoon in Police Court, Royal Williams, the owner of Portland's last distillery, and two other Anti-Dowites swore that they believed that the mayor was keeping liquor for illegal sale. Because Dow's law had eliminated judicial discretion, the reluctant Judge Henry Carter perforce agreed to issue a search and seizure warrant. But the judge refused to entrust the warrant to the constable brought by Williams and instead turned it over to a Dowite deputy marshal. The deputy spent about two and a half hours in consulting Dow and other superiors. Even after seizing the liquor at about 5:30 p.m., he did not remove it or arrest the mayor. [4]

While the deputy dawdled, Dow hurriedly tried to legalize his position. In mid-afternoon, as soon as he heard of the complaint against him, he called a special meeting of the aldermen at his office. By getting them to approve the city agent's bond, he at last established a legal liquor agency. He then asked the board to purchase the invoice for the controversial shipment of liquor. Some of the aldermen wished to delay. But Judge Carter, who had hastened over from his courtroom, helped to persuade the Republican majority to accept the liquor for the city. Before leaving for tea, as he called the evening meal, Dow asked a Dowite alderman to come back that evening. He intended, as he said, to go to Carter's court to be arrested and wished a surety. Having repaired his technical breaches of the law prior to the delayed seizure, Dow was ready to meet his foes' legal attack. [5]

That evening, when Dow returned to his office in the City Government House two blocks east of City Hall, he learned that at least part of his foiled enemies were threatening violence. In the afternoon, a crowd of several hundred men had gathered around the Agency's store in the City Hall to watch the seizure of the liquor. The bystanders, part of whom were Irish, had loudly damned the dilatory seizure and the failure to arrest Dow but had dispersed for their evening meal. Between 7:00 and 8:00 p.m., some city rowdies, young laborers, sailors and boys began to cluster around City Hall. Located in the angle formed by the intersection of Congress and Middle Streets, the three-story brick building overlooked Market Square. The legal liquor-store, which ran laterally across its ground floor, had doors on both of the side streets. Gathering at the Agency's Congress Street entrance, the youths began to shout threats to spill "Neal Dow's liquor." From the Saturday night crowd in Market Square, they soon attracted many spectators. Mayor Dow began to receive reports of the formation of a dangerous mob. [6]

As he had on numerous previous occasions, Dow decided to meet force with force. He knew that earlier Portland mayors had failed to cope with mobs. Believing in the power of government, he intended to succeed. Dow did not try to use either peaceful persuasion or organized arrests of trouble-makers to disperse the crowd. Instead, a little before 8:00 p.m., he sent the city marshal and a fourth of his thirty-two ununiformed police into the Agency with orders to "protect the public property at all hazards." The police, some of whom had revolvers, skulked well within the shop and merely called out to the people to go away. Dow also sent Sheriff Seward M. Baker to read the Riot Act. By the time that the sheriff reached the Agency's Congress Street entrance, a semicircle of rowdies was cursing the name of Neal Dow and throwing stones through the door's shattered glass panel. Behind the forty or fifty active rioters, a crowd of nearly a thousand onlookers, including some of Dow's influential foes, laughed, yelled and generally encouraged a liquor-dumping. In the uproar, few heard the sheriff shout an order to disperse. Dow had failed to use the fading twilight to prevent the discharge of Portland's accumulated hatreds.

Meanwhile, having no confidence in his politically-appointed police, the mayor had sent written orders for assistance to two of the city's militia companies. At about 9:00 p.m., he and four Republican aldermen had hurried from the City Government House to the armory of Captain Charles E. Roberts' Rifle Guards. Finding that only a few militiamen had gathered, he went to the room of Captain Charles Green's company on the second floor of City Hall. There, he found about twenty-four of the Light Guards. Green wished to wait for more men, but Dow, expecting the Rifle Guards to arrive soon, insisted that they had enough troops. A little after 10:00 p.m., Dow, Sheriff Baker and two aldermen led the handful of ununiformed Light Guards out under the City Hall's classic portico and down the stairs into Congress Street. In front of the Agency's door, Dow had the company form two ranks. With loaded "carnal weapons," the ex-Quaker faced his hostile constituents. 7

Brandishing a watchman's hook, Dow loudly commanded the crowd to disperse. From out of the darkness, the hated mayor received in reply a shower of oaths, hisses and stones. As missiles injured two militiamen, Dow flew into a frenzy. Without seeking the legally-required concurrence of the sheriff or an alderman, he shouted a command to fire into the dense mass of rioters and spectators. The militiamen, however, waited for their captain to repeat the order. Turning to Dow, Captain Green asked, "must I fire, for its hard to shoot our own citizens." The mayor replied, "wait a minute." He later claimed that he had intended only to frighten the crowd. At Green's insistence, Dow then led away the Light Guards to seek reinforcements. By his failure to arrest anyone or to carry out his own hasty order to fire, he had only encouraged the angry rioters to shout, "see the [damned] cowards leave."8

In Middle Street on the opposite side of City Hall, Dow and his small escort met Captain Charles E. Roberts with about thirty Rifle Guards. The mayor told the militiamen that this time he would give the order to fire through their captain. There would be no more indecision. ". . . I want every man of you to mark your man," Dow fiercely commanded. "We'll see whether mob law shall rule here, or whether your Chief Magistrate shall!" Since the Rifle Guards had no cartridges for their weapons, the mayor led them into the Light Guards' City Hall armory and peremptorily compelled Green's men to turn over their muskets to Roberts' company. From the Agency below, as a few of the more determined rioters finally worked up enough courage to

attempt an entrance, he heard the noise of battering and the crack of the policemen's pistols. While most of the spectators scattered, several mobsters
burst open the Congress Street door. From an alderman, Dow received a
report that the police were about to "fall a sacrifice to the fury of the mob."

The mayor and the Rifle Guards clattered down the stairs to the rescue.
Learning from his failure with Green's company, he did not expose his untried
troops to attack. Instead, leading them into the Agency's Middle Street entrance, he halted the militiamen within the darkened store. Several rock-
throwers were visible through the opposite door. Dow shrieked an order to
fire and three ragged volleys ripped along the length of the store into nearly-
empty Congress Street. During the shooting, Dow took three Rifle Guards
into the cellar to fire up through the window gratings but found no targets. He
then withdrew his men through the Middle Street door, helped them to reload
their muskets and finally ordered Captain Roberts to clear stragglers from
the neighborhood with the bayonet. The prohibitionist mayor had won his battle
to protect the legal liquor-store. 9

Shortly before midnight, Dow and his victorious followers gathered within
the bullet-riddled Agency and refreshed themselves with crackers, cheese and
cold water. A bystander, who saw Dow hungrily munching, later recalled the
glow of righteous exultation upon his face. When a doctor entered to inform
him that one of the crowd was dead, Dow casually asked, "if the body was
Irish." If the dead man were foreign-born, he could easily explain the killing
to his many Know-Nothing supporters. The doctor, however, identified the
corpse as that of an "American." The dead man, John Robbins, was the twenty-
two-year-old mate of a Maine vessel. Dow later learned that his police and
militiamen had also hit several Irish laborers. In putting down the riot, Neal
Dow had caused the death of Robbins and the wounding of seven other men. 10

All through the following day, June 3, 1855, excited citizens disturbed the
city's usual Sabbath calm as they gathered to examine the Agency's bullet-
pocked door. Hot-tempered John Neal, for one, began to declare openly that
his cousin Neal Dow should be hanged for murder. Although officials on the
scene easily persuaded the people not to linger in the fatal neighborhood, Dow
feared fresh trouble. That afternoon, he summoned the aldermen and city
officers to his house to consider calling out Portland's five militia companies.
They suddenly discovered that the Militia Law of 1844, under the form of which
Dow had ordered out the Light and Rifle Guards, was no longer in effect. Dow
and the aldermen could not persuade the militia to assist voluntarily. Finally,
they dispatched a messenger to ask Republican Governor Anson P. Morrill
to issue the needed order. Dow had lost none of his faith in force. 11

Yet, because of his violent repression of the riot, the master of propaganda
lost the initiative in the battle to sway national opinion toward prohibition. On
the morning of Monday, June 4, in their first editions since Saturday, the
Democratic EASTERN ARGUS and Whig STATE OF MAINE printed hostile
accounts of Dow's handling of the mob. ARGUS Editor John M. Adams blamed
Dow's high-handed prohibitory law enforcement for the whole affair and John

A. Poor, publisher of the STATE OF MAINE, decorated his office with a banner inscribed "Murder. " Through the Anti-Dow newspapers, exchange editors in other cities received their first descriptions of the riot. Because Judge Henry Carter's PORTLAND ADVERTISER, an afternoon paper, sold out its entire first edition in its home city, the Dowite version lagged far behind the opposition's attacks. Soon, Dow saw the result. From Rhode Island, he received a broadside showing soldiers massacring defenseless citizens. A Connecticut editor proclaimed Dow to be at best "a remorseless, unscrupulous tyrant, who wants only power to commit atrocities that would affright a Nero. " All over the country editors reported that the Portland mayor who had outlawed Rum had killed to protect the Demon. [12]

At home, too, Dow faced powerful propaganda. On June 4, after a hasty inquest over the corpse of John Robbins, a city coroner's jury dominated by his supporters declared the dead man to have been a member of a riotous mob. But the Anti-Dowites replied with an attempt to make a hero of Robbins. After the inquest, two seamen carrying an American flag at half-staff led about 300 of the dead sailor's admirers in a funeral procession. An anti-Maine Law editor later predicted that Robbins' grave would be honored when Dow's was "lost among the wild grasses and weeds that spring from carrion carcasses, in places hideous to human tread. " That afternoon at City Hall, the city's wealthiest Whigs and Democrats called a meeting "to allay the present excitement. " The gathering demanded the prosecution of those responsible for Robbins' death and called for Dow's resignation. At midnight, after receiving an order from Governor Morrill directing the militia to support him against an "Insurrection, " the embattled mayor called out two military companies. [13]

Dow used the troops to guard his trial on the original charge of possessing liquor with intent to make an illegal sale. On June 5, looking weary and jaded, he appeared before the Police Court in City Hall and pleaded not guilty. He himself had helped to place his judge, Henry Carter, on the bench. Prosecuting Attorney Nathan Clifford, however, was a hostile Democrat and a former United States Attorney-General. Clifford charged that Dow, by making an unauthorized purchase before the formal establishment of an agency, had broken the Maine Law. The mayor did not testify in his own defense. Instead his attorney, Republican Senator William Pitt Fessenden, used other witnesses to show that the seized barrels bore the Portland Agency's address. Fessenden contended that Dow had not personally acquired possession of the liquor. On the following day, Judge Carter, who had helped to persuade the aldermen to accept Dow's purchase, held that their action had wiped out any technical violations. Amid the cheers of Dowites, Carter announced their leader's acquittal. Next day, the mayor permitted the discharge of the militia. He had won both the street and the courtroom fights. [14]

But, as his opponents continued their assault on his reputation, Dow had to undergo another legal inquiry into the death of John Robbins. On June 9, 1855, a week after the riot, Dow's influential foes induced the county coroner to impanel a jury of virulent Anti-Dowites. While Dow and the aldermen denounced this second inquest as illegal and unnecessary, they sent counsel to cross-examine the witnesses. They also immediately countered by appointing a "non-partisan" committee of Dowites to investigate their own conduct. During the lengthy hearings conducted by the two investigating groups, most of the key officials appeared before both bodies and filled the newspapers' columns with their testimony. Dow was not a witness at the coroner's inquest. Instead, he gave an informal account of the riot to the "non-partisan" committee. Despite two opportunities, the mayor had not and would not testify under oath about the fatal riot. 15

While the investigators sought ammunition for use against their enemies, Dow finally organized his defense in the propaganda war. In a report on the riot dated June 9, 1855, he claimed that "men of influence" had for weeks encouraged and planned an "extensive combination" to raise a mob of "savage ferocity, "destroy the Agency's liquor and burn down the City Hall. He branded the dead Robbins as a ringleader of the riot. In words which hearkened back to his childhood training, the mayor declared that he had acted to uphold "the majesty of the law" and to suppress a plot "to let loose upon us all the horrors of anarchy and riot. " On June 11, his majority on the Board of Aldermen ordered the publication of Dow's "true history" of the Portland Riot. By his narrative, Dow generally satisfied the editors of Republican, religious and reform newspapers and drew demonstrations of confidence from his followers. Some temperance women of Biddeford, Maine, sent a silver pitcher. The New York State Temperance Society declared that Dow and the other suppressors of the riot deserved the "support and approbation of all good citizens. " The Maine Law chieftain could still rely on the loyalty of his prohibitionist army. 16

Through the controversy over the Portland Riot, Dow finally succeeded in making himself and his law the overwhelming issues in a state election. On June 21, 1855, when the Democrats nominated Samuel Wells for governor, they adopted a platform condemning the "intensified Liquor Law" but favoring "suitable prohibitory laws. " The remnant of the Whigs later nominated Isaac Reed on a similar platform and united with the Democrats in legislative contests. On July 4 at Paris Hill, Francis O. J. Smith, Dow's lawyer at the previous decade's Fire Department hearing, shouted to an anti-Republican rally, "Dow ought to be hanged, and if we succeed this fall, he will be hanged. " Only a few miles away at South Paris, Dow was addressing a Republican Independence Day rally and listening to the crowd of thousands cheer a resolution approving his conduct at the riot. His party had already renominated Governor Anson P. Morrill. But again and again throughout the campaign, the Democrats and Whigs told the electorate that "A vote for Morrill is a vote for Neal Dow, and a justification of all his illegal, tyrannical and murderous acts. "17

Both sides in the campaign could exploit the contrasting reports of the Portland Riot's investigators. On July 9 and 10, respectively, the Anti-Dow Second Inquest and the Dowite Investigating Committee brought in their findings. The former principally contended that Dow had ordered out the militiamen without legal authority and that one of them had shot Robbins. The latter claimed that Dow had really called upon the troops to fulfill an agreement to act as an emergency "armed police" and argued that, in any event, the regular police had done the killing. While the Second Inquest charged Dow with committing murder or manslaughter, the Dowite investigators adopted the reasoning of their leader's report to justify his firing into "an embruted mob." As proof of Dow's innocence, his apologists pointed to the grand jury's subsequent failure to indict the mayor. A Dowite editor branded the instigators of the Second Inquest as "a perfidious junta of civil pirates." On the other hand, the Anti-Dowites sneered at the mayor's "Whitewashing Committee." Dow and his enemies each published their own side's report, the former at public expense, and thereby made them campaign documents. [18]

In the September gubernatorial election, after weeks of stumping the state for his party, Dow met a disastrous defeat. Republican Governor Anson P. Morrill failed to get the required majority and lost control of the legislature. The hostile lawmakers later placed Samuel Wells, the Democratic nominee, in the gubernatorial chair. The Republicans, however, could draw comfort from the fact that their candidate had actually bettered by fifteen per cent his previous year's total vote. Pointing to the divisions in the opposition, a Bangor editor predicted a great Republican victory in the 1856 state and national elections. The Republican newspaperman blamed Morrill's defeat upon the "questionable legislation of last winter." Using words ominous to Dow, he proposed that the Republicans strengthen themselves by purging their party of the "men of isms" and the "partizans of humbug." Having been the most conspicuous causes of the Republican rout, Dow and his Maine Law suddenly became likely candidates for the sacrificial altar. [19]

As Dow admitted to the Reverend John Marsh of the American Temperance Union, he and the prohibitionists were "at first fairly stunned by the result of the election." He confessed, "We did not for a moment anticipate a defeat. . . ." Deciding that his fellow-Portlanders had "voted for rum," he even momentarily relaxed his enforcement of the Maine Law. His ally, Elder Benjamin D. Peck of the MAINE TEMPERANCE JOURNAL, frequently asserted that, as a "moral effect" of the Republican defeat, drunkenness at Portland was increasing. But, to reassure his followers in other states, Dow quickly found an explanation for his setback in a cyclical theory of temperance. In private and published letters, he contended that similar reactions had followed each of his past successes and had only been the preludes to greater victories. The next election, Dow optimistically predicted, would "bring all right again." [20]

Between elections, however, Dow spent a bleak winter suffering the penalties for defeat. Impotently, he watched the Democrats and Whigs in control of the 1856 legislature repeal his Intensified Maine Law. Although the Democrats had promised to enact "suitable prohibitory laws," the legislators passed a license law. Senator Phineas Barnes, the act's author and one of Dow's old Whig enemies, permitted innholders to offer liquor by the glass and allowed a limited number of retailers in each town to sell it for home use. On March 13, 1856, in an unsigned editorial in Elder Peck's newspaper, Dow pointed out to "our 'naturalized citizens'" the extremely restrictive character of the Barnes Law. Charging that the new license system only provided liquor for the ruffle-shirted aristocracy, the former Know-Nothing candidate quoted an Irishman as saying, "Neal Dow's law was honest, for it trated all alike, but this thing is a chate and we'll have none iv it." Dow would always oppose any intermediate course between "free rum or Maine Law." To encourage a return to prohibition, Dow's editorial supporters immediately began to report a frightful upsurge of debauchery. [21]

At the spring canvass of 1856, Mayor Dow did not run for re-election. Even without the man himself to oppose, the Democratic EASTERN ARGUS declared that the only issue was "DOWISM," the synonym for "governmental tyranny." Editor John M. Adams reminded his readers that William Willis, the Republican candidate, had headed Dow's "Whitewashing Committee" and had thereby apologized for "the murder of Robbins." On April 8, 1856, an Anti-Dow "Citizens' Ticket," which Elder Peck described as "a combination of the upper classes with money, rum, and the low Irish," swept to victory. As Dow left office, he found personal satisfaction in an unanimous vote of the City Council commending his performance of duty. In token of his followers' continued faith in him, he received from the Portland Ladies' Temperance Band four silver goblets on a matching salver. But, politically, he had sustained another loss. Dow's fellow-citizens had again indicated the peril of any connection with "Dowism." [22]

That summer, Dow learned the full extent of his new political weakness. Because of the influence of Maine's early state election upon the prospects of Republican presidential candidate John C. Fremont, he wished to woo enough opposition voters to secure a decisive majority. From even prohibitionists, Dow received advice against insisting on the party's endorsing his controversial Maine law. On condition that the Republicans would recommit themselves to prohibition in 1857, Dow reluctantly acquiesced in their making the prevention of the spread of slavery their only issue. In September, the bargain gave Republican gubernatorial candidate Hannibal Hamlin, who had finally quit the Democracy, an overwhelming popular election. As he had during the state canvass, Dow kept out of the subsequent national campaign. On November 3, however, he permitted Anti-Dowite John A. Poor, a convert to Republicanism, to introduce him to an election-eve rally on the very site of the Portland Riot. The temporizing prohibitionist leader helped to carry Maine but not the nation for Fremont. After watching a Democratic "rabble of Irish blackguards" parade victoriously by his house, the defeated Dow mused bitterly to his daughter about the country's future. [23]

In the winter of 1856-57, only two years after the season of the Maine Law's brightest prospects, Dow had good cause to feel downcast. While he resumed his propaganda for re-enactment of the Maine Law, he could hope for little from the Republican state administration. On January 8, 1857, in a message to the legislature, Governor Hannibal Hamlin spoke of the "implied, if not actual pledge" against immediately restoring prohibition. Moreover, to remove the issue from "the vortex of party politics, " the governor recommended the submission of any future prohibitory law to a popular vote. The Republican officeholders were wary of again becoming responsible for a Neal Dow law. Indeed, some of the Republican prohibitionists, who had charged the Democracy with placing a lust for office ahead of their reform, began to show similar inclinations. Dow's associate, Elder Benjamin D. Peck, received the lucrative post of State Treasurer and boasted in his temperance weekly of the success of the prohibitionists' bargain with the politicians. Dow obtained only the minimal satisfaction of the exclusion of the Barnes License Law from a new edition of the REVISED STATUTES. Even with his party victorious in his own state, he had lost most of the decade's gains for prohibition.[24]

Surveying his once-flourishing Maine Law empire, Dow found a similarly cheerless prospect. In July, 1855, he had personally watched a New Hampshire legislature elected before the Portland Riot bring the last New England state under his banner. Since then, however, he had made no new accessions. The people of other states had discovered that his Maine Law did not produce the almost magical results implied in his propaganda. Though prohibition had been effective in many rural areas, the enforcement problems with which Dow had struggled in Portland had proven even more difficult in Boston and other metropolises. Moreover, as in Maine, politicians had found that foreign-born voters were hostile both to prohibition and the Know-Nothingism often allied with it. By his conduct at the much-publicized Portland Riot, Dow gave many of his hasty converts a reason for abandoning his cause and turning their attention to the slavery issue. By early 1857, only five New England states and Michigan retained their unevenly-enforced Maine Laws. Ohio and Iowa also ineffectually restricted liquor-selling. Dow's earnest publicist, the Reverend John Marsh, mourned, "Where was the myrtle tree is coming up the brier. . . ."[25]

Neal Dow had both fertilized and blighted the Maine Law myrtle. With the aggressiveness which had helped him in his rise to power, he had insisted on spreading and strengthening his system faster than many Americans thought desirable. When the minority had resisted, he had characteristically resorted to force. By his fanaticism during the Portland Riot, he had darkened his political future and had weakened the roots of his cause across the nation. And, through his bargain with the Republican leaders, he had temporarily forestalled himself from even regaining the ground lost in his own state. Having blasted his prospects in the New World, Dow looked across the Atlantic to find fresh soil for prohibition.

Chapter IX

MAINE LAW MISSIONARY

In 1857, Neal Dow became a missionary to spread the gospel of prohibition in Great Britain. During the period of his Maine Law's greatest prestige in the United States, he had felt himself too busy with local campaigns to accept invitations to visit the land of his ancestors. By going when even his own state had no Maine Law, he made himself a target for anti-prohibitionists. An English editor sneered that "Mr. NEAL DOW has transferred himself to this country because his cause is already worn threadbare in his own."[1] Dow would attempt through his propaganda abroad and his political activity at home to refute such reports of his crusade's American decline. Broadening his interest to include the entire world, he would seek to promote a general Maine Law revival.

In attempting to convert Great Britain to prohibition, Dow could build on existing international cooperation between temperance men. In the late 1820's, the founders of the United Kingdom's original temperance societies had drawn their inspiration from the writings of Lyman Beecher and other Americans. The British temperance men, living in a country where beer-drinking was common, had early adopted the standard of total abstinence from all forms of alcohol and had repaid their American teachers by giving them the word "teetotalism" to denote the new principle. Close contact had continued between the American and British temperance crusades. In 1846, when the British had held a World's Temperance Convention, Dow had decided only at the last moment against joining the Reverends Lyman Beecher and John Marsh in attending. By the mid-1850's, substantial groups calling themselves the National, British and Scottish Temperance Leagues were urging their countrymen to abandon the Demon Rum.

But the British temperance men had not become as numerous nor as interested in politics as their American contemporaries. The Congregationalists, Methodists, Presbyterians and Quakers, among whom the temperance movement was strongest, were only a minority in Great Britain and few members of the dominant Church of England had taken the pledge. In Ireland, despite a campaign in the 1840's led by Father Theobald Mathew, the Catholic majority had remained mostly hostile or indifferent to teetotalism. And, unlike many areas of the United States where social and religious leaders had fostered temperance, the majority of British aristocrats and clergymen had not become abstainers. Even among the British teetotalers, few had advocated more than personal abstinence. The British had not followed the American shift from persuasion to prohibition. [2]

By his Maine Law, Neal Dow had planted the seed of a British movement against liquor-selling. In reply to a letter from Nathaniel Card of Manchester, Dow had sent the elderly Quaker manufacturer some of his early reports of his law's success. In 1853, Card had organized the United Kingdom Alliance for Obtaining the Immediate Legislative Suppression of the Traffic in All Intoxicating Drinks. While Card was a teetotaler, the United Kingdom Alliance had also accepted for membership drinkers interested in closing Britain's public houses. Through his statistics on the Maine Law's reduction of Portland's crime and pauperism, Dow had helped the Alliance to recruit wealthy taxpayers and thus obtain ample financial backing. Dow's foreign followers had begun to agitate for a British Maine Law.

Dow had become a regular correspondent of Thomas H. Barker, one of Nathaniel Card's first converts. Born in 1818, the son of a cabinet-maker, Barker had grown up to become a clerk. In hope of improving his delicate health, he had decided to shun both alcohol and meat and had then become ardently active in local societies of teetotalers. In 1853, he had abandoned his own small accounting business at Manchester to become the United Kingdom Alliance's paid secretary and central driving-force. He had proven to be an able organizer and propagandist. To advance the cause of prohibition, Barker and the Alliance wished the Maine Law's author to tour Great Britain. "Do not let any mere difficulty hinder," the professional prohibitionist wrote Dow in December, 1856. "Nothing short of the 'impossible' must keep you from us." [3]

While Dow wished to accept the Alliance's invitation, he needed someone to attend to his personal affairs in his absence. Though still active, his ninety-year-old father could no longer bear alone the burden of managing the family tannery. Neal Dow decided to have his oldest son, Frederick, help his father. Early in 1857, he summoned home the sixteen-year-old boy from the Friends' School at Providence, Rhode Island. By ending the youth's schooling, he caused Fred to complain later that he had shown little regard for his son's future. The father had, however, earlier made clear to Fred that he did not intend to send the boy to college. Despite Neal Dow's own previous desire for more schooling, he shared his Quaker parents' fear of the campus' temptation to dissipation. Living in an age of strong paternal authority, he could easily disregard Fred's wishes in the matter. And, in any event, Neal Dow had often subordinated his family to the good of his crusade.

To aid Josiah Dow in advising Fred, Neal Dow relied upon Eben Steele, his old business partner, upon George H. Shirley, his temperance associate, and especially upon Charles A. Stackpole. Like Dow himself, the fifty-nine-year-old Stackpole was short and slight. At the start of the 1850's, when Stackpole had come from Bangor to edit a Portland abolitionist newspaper, Neal Dow had made the older man an important part of his political machine. Both he and Fred had won Stackpole's friendship. During his frequent absences, Dow had permitted Stackpole to exercise great influence over his son. Reinforcing Dow's own teachings, Stackpole had helped make the boy an extreme abolitionist and prohibitionist. Dow often urged his son to seek the advice of his co-believer. [4]

Besides providing for the conduct of his personal affairs, Dow felt the need of preparatory propaganda for his trip. He recognized the problem posed for him by the repeal of the Maine Law. On March 23, 1857, to counter possible charges that his law had failed in the state of its origin, Dow had his Portland followers hold a public meeting. The Dowites recommended their leader to the British temperance men and predicted the re-enactment within a year of the Maine Law. On April 7, Republican William Willis, the chairman of the Dowite investigators of the Portland Riot, won the city mayoralty election. The MAINE TEMPERANCE JOURNAL AND INQUIRER claimed that in electing Willis the voters had endorsed Dow's suppression of "a rum mob." Dow departed amid his supporters' loyal applause. [5]

On April 8, 1857, after a tearful parting with his wife and two older daughters who had accompanied him to Boston, Dow sailed on the Cunard steamship Europa. Swallowing a few pellets of nux vomica, he blessed the poisonous medicine for his freedom from seasickness. Dow generally had great confidence in the efficacy of self-medication. When heavy weather drove other passengers below deck, the sturdy little man wrapped himself in a shawl, huddled in the lee of the smokestack and watched with interest the crew's activities. He also disapprovingly observed his fellow-passengers' drinking and gambling. Dow proudly noted that, because of his reputation as a reformer, no one asked him to join these pastimes. Indeed, he believed that by his presence he might have discouraged drinking. On April 19, at the request of all the passengers including those hostile to his principles, Dow delivered an address thanking the ship's captain for a safe and pleasant voyage. [6]

On the afternoon of April 20, 1857, at Liverpool, Dow stepped off the Europa and into a controversy. At a small reception in a temperance hotel, he heard an officer of the United Kingdom Alliance read a letter written by John B. Gough to a British friend. Gough, who had given up drinking during the Washingtonian revival, was one of America's most popular temperance orators. From Gough's letter, Dow discovered that his fellow-agitator considered the Maine Law to be "a dead letter everywhere." Gough's previous endorsement of the Maine Law made doubly damning a reference to "the universal failure of the law to produce the desired results." Gough also referred favorably to Dow's overseas mission and later denied any intention of adversely affecting it. Because of Gough's "dead letter" allegations, however, the Maine Law Missionary faced a serious threat.

Dow learned that Gough's statements on the decline of the Maine Law, which were similar to those of a number of other American temperance men, had become a weapon in an existing dispute among British temperance men. The National and Scottish Temperance Leagues, two of Great Britain's important total abstinence organizations, had previously criticized the prohibition policy of the United Kingdom Alliance. Gough had written his letter to a leader of the National League and was to lecture in Great Britain under the two Leagues' sponsorship. From his Alliance hosts, Dow heard that members of the hostile temperance groups were using the "dead letter" report to discredit prohibition and himself.

Reacting immediately, Dow admitted Gough's high reputation as a temperance advocate but claimed that the Washingtonian had not inquired deeply enough into the facts. He acknowledged a general but temporary decline in prohibitionist activity, a failure to enforce the Maine Law in many areas and considerable drinking among the foreign-born. But he claimed continued success in rural New England and saw the victories of the Maine Republicans as auguries of a new Maine Law. On these grounds, he branded as untrue Gough's statement that the Maine Law was "a dead letter everywhere. " To get further evidence to use on his overseas tour, Dow soon afterward sent a circular letter to Maine Law men in the United States. At the same time, by having newspaper accounts of his British activities republished in Maine, he tried to promote his cause at home. As on previous occasions, the master publicist sought to drown his critics in a flood of propaganda. [7]

On April 23, 1857, at Manchester's Free Trade Hall, Dow opened in earnest his campaign to convert Great Britain to the Maine Law. He was nervous, as he later confessed, at the prospect of speaking in the country's largest auditorium. But from the hearty cheers of the crowd of 4,000, which intensive publicity had prepared for his coming, he speedily gained reassurance. He listened with pleasure as a welcoming speaker ranked his name with those of Washington and Franklin. After the laudatory introduction, the small, nattily-dressed Dow rose and stood alone at the front of the platform. At fifty-three, he still retained his handsome, youthful appearance. His long brown hair, falling to the base of his neck, gave his head a look of Byronic grace. As he gazed through deepset eyes at his greatest indoor audience, he joyfully recognized his opportunity to exercise the widest influence.

After the cheers and applause had died away, Dow spoke for about an hour and three-quarters. His freedom from the nasal tones common among many of his contemporary American orators pleased one of the British reporters present. The little man strained his mellow baritone voice in an effort to reach all the great crowd but, by constantly walking back and forth on the platform, he deprived the listeners at his back of part of his words. Dow offered the British audience the Maine Law to repay America's original obligation to his "father land. " He emphatically denied that the law which he wished to give to them was a failure. Illustrating his speech with vivid word pictures and touches of humor, he held his auditors' attention. As an exciting conclusion, he told how a British captain had once led a fleet through seemingly impassable waters to safety. The men of Maine were flying a banner inscribed "Dirigo" or "I direct, " Dow cried, and were calling on the world to sail behind them into a prohibitory port. Listening to the cheering throng and reading the wide newspaper coverage of his speech, Dow knew that he had acquainted many Britishers with his cause. 8

Upon consideration, Dow decided that he could accomplish even more for British prohibition through speeches to small gatherings of invited guests. At select breakfasts and dinners, he could reach clergymen and other community leaders. On April 24, 1857, at a "Soirée" for about eighty people in Manchester, Dow delivered an address and answered questions. Seeking to persuade the reluctant British teetotalers to embrace prohibition, Dow boldly asserted, "We have no temperance men in America at all who are not Maine-law men:-none. " Since the 1830's, Dow had declined to recognize as temperance men any opponents of drunkenness who did not profess his entire creed. Some of his listeners at the Manchester soirée questioned the United Kingdom Alliance's consistency in accepting the support of wealthy wine-drinkers. Dow replied that these "influential gentlemen, " while fighting the social evil of drink, might also become teetotalers. He joked that "they will perhaps know more when they are older. . . ." At every meeting, large or small, Dow stressed the need for political activity to repeat in Great Britain the Maine Law's American success.9

On April 27, under the sponsorship of the United Kingdom Alliance, Dow and Doctor Frederic R. Lees set out on a lecture tour of the British Isles. Dow respected his forty-two-year-old traveling companion's reputation as an able advocate of the medical arguments against alcohol. Lees, a Scot by descent, had taken the pledge as a sickly adolescent and still retained an unhealthy appearance. His blue eyes, bright brown hair and fringe of beard contrasted sharply with his pallid complexion. A British temperance man later recalled that had Lees "been put on a white horse . . . he might have passed for death in the Revealations [sic] . " Partly because the doctor acted as an instructive guide to Britain's antiquities, the studious Dow became Lees' good friend. The two prohibitionist lecturers devoted special attention to the industrial regions of Scotland and of the west of England. There the Nonconformist Protestants, among whom the British teetotalers had been successful, were most numerous. For seven weeks in the summer of 1857, Dow also made a pleasure tour of the Rhineland, Switzerland and France.

While on his temperance travels through Great Britain, Dow usually ate and slept at the homes of sympathizers. By his descriptions of the more noteworthy households, he made plain his enjoyment of the opportunity to observe British family life. Occasionally he visited members of the aristocracy. More frequently he was the guest of business men and ministers. Often, as he informed his aged Quaker father, he met a warm reception from Friends. When at Manchester, he invariably visited at the mansion of Wilson Crewdson, a wealthy Quaker teetotaler, and became particularly intimate with Crewdson's whole family. Sometimes Dow received invitations from men opposed to his views. He declined to make a special visit to one Irishman who had remarked, "I have just laid in a barrel of the finest whiskey you ever saw." Whether staying with teetotalers or drinkers, Dow constantly and with some success proselytized for prohibition. [10]

In his public speeches abroad, as he had so often done in the United States, Dow emphasized claims of the economic cost of the liquor traffic. He repeated and embellished the allegation of British temperance men that drunkenness was their country's "national vice." By his tactics, Dow appealed to industrialists interested in sober workmen and taxpayers eager to reduce their bills. He himself believed that he was impressing "thoughtful men among the influential classes." Frequently, however, as he later confessed, he saw with mortification John B. Gough's "dead letter" statement used to counteract his Maine Law propaganda. Moreover, the London TIMES and most other important newspapers opposed him. One editor, hitting Dow directly for his economic arguments, maintained that the Yankee visitor made up "for temperance as to beer and gin by intemperance in assertion." The Londoner charged, "He is a perfect drunkard when he comes to statistics. . . ." Dow began to realize that he would not duplicate in Britain his speedy American triumph. [11]

Dow attributed the slowness of the British to adopt his reform to their unprogressive nature. He saw proof for his belief in this British characteristic in the operation of their railroads. On October 12, 1857, while riding on a train between Carlisle and Lancaster, he noticed that the baggage on top of the second car in front of his was afire. Because the British cars had no inside corridors or signal devices, he could not easily warn the engineer. Quick to act and courageous, Dow stepped from his compartment onto a narrow footboard and started forward along the outside of the train. Holding on to doorhandles, he nearly fell off when a door flew open. He had nearly reached the engine before some track-workers stopped the train. Dow afterward wrote a letter to the London TIMES describing the American system of running signal cords to the whistles of locomotives. Referring to the subsequent failure to adopt his suggestions concerning either railroads or liquor-selling, he sadly commented, "New ideas, new ways of life and new methods in all departments, make slow progress in England." [12]

On October 14, 1857, to climax his British tour, Dow returned to Manchester's Free Trade Hall for the annual meeting of the United Kingdom Alliance. He was angry at John B. Gough for refusing to retract the "dead letter" claim. In a stirring speech to the meeting, the prohibitionist orator denounced as ignorant or wicked those who claimed his Maine Law was a failure. Dow also saw the Alliance adopt its first specific legislative program. While continuing to praise the statewide Maine Law, Dow's hosts only asked their Parliament to permit a two-thirds majority of the taxpayers in each of Great Britain's local governmental units to ban liquor-selling. Under the provisions of their Permissive Bill, which was similar to earlier American local option laws, the prohibitionists might win immediate victories in the areas of their greatest strength. On October 24, when Dow started his thirteen-day voyage home, he left behind a British Maine Law movement united in policy and slowly increasing in power. [13]

To remove the hindrance of the "dead letter" story to the British prohibitionists, Dow set to work to resurrect the Maine Law in his own state. Even before making his overseas tour, he had begun to suspect that the Maine Republicans might be unwilling to take the final responsibility for restoring prohibition. He had heard a rumor that his party might advocate submitting any new Maine Law to a popular referendum. In an anonymous editorial, Dow had opposed "leaving the whole thing to Pat Murphy and Shandy O'Connell, to say whether grog-shops will be licensed or not. . . ." Yet he had not publicly attacked the plank of the 1857 Republican platform calling for such a referendum. Nor, after the Republican victory, did he ask the legislature to re-enact the unpopular Intensified Maine Law of 1855. In the winter of 1857-58 at local and state temperance meetings, he organized a drive for the elimination of the Barnes License Law and a return to his original Maine Law with its 1853 amendments. After two years of yielding to his party's chiefs, Dow was again making a specific though moderate demand. [14]

But the prohibitionist chief discovered that the Republican leaders were unwilling to become once again mere registers of his wishes. He learned that a legislative committee, headed by his old friend and business partner, William W. Thomas, was drawing a bill acceptable to the "rummies." Dow anonymously warned that, if betrayed, the prohibitionists would disrupt the Republican party. On February 17, 1858, when Senator Thomas reported a feeble prohibitory bill to the legislature, he realized his worst fears. Through public meetings and personal interviews with Thomas, he fought for amendments but secured only part of them. In the new Maine Law passed on March 25, the legislature provided few of Dow's stern penalties for illegal liquor-selling. The lawmakers even allowed the sale of native wine and cider. Dow openly expressed his abhorrence for the provision of the law permitting Maine's distilleries to reopen for limited use. He saw, however, that the legislature had re-established at least the principle of prohibition. He could use the Maine Law of 1858 to strengthen his national and international propaganda. [15]

Dow still faced a referendum on prohibition. The Republican lawmakers had provided that on June 7, 1858, the voters could choose between the Maine Law of 1858 and the repealed Barnes License Law. Dow, however, later admitted that, because of court decisions against the constitutionality of referendums, the prohibitory law would take effect regardless of the result. Nevertheless, to demonstrate the popularity of his cause, Dow took the stump to get out the vote. The Republicans refused to make a party test of the issue and the Democrats largely shunned the polls. Dow won 28, 864 ballots out of a light vote of 34, 776. In the subsequent state campaign, while the Democrats sought to make capital of the return to prohibition, Dow's party emphasized the slavery issue. Yet, to his foreign followers, Dow presented the Republicans' victory in 1858 as a final endorsement of the new Maine Law. The September election, he claimed, proved that "every Republican voter is either a Prohibitionist per se, or yields that point. "[16]

Dow hoped that the restoration of prohibition in Maine would stimulate "a general uprising of the people in all New England, and indeed through all the free States, for another vigorous campaign against the liquor-traffic." As after the enactment of earlier Maine Laws, he and his Portland faction wished to set a vigorous example of enforcement. But the city's Republican authorities delayed active enforcement till after the September election and then prosecuted only what one temperance man called "the keeper of an Irish rum hole." They spared the Republican proprietors of "fashionable drunkeries." "Grogshops swarm all over the city," complained the local temperance editor on September 16, 1858, "and there is no attempt at concealment on the part of the occupants. . . ." Correspondents reported similar conditions elsewhere in Maine. Dow was still offering little more than a "dead letter" as an example to the world. [17]

But, when writers outside the state pointed to the new Maine Law's shortcomings, Dow leaped to its defense. Late in 1858 in the organ of the British teetotalers opposed to prohibition, he read that the Maine Law of 1858 "has failed to do anything very effectual at home and thus far has been powerless in its influence abroad. . . ." The writer of the allegation, the Reverend Theodore L. Cuyler of New York, was defending John B. Gough against the prohibitionist critics of Gough's "dead letter" statement. Dow, like Gough, was a good friend of Cuyler's and had once received a testimonial silver pitcher from the minister's hands. None the less, Dow did not spare Cuyler. On December 20, 1858, in a public letter, he claimed that the mere threat of enforcing the new law had halved Portland's liquor-sellers and had driven the remainder into "dark back places." He had the non-enforcing Republican mayor endorse his claim. Three days later at a county temperance meeting, Dow helped draft a resolution calling authors of "false reports" like those of John B. Gough and Theodore Cuyler "practical enemies in disguise." Regardless of facts or friendship, Dow would uphold the Maine Law's reputation. [18]

The Maine Law Missionary was using his state's prohibition law mainly as an instrument of propaganda in distant areas. On his British tour, he had seen both the increasing strength of his foreign converts and the damaging effect of the charge that his law was a dead letter. As a means of refuting criticism, he had sought to resurrect in Maine at least the principle of prohibition. In lieu of an effective ban on liquor-selling, Dow had reluctantly accepted and even defended the feeble Maine Law of 1858. While grumbling at the Republican leaders' failure to grant his wishes, he had not broken with his party on the issue. The reformer would seek the politicians' reward for his compromising course--and would receive unexpected retribution.

Chapter X

A FEARFUL FALL

"The cordial support of Mr. Dow at this time, by those who so firmly opposed him on past issues," remarked a Republican journalist in November, 1858, "may be hailed as conclusive evidence that an 'era of good feeling' has been inaugurated among the Republicans of Portland. . . ." With these words, the editor of the PORTLAND ADVERTISER urged anti-Maine Law men to reward Dow with a legislative seat for postponing effective prohibition in the interest of party unity. Dow was running, the editor emphasized, not as "specially the exponent of prohibition" but "simply as a Republican." Putting aside for the moment his attempt to stamp out Maine's liquor-sellers, the reformer again sought to realize the ambitions frustrated by the Portland Riot. Once more, he reached for political plums and gathered bitter fruit.

Dow and his Republican friends carefully arranged his return appearance before the Portland electorate. One of the Republicans elected in September, 1858 to the lower house of the state legislature declined to serve. On November 16, Dow obtained the Republican nomination to run for the post in a special election which he regarded as "an opportunity for a popular vindication." He later recalled that the Democrats, who had suffered a thorough defeat in September, "deemed it only fair to pay me the compliment of declining to nominate a candidate against me." On November 18, Charles Q. Clapp, the wealthy Democrat, kept alive the memory of the Portland Riot with a vote for "martyr" John Robbins. But with only 772 Republican votes, Dow easily overcame 56 scattered opposition ballots. To his British followers, he hailed his victory an an indication of the prohibitionists' strength. "The politicians are astonished now, and bow to us very respectfully," he arrogantly crowed, "and say, that we must have the Governor in 1859, and the Member of Congress in 1860." Ambitious Neal Dow still dreamed of power. [1]

Early in 1859 at Augusta, while attending his first legislative session, Dow followed a path well suited to lead him to the governor's chair. While on the floor of the House of Representatives, he shunned as he would a tippling shop the controversial Maine Law question. Instead, as chairman on the part of the House of the Joint Committee on Mercantile Affairs and Insurance, the businessman-lawmaker introduced routine incorporation bills. In debate, he loyally upheld his party. With a deceptively genial smile playing around his thin lips, the Portland Republican sarcastically slashed opponents. Dow, as a reporter noted, indeed had "a very smooth way of saying very harsh things . . . ." By his course, Dow avoided antagonizing anti-prohibitionist Republican politicians and inspired "intimations from many quarters" that the "old prejudices" against him were wearing away. At the same time, he addressed temperance meetings and continued to lead the state's Maine Law men. He had, in the words of a Democratic observer, the backing of the "old abolition and ramrod" prohibitionist Republicans. In the Democrat's opinion, when Governor Lot M. Morrill retired, Dow might well win the succession.[2]

In line with both his personal interest and that of his prohibitionist Republican faction, Representative Dow worked for the re-election by the legislature of State Treasurer Benjamin D. Peck. In the early days of the Maine Law movement, he had used the ex-minister's Portland temperance weekly to spread the Maine Law and to vilify its enemies. After early 1857, when Peck had received the treasurership, Dow had increasingly disapproved of the office-holding reformer's willingness to compromise with the anti-prohibitionists. In September, 1857, he had sorrowfully confided to his daughter, Louisa, that the fat, cigar-smoking Peck was an unprincipled politician. "Mr. P. richly deserves the 'blowing up' you mention," he had admitted, "but I shall not even reproach him. I have no heart for it. . . ." Dow did not mention to his daughter a hidden tie which bound him to the prohibitionist politico. Despite his misgivings about Peck, he had entangled himself with the State Treasurer in a web of intrigue.

When Peck had taken office in 1857, Dow had become one of his bondsmen. He had then learned that Peck was planning to lend the state's money to private citizens. While previous treasurers had often made such profitable loans, the 1856 legislature had forbidden the practice. Nevertheless, Dow had merely urged Peck to get good security for his loans and, in 1857 and 1858, had himself borrowed and repaid about $8000 in state funds. In October, 1858, another borrowing bondsman, Congressman-elect Daniel E. Somes, had gone into bankruptcy. Though Dow had made five trips to Somes' town of Biddeford to investigate his fellow-Republican's finances, he had been unable to recover enough money to repay Somes' debt to the State Treasury. At the year's end, Bondsman Dow and his friends had endorsed notes to help Peck conceal the large deficiency. Dow was out of town when the House Finance Committee, to which he belonged, made a perfunctory examination of Peck's fraudulent accounts, but he joined the rest of the 1859 legislature's Republican majority in re-electing the State Treasurer. Again signing Peck's bond, Dow quickly borrowed $11,500 from the treasury. The reformer was behaving like many of the politicians whom he had so often attacked.[3]

By borrowing again from the State Treasurer, Dow unwittingly drew closer to a financial precipice. Since 1858, Peck and several Bangor businessmen had been buying timber and building a sawmill in Canada. To the project, the

Bangor men had contributed worthless personal notes and bills embezzled from their city's Norombega Bank. Peck, however, had invested nearly $100,000--the bulk of the State Treasury. In the fall of 1859, with no profits in hand and an accounting drawing near, the State Treasurer turned to Dow for help in raising funds. Dow, who still owed the treasury $11,500, endorsed $10,805 of Peck's personal notes. He agreed in writing that, if Peck repaid the notes, he would still owe the treasurer the full amount of the original loans. While Dow later admitted knowing that Peck was buying timber "to a limited amount" and with personal funds, he claimed that he had believed that the State Treasurer was using for official purposes the $10,805 raised through the notes. The usually shrewd Dow surely had no inkling of the depth of the financial pit that Peck had dug for them. [4]

Toward the end of December, 1859, Dow began to hear from Portland financiers rumors that the State Treasurer's situation was perilous. To protect himself against loss, he induced Peck to give him title to the latter's house and personal property. The collapse of the looted Norombega Bank on December 28 exposed the Peck frauds and the broken treasurer went to Bangor to arrange for the transfer to his bondsmen of his Canadian property. On January 2, 1860, Governor Lot M. Morrill proclaimed the State Treasurer to be a public defaulter. As Peck's bondsman, borrower and intimate associate, Dow faced involvement in his ruin. [5]

On January 3 or 4, 1860, Representative Dow rushed to Augusta. Though he had won routine re-election to the legislature which was about to meet, he was more concerned with his role as representative of the Portland bondsmen. He recognized that their financial loss, unless somehow reduced, might be ruinous. On January 4, 1860, he called on Governor Morrill to learn the state administration's policy toward the bondsmen. As Dow told his wife, he found Morrill "everything I could wish." He learned that the Republican governor would not call for public proceedings against Peck, who had been chairman of the party's State Committee, nor for immediate payment by the equally influential bondsmen. Indeed, Dow understood Morrill to intimate that "by and by . . . if it should be necessary for the State to share the loss with the bondsmen, it could be very easily done." The relieved Dow felt "delighted to hear this as it was so proper and right." Two days later, Morrill assured the legislature that that bondsmen's obligations would "be honorably met, without embarrassment to the Treasury. . . ." But, while the governor had been indulgent with the bondsmen, the legislature appointed a special committee to investigate Peck's peculations. For Dow, who had borrowed from the State Treasurer, such a probe meant possible exposure. [6]

Dow had already begun to take desperate measures to hide his connections with Peck. He had first sent George H. Shirley, his trusty temperance lieutenant, to induce Peck to complete the transfer of the Canadian timberland to the bondsmen. On January 4, 1860, at Peck's temporary residence in the Bangor jail, the hapless State Treasurer had given Shirley the key to his safe and permission to remove the papers relating to Canadian lands. On the following evening at Portland, Dow's agent had taken from the safe not only the Canadian documents but also several other papers including Dow's acknowledgment that he had endorsed $10,805 in notes for Peck. These, together with the key to the safe, Shirley had turned over to Dow's wife. Dow later destroyed the memorandum of his endorsements and then paid off the notes in advance of their maturity. He eliminated the evidence of his dealing with Peck because, as he later explained, "he did not desire his name to be mixed up in any way with the matter."

On Saturday, January 7, 1860, while home from the legislature for the weekend, Dow acted at the behest of the other bondsmen to take possession of the rest of Peck's possibly valuable papers. After consulting two lawyers, he found ground for taking Peck's safe in the title which he had previously obtained to the latter's house and furniture. To aid him, Dow summoned his abolitionist lieutenant, Charles A. Stackpole, a teamster who was one of Dow's tenants and some tannery workmen. After dark, Dow loaded his party onto the teamster's sled and drove through the cold winter night to Peck's house. There, in an effort to avoid attracting public notice, he scattered his men. He sent Stackpole inside to persuade Peck's wife to give up the safe. After Stackpole's persuasion had overcome her objections, he had his men take the heavy iron box to the Merchants Bank and, two days later, move it to Director Neal Dow's own Manufacturers and Traders Bank. Dow and his fellow bondsmen had thus eliminated the chance that Peck might have hidden from them some remaining assets. 7

But Dow's attempts to avoid scandal and financial loss had not escaped the eyes of his many enemies. In January, 1860, some of these were already spreading a canard, perverted from a newspaper account of a recent fall by Dow from a beam in his tannery, that the Prophet of Prohibition had "fallen" into drunkenness. The Portland temperance newspaper inaccurately blamed Editor John M. Adams of the EASTERN ARGUS for starting the story on its rounds through the nation's press and accused Dow's old enemy of concocting "a little army of falsehoods" about him. The angered Adams took this as a challenge to begin on February 16 to publish rumors about Dow's borrowing from Peck and about his surreptitious removal of the safe. Adams, who had smarted for years under Dow's denunciations of Democratic misdeeds, vengefully jeered, "What a pillory for a moral reformer to be in." The effort by Dow to conceal his ties with Peck had merely provided his detractors with more missiles to hurl at his pillory. 8

Benjamin D. Peck, embittered by the seizure of his safe, confirmed in his testimony before the legislative investigation that he had loaned Dow $11,500. Appearing before his fellow-legislators, Dow claimed that he only owed the state the difference between the amount of the loan and the $10,805 worth of notes which he had endorsed and paid for Peck. The committee decided, however, that Peck had used the proceeds of the notes for speculation rather than for state business and demanded that Dow repay the entire $11,500. Dow then paid back all but $3000 representing the yield of one note that Peck had actually deposited in a state account. He submitted the question of his liability for that sum to the Maine Supreme Judicial Court which in 1866 ruled in his favor. But, by paying for Peck's notes and then repaying part of the original loan, Dow had lost $7, 805. Referring to Peck, the shrewd banker groaned that he was ashamed to have to have let himself "be imposed upon by such a knave."

Dow took comfort, however, in the committee's determination of the bondsmen's liability. "We shall have plenty left by favor of a kind Providence, for an economical housekeeping. . . ," he assured his wife. According to the committee's report of March 5, 1860, he and the other bondsmen for the year of 1858 shared a liability for nearly $15, 000 of the embezzled money. As an 1859 bondsman, he owed part of over $62, 000. In April, 1860, however, the commissioners appointed by the legislature to settle with the bondsmen decided that the responsibility of the 1859 bondsmen had not begun until the date on which the legislature had approved their bond. Seizing the opportunity to reduce their liability, Dow and the other bondsmen of 1859 quickly got the commissioners to release them for $37, 000. Since the bondsmen had already forced Peck to disgorge $30, 000 worth of timberland, Dow lost only $1, 666. 60 in the settlement of the 1859 bond.

Through the liberality of Republican officeholders, Dow also avoided ruinous losses under the 1858 bond. He and the other signers of the bond, who included prominent men of both parties, suddenly remembered that they had not personally attached seals next to their signatures. To his wife, Dow confessed doubts about the righteousness of quibbling about the seals but, because of his previous losses on the notes and on the 1859 bond, he decided to join the other sureties in resisting the state's suit against their bond. Successive Attorneys-General permitted the state's claim to twist through the courts like an interminable worm of red tape, growing ever larger as unpaid interest accumulated. By the time the bondsmen lost their case, only Dow and one other among them were still alive and solvent enough to be able to help pay a staggering total of over $64, 000. Dow was fortunate indeed that the two bondsmen obtained from the Republican-controlled 1872 legislature releases upon payment of $5, 026. 11 apiece, their proportionate shares of the original sum owed the state. Twelve years earlier, Dow had probably correctly estimated the total cost to him of the Peck frauds at from $12, 000 to $15, 000. While he had escaped complete disaster, he had paid dearly for his ex-friend's favors. [9]

Besides his direct financial losses, Dow lost in many other ways through his part in the scandal. Since the first published rumors of the fraud, the reformer had tried to keep himself stainless. But, in March, 1860, when he read the investigating committee's detailed description of his loans and of his attempts to conceal them, he saw his reputation plunged into the mire. "It is really diabolical," Dow moaned about the exposé, "but eventually will do me no harm, as I will be understood." While awaiting such understanding, however, he staggered under a barrage of abuse based on the report's revelations. ARGUS Editor John M. Adams vindictively reminded him that proud Lucifer had sought to "reform" Heaven and had gone to Hell. "From 'Silver Pitcher' heights to the purlieus of Peck's safe, is a fearful fall, " gloated Dow's Democratic enemy, "but a 'lower deep' still yawns!" At the time of the Portland Riot, the Republican press had sprung to Dow's defense against similar attacks but this time not even his political friends endorsed many of his actions. Never before had he fallen so low in public esteem. [10]

Though even some former friends had become cool, Dow could still find consolation in his family. He assured his wife, using an expression incongruous for a teetotaler, that her courage in the face of possible financial disaster was "a cordial" to him. He attempted, however, to shield her from the criticism of his own conduct. In the spring of 1860, when she went to Philadelphia to escape the damp cold of Portland, he admitted deliberately refraining from sending her a copy of the legislative committee's "malignant" report. Seeing the sadness over his troubles of his daughter, Louisa, Dow tried to strengthen her with advice to "trust in a gracious Providence" and to "thank God that he has preserved us to each other. " The reform leader, while usually preoccupied with problems outside his family, tried to be a good husband and father. [11]

By his interest in the marriage plans of one of his daughters, Dow revealed both his fatherly wish to be sure she found a good husband and his inability to give this parental desire priority over his other affairs. His oldest girl, Emma, had already married William Edward Gould, the son of the cashier of Dow's bank. Then, in February, 1860, Dow discovered that twenty-eight-year-old Louisa also had a suitor. When he received a letter from Jacob Benton, a New Hampshire lawyer, businessman and Republican politician, asking permission to propose to Louisa, he replied that he would make such inquiries as he thought "necessary and proper. " He wished to send George H. Shirley to Benton's home town to interview the local minister about the character of his prospective son-in-law. But he was already using Shirley as his agent in connection with the Peck frauds, business matters and Portland politics and therefore decided that Benton would have to wait until his lieutenant was less busy. Not until two months later, when Shirley was free to investigate and make an enthusiastic report, did Dow refer the matter to Louisa for her affirmative decision. [12]

While helping to slow the progress of a courtship, Dow's involvement with Peck set back far more gravely the Maine Law movement. In the fall of 1859, the Maine prohibitionists had begun agitating for the strengthening of the ineffective 1858 Maine Law. With an eye toward the requirements of his continuing overseas propaganda, Dow had wished to set a better example of enforced prohibition. Like a millstone, the Peck embezzlement dragged down his hope. After the disclosure of the State Treasurer's thefts, one temperance man moaned that "every grogshop in Maine resounds with fiendish scoffings. . . . " On January 18 and 19, 1860, when the scandalous news was still fresh, Dow and the other delegates to the State Temperance Convention confined themselves to innocuous resolutions. True, one of Dow's followers challenged the "vilest and most unscrupulous rumseller . . . , with all the magnifying glasses he can put upon his bleared eyes" to find that Dow him-

self had done a single dishonest deed. But the editor of the MAINE TEMPER-
ANCE JOURNAL admitted that even "some tender-footed temperance men"
were failing to defend their leader. Throughout the next fruitless legislative
session, Dow tried in vain to reinspire and reinvigorate his cold water cru-
saders. [13]

Partly because of the Peck frauds, Dow as a Portland Republican also suffered defeats. Before the municipal election in April, 1860, in Peck's home
city of Portland, the Democrats made a leading issue of the State Treasurer's
corruption. They also criticized the connection of two of Peck's Republican
associates, Dow and George H. Shirley, with the Portland Gas Light Company.
In 1855, while mayor, Dow had combined the city's fifty per cent interest in
the Gas Company with his own small holding of its stock to make himself one
of its directors. Four years later, with the backing of the Republican city
government, he had won the company's presidency. His aide, George H.
Shirley, had then replaced the Democratic company treasurer. Charging a
Republican plot to control the Gas Company, the Democrats gained the backing of wealthy stockholders belonging to both parties and won the 1860 city
election. Neal Dow joined his ardently Republican son, Fred, in grieving
"that the wicked are to triumph even for one year." The Gas Company president faced political decapitation.

While awaiting the fall of the Democrats' axe, Dow worked hard to increase
the Gas Company's efficiency. Always interested in mechanics, he personally
did much technical research into the quality of gas-making apparatus. In May
and June, 1860, Dow travelled over 1,200 miles through the northeastern
United States to inspect gasworks and to contract for 150 miles of new pipe.
He privately expressed contempt for one old company president who knew only
"that there is to be a good dividend twice a year. . ." and who did not realize
that, by energetically cutting costs and prices, business volume and profits
could be increased. Bustling Neal Dow was ever an advocate of growth for
his enterprises and for his whole native city. Yet even as he planned for the
future of the gasworks, he had his neck on the political headsman's block. On
July 18, 1860, when the agent of the recently-elected Democratic city government took control of the Gas Company's annual meeting, President Dow and
the Republican directors lost their official heads. They were partially victims
of the harm done to their party by the scandal in the State Treasury. [14]

Since the Republicans were eager to disassociate themselves from the treasury fraud, Dow found that his relationship with Peck had blighted his prospects
for high political office. During the legislature's 1860 session, the Portland
representative had little opportunity to continue establishing a record of conservative statesmanship as he devoted much of his time to his problems as a
bondsman. After the revelations of the investigating committee, the reform
leader no longer figured in speculation about future governors. Indeed, according to a Democratic editor, he escaped expulsion from the legislature
only because the Republican chieftains were fearful of "disaffecting the temperance cohorts." In September, 1860, he did not run for re-election. He

had gained little from his "opportunity for a popular vindication."[15]

Once again Dow's strong qualities had led to his downfall. When he had reacted with characteristic violence to the Portland Riot, he had helped to ruin his national Maine Law crusade. In like fashion, driven by the acquisitiveness that had enriched him, he had borrowed from Peck and had thereby unwittingly involved himself in the scandal of the State Treasurer's own speculation. He had shown his usual boldness in his attempts at concealment but, when they had failed, his reputation had fallen to an unprecedented low. True, he had held the loyalty of a Praetorian Guard of prohibitionists. But the general public had judged the reformer less by the business and political standards of his day than by his own previous moral pronouncements--and had found him wanting. To re-elevate Dow to a position from which he could seek to gain broad respect would require a great civil explosion.

Chapter XI

REFORMER IN UNIFORM

In the summer of 1860, Neal Dow eagerly listened to the rumblings herald-ing the eruption of the Civil War. The Maine abolitionist, who had for a decade scornfully read the threats of Southern fire-eaters to disrupt the Union, hoped "that the crisis whatever it may be, may come soon." Thinking of the antici-pated election of Abraham Lincoln, whose race for the presidency he was sup-porting, he grimly predicted that the South would "have an opportunity soon, to make up its mind--What it will do about it!" After the Republican victory, when protesting Southern states began to secede, Dow stood for coercion; not compromise. The man who had broken with the Quakers over his support of war was ready to help lead the fight against the secessionists. In January, 1861, he sent word to President-elect Lincoln that he was ready to raise "a regiment of teetotalers."[1] While he had no military experience, Dow, like many other civilian leaders, proposed to recruit among his own particular followers and on this basis would receive high military rank. He would at-tempt to use his new authority not only to crush "traitors" but also to advance himself and his favorite reforms.

Dow believed that the secession crisis might serve the end of the anti-slavery reformers. On January 19, 1861, he predicted that, if an outraged North marched into the South, "she would not return from her mission, until the question of slavery should be settled forever." He opposed the proposal of a Portland Union Meeting, conducted by businessmen and politicians of both parties, to abandon the Republican principle of opposition to slavery in the territories. Dow warned that such conciliation of the secessionists might demoralize "the party of freedom." On January 26 in an anonymous editorial, he cried, "Down with tyrants and tyranny though the land be deluged in blood . . . ." Even after April 12, when the Civil War began at Fort Sumter, South Carolina, he confessed to "a constant dread of compromise." Others might fight merely to restore the old Union. Dow would have no peace without the destruction of the South's "peculiar institution" and political power.[2]

The antislavery fire-eater did not immediately join the militiamen hurrying to conquer the new Southern Confederacy. With streaks of grey appearing in his long, curly hair, he was beginning to show his fifty-seven years. As he later recalled, he felt almost too old to expose himself to military hardships. Moreover, he wished to give his attention to paying debts incurred as a result of the Peck frauds. Finally, he was particularly anxious not to leave before the imminent death of his ninety-four-year-old father. In his civilian capacities, however, he at once aided the North. He hurriedly arranged with his fellow Portland bank directors to loan $250,000 to finance the raising of the state's first troops. Throughout the war, he also wrote and had his British disciples publish in their newspapers many articles upholding the Northern cause.

While delaying his own journey to the field, Dow positively forbade his oldest son, Frederick, to answer President Lincoln's first call for troops. He felt that Fred, a handsome twenty-one-year-old who resembled him, was too sickly to take the field. He promised his son that, if the war continued, one of them would don the blue United States uniform. On April 15, 1861, Neal Dow offered his own services to the governor "in any capacity in which I might be useful." And, after Josiah Dow's death on June 1, he made Fred a partner in the family tannery. As in 1857, when he had overridden Fred's wish for more schooling, he was tying the would-be volunteer to the ledgers and freeing himself to take the path to glory. [3]

Early in the fall of 1861, in belated response to his offer to serve the state, Dow received a colonel's commission from Governor Israel Washburn. He knew from the Republican governor's explanation that he owed his military rank to his leadership of the prohibition crusade. Colonel Dow, the governor hoped, would help revive lagging recruiting by attracting his temperance followers into the Thirteenth Regiment of Maine Volunteer Infantry. Dow quickly selected company officers throughout the state to help him fulfill the governor's expectation. His subordinates appealed for sober "young men of christian character" to flock to the colors of "the Champion of Temperance, Col. Dow." In the winter of 1861-62, as an anti-alcohol writer boasted, Dow rallied more than enough "men of the right stamp--steady, temperate--total abstinent, and even religious." [4]

Colonel Dow, with his accustomed sense of responsibility for his inferiors' welfare, paid close attention to the moral and physical condition of his command. Among the thousand men in his regiment's camp at Augusta, he found some who did not measure up to his cold water standard. Dow had one drunken recruit stripped of his uniform and driven from camp. While the temperance chieftain was unable to prevent other men from smuggling in canteens of liquor, he preserved the 13th Maine's reputation for being "the most temperate and moral of all regiments raised in the state." As both his sober and backsliding teetotalers shivered in the cold of the bitter Maine winter, he also contended with the problems of caring for hundreds of sick soldiers. Despite his difficulties, Dow disciplined and drilled his recruits into a military organization. After decades of leading verbal attacks, the ex-Quaker was in command of a unit armed with "carnal weapons" and eager for the fray. [5]

Early in 1862, Dow fought a losing battle to avoid serving under the command of Major-General Benjamin F. Butler of Massachusetts. The Republican abolitionist regarded Butler, who had sided with the Southerners at the 1860 Democratic National Convention, as one of "the extreme pro-slavery and pro-rum democracy." After the outbreak of war, Butler had led the Massachusetts militia to rescue Washington from the Confederate threat. Even then, Dow had feared that "poor Butler" would protect slavery. When he learned that Butler was raising an army commanded mainly by New England Democrats to invade the Gulf Coast, he decided "to decline going." But the uniformed Republican leader's appeals to Maine officials failed to save him and the temperate Thirteenth from inclusion in Butler's command. On February 11, 1862, Colonel Dow received his preliminary marching orders. By his effort to escape Butler, of which the general was well aware, Dow had only assured his commander's enmity. 6

On February 18, 1862, at Augusta, Dow loaded his regiment aboard a long train and rode with them to Portland. At his native city, he enjoyed a moment of martial glory. Riding "Billy," a family pet which he had chosen as his war horse, the little colonel led his blue clad soldiers on parade past cheering crowds. At his side jingled a fine sword presented by the city's businessmen and in his holsters were deadly-looking revolvers which expressed the patriotic pride of the Sons of Temperance. Resplendent in blue and brass, Dow began to feel, as he later told his wife, that he was fulfilling his early daydreams of military command. Before boarding the train to Boston, he dramatically signed his will. At the Massachusetts port, reluctantly obeying Butler's order to divide his regiment, he led four companies aboard the steamer Mississippi and sent the remaining six to take ship at New York. On February 21, Dow sailed down the coast. Within six months, he expected to return victorious or dead. 7

Four days later, on the morning after the Mississippi had anchored at Fortress Monroe, Virginia, Dow shrank from his first contact with General "Ben" Butler. According to the hostile colonel, Butler stormed aboard "in a very bad temper, and made a fool of himself." Dow contrasted his own quiet orders with the general's shouts, curses and threats to arrest subordinates. Examining his commander with fastidious distaste, he saw a paunchy, middle-aged man. Butler's long, stringy hair refused to mask the general's great bald dome. Dow immediately noticed with disgust the cigar protruding from under Butler's curved mustache. He also observed his cockeyed superior's deep-pouched eyes glaring like coals from under drooping lids. Dow scornfully speculated, ". . . why should not moral obliquities be petrified into a squint?" In his disgust with Butler, he began to consider quitting the expedition. 8

But before Dow had time to do more than fume indignantly, he was steaming southward with Butler. In a storm off Hatteras, followed by a temporary grounding near Cape Fear, North Carolina, the colonel directed his men in assisting the ship's crew and won the praise of even the hostile Butler. From

March 3 to 10, 1862, while Dow's superior tried to repair the damaged <u>Mississippi</u>, he and his men rested at Seabrook Landing, South Carolina. There the reformer in uniform relished the opportunity to drive off with fixed bayonets a liquor-selling sutler. "We are not embarrassed here by lawyers quibbles, and bonds and appeals," Dow exulted. "There is no appeal!" Loading his command aboard another steamer, he resumed his voyage down the coast in company with Butler's ill-fated <u>Mississippi</u>. On the way, he threatened to cut off a sergeant's chevrons for using profanity and delivered an address against swearing. At last, he could freely impose his moral views upon a segment of society. On March 20, when he sighted the expedition's base at Ship Island, Mississippi, he regretted returning to Butler's immediate control. 9

Dow would have scant cause, however, to complain of intimate contact with his commander. In April, 1862, when Butler ordered away the other regiments to attack and occupy New Orleans, the colonel remained behind on the seven-mile-long sand bar. Dow kept the 13th Maine, reunited for the first time since leaving Boston, busy loading supplies for the expedition. And, though his men were mentally cursing the midges and sand fleas, he held compulsory evening religious services to uphold the regiment's moral character. Inwardly, Dow himself seethed at his monotonous exile. He believed that Butler knew that he had urged Maine's congressmen to win for him a brigadier-general's commission and felt that Butler's purpose in making him commander of insignificant Ship Island was to deprive him of opportunity for glory. He bitterly remarked of Butler, "A bully and a beast cannot be anything else except by constraint. . . ." Even after receiving the coveted brigadier's commission in May, 1862, General Dow loathed his superior and his situation. 10

While consuming time on his isle, Dow had ample leisure to develop war objectives in accord with his social, sectional and political ideas. He opposed any compromise which might save slavery, lead to speedy reconstruction of the Union and restore the national power of "the old Democratic party pro-slavery party." Instead, he urged the freeing of the slaves, encouraged fugitives to escape to Ship Island and gave them work. He also favored confiscating other property of the "rebels." In June, 1862, in line with this policy, General Dow sent two expeditions to the Mississippi mainland to overawe the inhabitants and seize supplies. Finally, he suggested reducing the Southern states to territorial status. He believed that "a deluge of Northern people" would then pour "into this delicious clime with their capital, their churches, their schools, their free thought, free speech, free labor. . . ." Dow, like many another Yankee, wished to make New England's way of life the national standard. 11

Before the general had much opportunity to apply his theories to the Southerners near Ship Island, he received an order from Butler to take command of the forts in the Mississippi River delta. Butler also scattered the companies of the hapless 13th Maine among the several posts. At Forts Jackson and St. Philip thirty-five miles up the Mississippi River, Brigadier-General Dow would have only six companies under his immediate command. "This is an insult so gross and palpable that I shall try to be speedily relieved from it," he fumed to his wife. Dow instructed her to have Charles A. Stackpole, his Portland political lieutenant, request Vice-President Hannibal Hamlin and other prominent Maine Republicans to arrange for his transfer from Butler's department. But, while waiting, Dow could only obey. Late on July 11, 1862, he and two companies boarded a steamboat for the voyage from Ship Island to the mainland. By the following noon, he had steamed through a chain of sounds and lakes to reach New Orleans. [12]

While pausing for the Sabbath at the Crescent City, Dow unwittingly endangered his fame as a foe of alcohol. Before lunch on July 13, 1862, his landlord sent a complimentary mint julep to his room. Dow permitted the drink to stand until the soggy heat had consumed its frost and wilted its leaves. When the waiter returned to announce lunch, Dow had him remove the bedraggled julep. As the general fully anticipated, the thirsty servant emptied the glass before returning it to the bar. Dow had not, however, expected a newspaperman to see the julep glass apparently brought empty from his room. After the journalist sent North an account of the incident, the temperance leader began to receive clippings from American and British newspapers reporting that he was "succumbing before the seductive influence of a mint julep." He hastily denied that he had taken to drink. Throughout his career, the controversial prohibitionist was often the butt of such widespread canards. [13]

Leaving New Orleans on the following day, Dow rode a steamboat seventy-five miles down the Mississippi to his new command in the delta swamps. Early the next morning, he landed on the river's east bank at Fort St. Philip and looked about in horror. Everywhere he saw rubbish, weeds, rat-holes and swamp-growth. Moreover, he found that the massive earthwork and its consort across the river still bore the scars received during the Union capture of New Orleans. He despairingly felt that "the whole concern looked like a golgotha. . . ." Dow doubted that he could survive the summer in the pestilential ruin.

Helpless against Butler, the author of his misery, Dow vented his wrath in a petty quarrel with his second-in-command, Lieutenant-Colonel Frank S. Hesseltine. He had already decided that Hesseltine was a boor with atrocious table manners and a sneak who would pry into others' correspondence. "He is rude, hoggish and selfish to an extent that I have rarely seen equalled. . . ." Dow complained. At Fort St. Philip, Hesseltine demanded that Dow give all orders through him and twice countermanded the general's instructions to enlisted men. For this, Dow banished the colonel to the even more uncomfortable Fort Jackson. Noticing that Hesseltine was firing morning and evening guns before those of Dow's fort, the general deprived his subordinate of the right to salute the colors. In or out of the army, Dow reacted strongly when treated with what he deemed to be disrespect.

Several weeks after his arrival in the swamps, Dow contracted an illness, as he had feared, and took to his bed. At first, he thought that he was suffering one of his frequent headaches and "bilious turns." But he soon learned from a Southern physician that he had "intermittent fever." For ten days, the feverish, sweat-soaked little man tossed and turned. At the insistence of the doctor, he reluctantly swallowed three draughts of "'Scotch ale'" as a remedy. The teetotaler was sure in advance that an unfavorable reaction would more than offset any benefits of the drink. Easily satisfying himself that he was right, he recovered without drinking more of the medicinal Demon. He believed that the experience justified his opposition to all uses of alcohol.

Aside from the period of his illness, General Dow found his service at the river forts more pleasant than he had expected. Since 1841, when he had wished to superintend the repair of Portland's defenses, he had occasionally read about fortifications. Putting his knowledge to use, the industrious Dow found the opportunity for increased activity a welcome change from the monotony of Ship Island. He set his men to work cleaning and repairing the forts and personally taught the Maine infantrymen to load and fire the heavy cannon. When they had learned the lesson, he began to stop and inspect passing vessels. Dow also acted as jailer for the mayor of New Orleans and other political prisoners of Butler. As he did in most roles, Dow began to inflate the importance of his position. In early August, 1862, he predicted that the capture of his forts "might prove fatal to our cause. . . ."[14]

As commander of the river forts, domineering Neal Dow was king of the Louisiana swamps and bayous. He was far from his commander and enjoyed considerable independence. He even doffed his hot woolen uniform for light civilian clothing. Though out of uniform, he freely applied martial law to further his reform interests. The prohibitionist general sent troops to dump liquor and arrested one dealer. "How I wish I had the Maine rumsellers out here . . . ," he wistfully yearned. Heedless of the fact that slavery was still legal in Louisiana, he encouraged slaves to come to the forts and refused to return them even to pro-Union owners. He fed the Negroes government rations and used them as laborers, personal servants, cannoneers and guards for Southern white prisoners. Dow, a ruler in Northern society, was fostering social revolution in the conquered section. He was contemptuous of President Abraham Lincoln's slowness in adopting his abolitionist policy. On September 17, 1862, he predicted that History's verdict on Lincoln would be "'Honest intentions, opportunities lost.'"[15]

The vengeful zealot strongly approved, however, of Lincoln's authorizing commanders after July 22, 1862, to seize needed Southern property and employ captured Negroes. ". . . I have done so all along," he admitted to his wife, "but not freely." On August 17, he led a steamboat-load of soldiers and armed Negroes 40 miles upriver to Point á la Hache. There he arrested a planter whom he believed was recruiting guerillas, freed all the slaves in the parish jail and seized supplies for his garrison. On September 6, wishing to make lemonade to ward off scurvy in the teetotaling Thirteenth, he sent an expedition to confiscate sugar. He would later regret that his officer seized twenty-four hogsheads of sugar at a plantation belonging to a Union man. Indeed, Dow confessed to qualms at taking the property even of Confederates. But he finally decided that "Rebels have no rights, except what they may claim as a matter of humanity."[16]

As he reached this conclusion, Dow found it increasingly easy to seize "rebel" property. At first, he wanted only some furniture for his camp and "some nice trophies" to display at home after "the great war of Emancipation." While seizing sugar, he collected two fine chairs, several guns, some bed-linen and a large silver pitcher belonging to a reputedly rich and "bitter Rebel." Though he carefully cautioned his family not to let the Democratic Portland EASTERN ARGUS hear of it, he professed to have no scruples about sending home these "trophies and souvenirs." He argued that many other officers in Butler's Department of the Gulf had gathered much greater quantities of household goods. The usually property-conscious Dow was imbibing the spirit of a command in which looting and rumors of looting were reaching epic proportions. Yet Butler blocked his hopes for greater gain. When in September, 1862, Dow raised forty tons of the great chain used by the Confederates to block the river, he applied in vain to his commander for salvage money. And, when he sent officers to supervise the harvest on three abandoned plantations and dreamed of a share of the proceeds, General Butler transferred him from the region of potential profit.[17]

On October 4, 1862, Dow received Butler's order to take command of the District of Pensacola and expressed pleasure at the prospect. He would be further from and more independent of his hated commander. Two days later, he boarded a steamboat and watched the malarious forts vanish around a bend of the Mississippi. Stopping at Ship Island, he took aboard Butler who was inspecting the Department. On October 9, Dow sailed through the narrow entrance to beautiful Pensacola Bay and glimpsed his new headquarters through the lush, sub-tropical greenery. Indeed, he could see at a glance his entire domain since for practical purposes the District of Pensacola was only a fortified enclave around the town. Dow, however, looked beyond to greater possibilities. Even before he set foot on Florida soil, he requested his political aide, Charles A. Stackpole, to ask their allies in Washington to make him the state's military governor.

Dow had heard that his new subordinates at Pensacola were a hard-drinking lot. The prohibitionist general had resolved to "be moderate in my reforms and draw up the reins gradually. . . ." Reviewing the garrison with Butler, he confirmed his expectation. His senior colonel, William Wilson of the 6th New York Infantry, was a former Tammany politician. "Billy Wilson's Zouaves" were notorious for their drunkenness and lack of discipline. Besides Wilson's unit, Dow took command of two other volunteer infantry regiments and six regular army companies in the harbor forts. After inspecting the troops, the frustrated Dow watched Butler order up a gill of whiskey for each man and then adjourn to a "drinking room" in the commandant's house. That night, after Butler's departure, Dow angrily forgot his intended moderation. He closed the drinking room and then the taps of the commissary whiskey barrels. Heedless of his inferiors' resentment, he put Pensacola under prohibition. [18]

As at earlier posts, Dow also advanced his other interests. He told Pensacola's slaves that they were free and put them to work building an elaborate stockade around the town. Unofficially and without authority, he permitted some of his officers to drill Negro military companies. The general laid a heavy hand upon the white "rebel" population. He imprisoned several leading men for refusing to take the oath of allegiance and banished their families into the deserted countryside. He intensified his confiscation policy. During his first few weeks in Florida, he sent expeditions to abandoned villages nearby to collect livestock, forage and furniture. Professing strict observance of regulations, he warned that he would deduct from foragers' pay "the value of a dime stolen" for personal use. Dow filled his quarters with captured furniture, including rosewood pianos, and toyed with the idea of sending home the best pieces. He ate with "rebel" silver and even read a "Rebel Bible." "I could not endure," he proudly admitted, "that Portland . . . should lie prostrate and helpless before a Southern General, as this place does before me. . . . "[19]

Once again, however, the Republican general ran afoul of his old nemesis. From both Dow and dissatisfied subordinates, "Ben" Butler quickly learned of Dow's seizures. In late October, 1862, Dow received a warning from the departmental commander that "any officer" who sent goods North for his own use would be guilty of "plundering." Butler also countermanded as improper several of Dow's orders for the sale of seized property. And, in December, Dow learned that the Democratic ARGUS of Portland was denouncing him as a piano thief. The prohibitionist believed that "rum Democratic officers," angered at his stoppage of whiskey-drinking, were instigating such attacks. While charging his Democratic critics with the grossest corruption, Dow averred that he himself had intended to auction off the confiscated furniture for the benefit of the United States, in accordance with Butler's departmental procedure, and then legally buy any wanted items. Though he sent home a few more small articles, he conceded that "Rebel mementoes cost vastly more than they are worth in vile insinuations. . . . " Neal Dow had once again found that men whose morals he had denounced would quickly condemn any lapse on his part from his own professed principles. [20]

In mid-December, 1862, Dow had a momentary vision of relief from the hostility of his departmental headquarters. He heard that General Nathaniel P. Banks, a dashing dandy of a commander, had replaced Butler. Before the war, both Dow and Banks had fought against rum, foreigners and slavery. Both were Republicans. Dow thought it would be "grand" to have a friendly superior. But he found Banks' first moves disappointing. To clean up corruption and appease the Southerners, Dow's new chief immediately suspended sales of confiscated property. Dow vainly protested that without sales the "poor whites" at Pensacola would eventually steal the furniture which he had collected there. Then, he received Banks' order to leave his most controversial but happiest military post. On January 25, 1863, the general arrived at New Orleans and learned that he was to take command of a brigade of four untrained regiments stationed behind the city's massive upriver earthwork. He feared that he might have to live in a tent. Unhappy, "bilious and miserable," Dow began to doubt that he liked Republican Banks better than Democrat Butler. [21]

The "Abolition General," as enemies sometimes called him, soon had an additional cause to regret his return to Louisiana. In late January, 1863, he learned that Brandish Johnson, the Union man from whom he had mistakenly seized twenty-four hogsheads of sugar for Fort St. Philip, was suing him for their value in a Louisiana court. Johnson also demanded damages for silverware stolen by the raiders. For the first time, Dow discovered that the silver pitcher which he had sent home as a "rebel" trophy had come from the Union man's plantation. He asked his family to send back the pitcher and expected his government to pay for the sugar. But he was not to satisfy Johnson so easily. By giving refuge at the river forts to the planter's runaway slaves, he had so embittered Johnson that the latter was determined to strike at Dow's personal pocketbook and reputation.

Dow flatly refused to appear in the Louisiana court to answer Johnson's suit. He believed that, if he acknowledged the jurisdiction of a state court, he and other Union officers would face a barrage of suits for confiscated property and liberated slaves. In April, 1863, when he heard that Johnson had obtained judgment for $1,454.81 against him, he threatened to see whether the state court's "writ would resist my bayonets." He also won Banks' promise to annul the court's action. The persistent Johnson, however, later tried to collect the judgment through the federal courts and Dow placed his defense in the hands of the national government. In 1880, the United States Supreme Court ruled that Dow and other commanders in occupied territory had been subject only to military courts. Besides avoiding financial loss, Dow had established an important legal and constitutional principle. But, because the Democratic press widely circulated Johnson's charges of theft, Defendant Neal Dow paid a heavy fine in the court of public opinion. [22]

The harried general began to feel surrounded by hostile eyes and ears. He realized that, while he had the respect of the relatively few military men who shared his abolitionist and prohibitionist views, he often antagonized the rest. Soon after his arrival at New Orleans, he found that junior officers on Banks' staff were harassing him with extra duties. As for his superiors, he quickly decided that General Thomas West Sherman, the commander of his division, was no friend. He resented Sherman's scoffing at his teetotalism. Once, when Sherman tried to pour whiskey in Dow's glass, the prohibitionist general pulled it back and let the hated spirits spill. He sorrowfully reported that General Nathaniel P. Banks too, "though a Son of Temperance, habitually drinks now." Dow also was thoroughly hostile to Banks' policy of compelling unemployed Negroes to return to the plantations. In March, 1863, he supplied Northern abolitionists with ammunition for use in attacks on his commander. He thought continually about obtaining a transfer. [23]

But in the late spring of 1863, when Banks resumed the Union offensive up the Mississippi River, Dow cheered up at the prospect of service outside the delta swamps. On May 19, he expressed pleasure at receiving Banks' order to join the main army near the tiny village of Port Hudson, Louisiana. Confederate cannon mounted on the bluffs of the Mississippi's east bank at Port Hudson and at Vicksburg to the north blocked free use of the great river. Like one jaw of a steel vise, General Ulysses S. Grant was pressing down on Vicksburg. As part of Banks' force, Dow would assist the vise's southern jaw to crush Port Hudson. On the night of May 20 at Carrolton, the New Orleans suburb in which he had his headquarters, he directed the loading upon five steamboats of his brigade's four regiments. Next morning, belligerent Neal Dow rode up the Mississippi toward his first battle. [24]

Early in the afternoon of May 22, 1863, General Dow landed his brigade a few miles below Port Hudson. Hearing distant firing, he mounted "Billy" and hurried his men toward the sound of the guns. Back and forth he rode along the column to close up the ranks of his green troops. After a ten mile march through blazing sun and tepid rain, Dow learned that no battle was in progress. He bivouacked his tired men about five miles below Port Hudson and spent the night scratching fleas in a log cabin. During the next two days, he formed his men in line of battle and advanced over the Confederates' forward rifle pits. To his left, the Third Brigade of Sherman's Division anchored Banks' army to the impassable ground below Port Hudson and near the Mississippi River. To the right of Dow's position, Banks' center and right curved in a broken circle around the main Confederate works. Port Hudson lay besieged. [25]

General Neal Dow soon showed his lack of battlefield experience. Though warned that Banks would probably order an assault, he did not reconnoiter the main line of enemy fortifications in front of his brigade. Instead, complaining that he felt "too ill with headache to do anything," he stayed near his quarters in a crude shanty. He vainly tried to maintain garrison routine. On the afternoon of May 25, he ordered a band to play at a formal guard-mount. When the band leader suggested that the music might betray their location to the Confederates, the elderly general petulantly exclaimed, "If you're afraid to play, you'd better go home." But, as the cowed musicians struck up "Yankee Doodle," an unexploded shell ricocheted through the trees and another burst near Dow. He ordered an abrupt silencing of the fifes and drums. The reformer in uniform was beginning to discover differences between attacking liquor-sellers and besieging a fortress. [26]

Early on May 27, 1863, General Dow read with dismay General Banks' vaguely-worded order for a general assault sometime after 6:00 a.m. He had hoped to use siege tactics to win a bloodless victory but found that Banks, hungry for glory and fearful of a Confederate attack on the Union rear, had insisted that before midnight "Port Hudson must be taken. . . ." After a hasty breakfast, Dow rode forward through the woods which sheltered his brigade and looked for the first time at the main defenses of Port Hudson. Peering across about 500 yards of open ground, he saw a deep ditch in front of dirt parapets and gun emplacements. He felt sure that an attack against such a position would be a disaster. Believing likewise, Dow's division commander, General Thomas W. Sherman, took advantage of Banks' failure to set a specific time for the assault. All morning long, while Banks' right wing vainly threw itself into concentrated Confederate fire, Dow awaited Sherman's order to attack. Not until Banks had furiously ordered Sherman to advance the Union left or face arrest did Dow's commander act.

Early in the afternoon, under Sherman's direction, the equally unenthusiastic Dow formed his brigade for the assault. Though ordered by Sherman to organize his four regiments into a long, narrow column, Dow used a broad formation to prevent the Confederates from concentrating their fire and accomplishing "a universal murder of our men." Shortly after 2:00 p.m., he rode with Sherman to a place just behind the advance guard and ordered his men forward at the double-quick. As Dow emerged from the cover of the woods, he felt surprised to find himself so well able to control his fear of the whirring death that filled the air. He later claimed to have passed several dead soldiers as indifferently as if they were "harvest laborers, lying down at noon to rest." In crossing several fences near the Slaughter or Schalter plantation house, his men broke ranks and some lay down behind the fences and underbrush. General Dow, who himself believed that failure was certain and death likely for most of the attackers, reluctantly drove the skulkers forward. Amid the bursting shells, he could not control his frightened horse and therefore dismounted to climb the last fence between him and the enemy parapet. After the battle, he compared the spent balls striking around him in the Slaughter plantation field to "big drops of summer rain upon the dusty streets." As he urged his brigade forward, he felt the painful twinge of a spent shot bruising his right arm and then the sharper agony of a bullet drilling through his left thigh. Helped to the rear, Dow remounted "Billy" and rode slowly away from the field of slaughter. [27]

At the hospital, the wounded general learned to his relief that in passing through his thigh the Confederate bullet had missed both bone and artery. As for his brigade, its 354 casualties in the unsuccessful charge were less than he had expected but the toll among the officers had been heavy. Dow hoped to succeed the badly-wounded Sherman as division commander. Nursing his wound in a small house near his troops, the prohibitionist consistently wet his bandages "with water, no rum." He soon learned that Banks had chosen another brigadier who was Dow's junior in date of rank to replace Sherman. Rather than serve under the new commander, the Republican general decided to visit his friends in Maine to seek a transfer and perhaps a promotion. On June 12, 1863, two days before a second futile assault, he exasperated Banks with an application for leave.

Dow had already moved away from close proximity to the army besieging Port Hudson. He had disliked the dust and teamsters' oaths "in the Irish brogue" which filled the air around his house and had therefore moved by ambulance-wagon on June 6 to a small plantation home several miles in the rear of the Union army. He realized that Confederate cavalry operating in the vicinity made his more comfortable quarters extremely dangerous. Indeed, believing that the Southerners had captured two of his few bodyguards, he spent the night of June 29 hiding in a cotton-shed. Next day being again able to mount his horse, he visited his brigade and decided to rejoin the main body of the army that night. After dark, he rode Billy back to the plantation to retrieve his possessions. Entering the moonlit yard, he found himself covered by Confederate carbines. "Surrender, or I'll kill you," he heard one of the raiders shout. "I'll surrender, sir--I'll go with you," the unarmed general meekly replied. On June 30, 1863, Neal Dow had abruptly ended eighteen months of military command. [28]

Commissioned primarily because of his leadership in reform and politics, Dow had succeeded in attracting to the colors many of his like-minded followers. But, by seeking to advance the principles which had attracted his first recruits, the reformer in uniform had angered many other members of the army. He had lacked that natural ability to lead men of diverse backgrounds which enabled a number of other Civil War commanders to compensate for deficient military training. Through his quarrels with men who disagreed with his views, he had assured maximum exposure of failings common among his contemporaries but ill becoming a regulator of morality. Altogether, despite his personal courage and his battle wound, he had gathered few laurels. Dow would, however, need no martial skill to undergo the martyrdom of captivity. The imprisoned general would have a fresh chance to strengthen his prestige among his friends and his hatred for his foes.

Chapter XII

BEHIND THE CURTAIN IN REBELDOM

A prisoner of war, thought Neal Dow, was "like a sick man in a charity hospital dependent on nurses who have no interest." The imprisoned general explained, "He cannot help himself and nobody cares."[1] He felt keenly the complete reversal of his position. The proud conquerer who had proclaimed that Rebels had no rights was at their mercy. He who had enforced his principles upon his military inferiors would have to mingle on terms of equal lowliness with his fellow prisoners. For the first time in fifty-nine comfortable years, he would face real hardships. Yet, as a prisoner, Dow would also have unusual opportunities. By enduring captivity, he could regain popularity in his own section of the nation and help determine its attitude toward the South.

In the first hours after his surrender on the evening of June 30, 1863, however, Dow was most conscious of the ignominy of his position. Largely through his own carelessness, he had permitted six youthful raiders to capture him without resistance and far from the glamour of the battlefield. As his captors hurried him off on horseback along woodland paths, he seethed with both mental anguish and the pain of his barely-healed leg wound. Next morning, to add to his torture, thrifty Neal Dow watched the raiders cast lots for "Billy", his favorite horse, and for his fine sidearms. A few hours later at Confederate cavalry headquarters near Clinton, Louisiana, he poured his feelings into a letter to his wife. "I am very much chagrined and vexed that I am obliged to direct to you from this place under such circumstances," he moaned. While he admitted that most of his captors were courteous, the domineering general would not enjoy being subject to their will.[2]

Under guard, Dow journeyed by wagon and slow train across the South to Richmond, Virginia. On July 11, 1863, he arrived at the Confederate capital and soon was inside the thick brick walls of Libby Prison. A former warehouse overlooking the James River, Libby was the Confederates' principal prison for Union officers. In the commandant's office, the general found a crowd of Confederates curious to see "'the Neal Dow of Temperance and Maine-Law fame.'" Recovered from his initial gloom, he accepted in good spirits their banter about the honor of entertaining him. Dow humorously remarked that "under the circumstances their hospitality would be so pressed on me that I could not avoid it. " Learning that the belligerents had ceased the regular exchange of prisoners, he settled himself for an indefinite stay and jokingly begged his jailers "not to let me wear my welcome out. "[3]

The former ruler of conquered territory soon left Libby to face the charges of his subjects. An obscure Louisianian sent the Confederate Secretary of War an account of one of Dow's raids in 1862 along the Mississippi River. The Southerner told how the abolitionist general, aided by armed Negroes, had liberated slaves and taken them back to his river forts. On May 1, 1863, the Confederate Congress had resolved that any commissioned officer leading Negro troops or encouraging slaves to revolt would be liable to the death penalty. In accordance with these Joint Resolutions, Confederate President Jefferson Davis referred the accusation against Dow to a military court at Mobile. On August 1, 1863, in custody of two "officers of the Confederate police, " Dow himself set out for the Alabama city. He never learned from his captors the reason for the trip. [4]

Dow's family and friends, on reading in the newspapers of his transfer, began to worry. They heard rumors that the abolitionist general was to suffer shooting or hanging for "stealing negroes. " Even Dow's bitter personal enemy, John Neal, became concerned and at a Portland prayer-meeting besought the captive's safe return. In mid-August, 1863, thirty-three Maine citizens residing in Washington petitioned President Abraham Lincoln to take "special and exceptional" action to protect the hero of "the friends of temperance and virtue. " The United States authorities then warned the Confederates to treat Dow in accordance with the laws of war. On August 28, Secretary of War Edwin M. Stanton ordered Confederate General John H. Morgan, who was then a prisoner, held in close confinement as a hostage for Dow's safety. Meanwhile, unaware of the concern over him, Dow was living in the relatively-comfortable Provost Guard House at Mobile and suffering only from a lack of letters. [5]

The captive general none-the-less was under the shadow of the gallows. Unknown to him, the military court of Maury's Corps was investigating the original charge against him. The Southerners also took evidence that Dow, while in command at Pensacola, had freed and armed slaves. On the other hand, Judge Victor Burthe, a Louisiana refugee whose son Dow had held prisoner, testified to the Yankee general's kindness. On August 22, 1863, because its judges could find no proof of Dow's antislavery actions after the date of the Confederate Congress' Joint Resolutions, the court reported its failure to convict him. Confederate Secretary of War James A. Seddon ordered the abolitionist returned to Richmond and on October 12, Dow once again stepped into Libby's grim maw. [6]

After passing through the office of Captain Thomas P. Turner, Libby's youthful commandant, Dow climbed the stairs leading to the building's second story. He found himself in a low room about 45 feet wide by 110 feet long. In six such rooms on the prison's second and third floors lived over a thousand

Union officers. Dow, like all newly-arrived prisoners, heard their cries of "Fresh fish!" and became the center of a knot of men hungry for news of the outside world. Since their incarceration in Libby, none of the other prisoners had shared the general's opportunity for an excursion outside its walls. As the introductory excitement died, Dow quartered himself on the floor at one end of the second floor's middle room and became a member of a crowded, noisy and uncomfortable community. [7]

Even at Libby, Dow enjoyed better living conditions than most of his fellow inmates. Though the prisoners paid little heed to rank, Libby's lone general received some privileges. Instead of huddling in a close-packed row at night, he received adequate floor-space in the only room with glazed windows. From other prisoners, the general borrowed two coats and three old blankets to reduce the chill and soften the hard boards. He also borrowed from one comrade all the money he needed to purchase extra food in the local market. Because of his age and rank, he received exemption from the onerous chore of helping to cook his meals in the prison's smoky kitchen and was able to spend his waking hours writing letters, playing chess and reading the books of such diverse authors as Thucydides, Blackstone and Thomas Hughes. While Dow disliked his stay at Libby, he did not suffer extreme physical privation. [8]

General Dow soon discovered that two factions divided the disorganized Libby community. Lieutenant-Colonel James M. Sanderson, a bald, white-bearded New Yorker, was the center of one group. Because of Sanderson's experience as a hotel steward and corps commissary officer, some of the Libbyans had asked the colonel to supervise the prison's kitchen and mess system. Sanderson had efficiently brought order out of the cooking chaos. He himself had set so good a table that envious prisoners called his mess the "Royal Family." But, by his strict discipline, he had angered many of his comrades and had especially antagonized Colonel Abel D. Streight of Indiana. A profane, burly braggart, Streight had arrived under a cloud of rumors that he had made a dishonorable surrender of his command. To demonstrate his loyalty, he had loudly complained about the prison conditions. After early September, 1863, when Sanderson had endorsed a denial of some of Streight's allegations, the Indiana colonel had become the leader of a venomous anti-Sanderson cabal.

Dow quickly chose sides. He found that, while Streight was a Radical Republican like himself, Sanderson was a Democrat. The former hotelman also liked liquor and despised prohibitionists. To an officer who became one of Dow's intimates, Sanderson had remarked that the temperance general was "neither a soldier nor a gentleman. . . ." Moreover, Dow noticed that Sanderson who in peacetime had often catered to Southern travellers was on friendly terms with the jailers. This Dow interpreted as disloyal fraternizing. Shortly after his arrival, he heard and believed an unsupported rumor spread by Streight that Sanderson had betrayed an escape plot to the Confederates. The general decided to have nothing to do with the New Yorker and the policy of conciliating their captors. Allying himself with the Streight faction, he became one of the most vocal critics of the Confederacy. [9]

Shortly after his return from Mobile, Dow attempted to encourage his fellow prisoners with a speech predicting a speedy Southern collapse. Before beginning, he posted sentinels. When they warned of the approach of a Confederate officer, he quickly shifted his verbal attack from the "rebels" to the "rumsellers." In all, during his stay in prison, he spoke five times on the war and temperance and pleased those prisoners who shared his political and prohibitionist views. The able orator persuaded even some who were normally unenthusiastic for temperance to sign the teetotal pledge with such mental reservations as "'till we get where whiskey is cheap.'" But, by advocating total abstinence in a place where canal water was the usual drink, he confirmed Sanderson's friends in their belief that he was an "oldwomanish" fanatic. [10]

The general also described life "behind the curtain in rebeldom" to his President and Secretary of War. He had specially exchanged prisoners smuggle out his letters in which he told of the South's increasing desertions, depreciating currency, weakening rail network and failing morale. Though he recognized the Confederates' shortages of food and transportation, he also complained most bitterly about the meager prison rations of rice or beans, bread and beef. On several days in late October and early November, 1863, as he pointed out, he received only a few potatoes, some cornbread made of unsifted meal and no meat. He vividly portrayed the hungry prisoners huddled together for warmth on the hard, cold floor. He entreated that, in retaliation, Southern officers in Union hands "may at once be subjected to the same treatment that we suffer." [11]

Dow, Streight and other complainants about prison conditions aroused great sympathy in the North. At the end of October, 1863, they began to receive blankets, clothing and food from their government, the United States Sanitary Commission and private friends. As the senior Union officer at Richmond, General Dow distributed the supplies to the Libbyans. He then got the Confederates' permission to divide the remainder of the first shipment among the imprisoned Union enlisted men. On November 5, after giving his parole, Dow rode in an ambulance wagon over the nearby bridge to Belle Isle in the James River. On the low island within sight of the Confederate Capitol, he found 5,400 cold, hungry and indescribably filthy prisoners. Some, having no tents, slept like animals in holes in the earth. Dow confessed that Libby's privations, compared with those of the Belle Isle camp, "were as joys of Elysium."

Moved to sympathy, General Dow made a speech to the ragged prisoners. He assured them that the Union officers shared the same inadequate rations and that their government had sent an ample supply of clothing. In conclusion, overlooking the prisoners' desperation and lack of discipline, he urged all who were in need to come to him. As the sufferers rushed forward and crowded around the boxes of stores, the elderly general desperately attempted to supply them. In the confusion, as Dow later understated, he had "reason to believe that many articles were unaccounted for." When a guard lunged with a bayonet at one close-pressing prisoner, he remonstrated with the Confederate.

But, because he lacked enough clothing for all, he finally needed the guards to protect him from the disappointed, cursing prisoners. The former nativist angrily remarked to the island's commandant that some of the Union enlisted men were "the rakings and scrapings of Europe." Despite good intentions, Dow had once again demonstrated his inability to deal with men unlike himself.

Safely back at Libby, Dow gave the other officers and his superiors at Washington a lurid account of Belle Isle. He claimed that the prisoners there were dying at the rate of eight or ten a day and predicted a daily loss by January of one hundred. On November 8, 1863, Dow asked Brigadier-General John H. Winder, the Provost Marshal of Richmond, to improve the Union enlisted men's "very wretched" condition. He further requested the Southerner to permit him and six Union officers to make a more efficient distribution of an additional supply shipment. From subordinate Confederate prison officials, Winder also received complaints about Dow's "contemptible and false" description of Belle Isle and about his "unsystematic and loose" method of distribution. A choleric old martinet, Winder summarily revoked Dow's authority to visit the enlisted men's prison. Dow had another score to settle with the "rebels."[12]

To Dow's disgust, he soon learned that the Confederates had placed Lieutenant-Colonel James M. Sanderson in charge of distributing supplies. His initial hostility toward the New York colonel thereafter grew apace with his hatred for the prison authorities. Through some of his friends, whom Sanderson sometimes took to Belle Isle, he collected reports of his replacement's activities. He learned that Sanderson was displaying courtesy toward the prison authorities and demanding from the undisciplined prisoners at least a show of military respect. Already sure that Sanderson was a pro-Southern traitor, Dow readily believed false rumors that the colonel was kicking, cursing and generally oppressing the Belle Islanders. In his diary, he began to compile a "black list" of Sanderson's misdeeds against a day of vengeance.[13]

As for the Confederates, Dow intensified his earlier feeling against them to a deep and consuming passion. By his earlier demands that his government worsen the condition of imprisoned Confederates, he had helped to increase the Libbyans' own hardships. From mid-December, 1863, to late February, 1864, because the retaliating United States prison officials had stopped delivering packages to Confederates in the North, the Southerners cut off shipments to their captives. Before the ban, Dow had laid in an ample stock of blankets and food. He shared his store with his friends but appeared selfish to those outside his circle. Dow blamed the Confederacy for the privations of some friendless prisoners and began to regard every action of his jailers as a deliberate oppression.[14]

Dow particularly resented the Confederates' interference with his mail. He had early found a way to evade the prison's censorship. After warning his family through a smuggled letter, he had begun to fill blank portions of his regular correspondence with notes written in lemon juice. Through these invisible messages, he was able to discuss in privacy such home matters as the engagement of his son, Fred, and the accidental burning of the family tannery. But another prisoner, before beginning to write in lemon juice, included an open instruction to heat the letter and thus revealed to the prison censor the method of making the hidden writing visible. On February 1, 1864, to provide for more thorough censorship, the Confederates limited each prisoner to writing one letter of six lines each week. Dow complained that the "intensely mad" officials were seeking "every and any opportunity to vent their wrath."15

The general became even more irritated at Confederate precautions against escape. He himself had donated a long rope taken from a bale of blankets to aid a group of prisoners digging a tunnel out of Libby's basement. But, when they escaped on the night of February 9, 1864, he felt too old and infirm to go along. He stayed to endure the Confederates' numerous roll calls, searches of the prison and other attempts to prevent a repetition of the escape. Like most of his fellow prisoners, he associated none of the jailers' new measures with the Libbyans' own conduct. Instead he commented, "Everything done here is calculated, and we believe, intended to annoy us and make us suffer."16

In early March, 1864, when Union cavalry raided near Richmond, Dow found confirmation for his worst suspicions. On March 1, he learned that Libby commandant Thomas P. Turner had ordered his men to shoot any prisoner seen at a window. As Dow later admitted, the Libbyans had been signaling to Union sympathizers in the city. Two days later, the general heard accurate rumors that the Confederates had buried several hundred pounds of gunpowder in the Libby basement. From several Southerners who hoped to overawe the prisoners, he learned that the jailers intended to blow up the building, if necessary, to prevent its inmates from breaking out to join the attacking cavalry. The failure of the Union raid averted the danger. Dow, however, urged his government not to defer any future attack for fear of the prisoners' safety. Flaming with fury against the Confederates, he relied upon a threat of "the entire desolation of the Rebel States, with fire and sword . . ." to dissuade the jailers from lighting the fuse.17

The bitter old general hoped for a speedy opportunity to expose and punish his enemies. In late January, 1864, he had hurriedly sent word to his son, Fred, and to Maine Republicans in Washington that the Confederates might be willing to exchange him for the also imprisoned General Fitzhugh Lee. Fred had personally visited President Abraham Lincoln to urge the exchange. On February 24, Dow had learned that his government had agreed to the Confederate proposal. While awaiting his freedom, Dow began preparations for vengeance. He jotted down the names of witnesses to Confederate atrocities and carefully noted the location of the home of Libby commander Thomas P. Turner. By the time he received his order to leave, he had made his intention obvious to the Southerners. One of them joked, "We suppose you will give us [Hell] when you get North of the Potomac!"18

At the moment of his departure on March 14, 1864, thrifty Neal Dow furnished his enemies with final proof of what they regarded as his "selfishness." Filling two large trunks with his pile of blankets, his palate-tempting delicacies and his other possessions, the tightfisted Yankee asked another officer being exchanged to help carry them out. The man scornfully replied that he had left his own supplies for the remaining prisoners and "must decline the honor" of aiding the general. Dow was also unable to get a dray from the Confederates. Finally, he persuaded several other Union officers to help him move the trunks from Libby to a nearby dock on the James River. After resentfully submitting to a final search of his person, he then boarded the Confederate flag-of-truce steamboat and set off downriver to freedom--and to revenge.

That evening at City Point, Virginia, General Dow set foot on the New York, the United States flag-of-truce boat, and stood once again under the stars and stripes. Having had no food since breakfast, he had a headache. He heard Major John E. Mulford, the Union Commissioner of Exchange, direct a Yankee sergeant to carry the small valise of General Fitzhugh Lee, his Southern counterpart, aboard the Confederate steamboat. Exploding, Dow ordered the sergeant to put down Lee's bag. "When I left Richmond," he peevishly complained, "the Confederates would give me no assistance, and you shall give him none!" But Mulford, despite the old general's ruffled feelings, had the sergeant carry Lee's handbag. Balked in his first attempt at revenge, Dow devoted part of his journey North to collecting from other exprisoners evidence which he could use to expose the secrets of Richmond's "horrible Prison House."19

On March 18, 1864, Dow reached Washington. After collecting nearly $3,000 in back-pay, he went to the Capitol, thanked several of the influential politicians who had helped to arrange his exchange and visited the floor of the House of Representatives. Wearing his makeshift prison garb which included a captain's coat and a private's trousers, the little man appeared incongruous amid the expensively-dressed congressmen. As they crowded around him to hear of his experiences, Dow saw a chance to further his desire to humble the South. He had come to believe, through conversations with Confederates, that the re-election of President Lincoln would complete the destruction of enemy morale. Despite his past distrust of Lincoln's moderate policy toward slavery, he urged the Republican politicians to support the president's renomination. He also arranged to supply a congressman with an account of the Libby "Gunpowder Plot." Before going home to a round of public receptions, he had begun his vengeance.20

Two days after an affectionate reunion with his family at Portland, the former prisoner continued his attack on his ex-captors. On March 24, 1864, at a rousing meeting at Portland's New City Hall, Dow arraigned the slaveholding Southern "semi-barbarians." Forgetting his earlier good treatment at Mobile, he dwelt on his jailers' recent short rations, strict regulations and threat to blow up their captives. He exaggerated even the horrors of Belle Isle. The embittered general aroused cheers with a rhetorical promise to the Southerners that the North would "strike a balance with them one of these days." Turning to the forthcoming presidential campaign, he made a thinly-veiled assault on the Northern Democrats and again urged Lincoln's re-election. Dow mailed out many newspapers containing his diatribe and permitted its use as a Republican campaign document. Through his period as a prisoner of war, he had renewed his popularity and influence. [21]

In his vengeful mood, Dow remembered his replacement at supply distribution, Lieutenant-Colonel James M. Sanderson. Colonel Abel D. Streight, leader of the anti-Sanderson faction, had already attacked the recently-exchanged commissary officer. On April 4, 1864, in response to a War Department request for additional evidence against Sanderson, Dow charged his old foe with betrayal of an escape plot, cruelty to the Belle Isle captives and sympathizing with the enemy. As Dow himself admitted, he based his damning indictment on hearsay evidence but he none the less won Sanderson's dismissal from the service. A year later, Dow's opponent succeeded in getting a military commission to review the case, acquit him and censure Dow for making unsupported accusations. By publishing the commission's verdict and other documents, Sanderson also attempted to arraign Dow before the "great bar of Public Opinion" for "knavery and sneaking." [22]

While continuing prison quarrels, Dow felt too old and infirm to resume fighting in the field. His long hair and the bushy sideburns which he had begun to wear had turned grey. Weakening eyesight had compelled him to use reading glasses. After his release from Libby's cramped quarters, the aging general had tired himself by the sudden increase in exercise and had contracted a bad cold. For some months, he also had attacks of vertigo. Though soon well enough to supervise the rebuilding of his tannery on a site outside the residential district, Dow was beginning to feel the weight of his sixty years. Through the bloody summer and fall of 1864, he remained on half pay in Portland and left to younger men the pursuit of martial glory. [23]

Until the end of the fall electioneering season, Dow obtained extensions of his leave from the War Department. At "Union" meetings prior to the state and national elections, he delivered speeches against the Democracy or, as he called it, the "infamous, infernal Copperhead party." Learning the result of the presidential election, the ardent Republican rejoiced, "Lincoln re-elected by an immense majority and the country saved." But, after the election, he received no more extensions of leave. While he often considered returning to the field, he finally decided that he was too broken in health. On November 28, 1864, Brigadier-General Dow resigned his commission and thus ended his active role in the national conflict. He continued, however, to wage his personal war against the South. [24]

Dow carried his wartime spirit into the peace. In the spring of 1865, as the Confederacy sank down in defeat, he considered ways to safeguard the Northern victory. He proposed executing "a very few" of the "rebel" leaders, exiling the rest, disfranchising all officers of the rank of colonel or above and confiscating their property "to make good the losses of Southern and Northern loyal men." Shortly after the assassination of Abraham Lincoln on April 14, 1865, he privately opined that the death of the "illustrious martyr" was "fitting and opportune. " According to Dow, only a president without Lincoln's "kind, generous and magnanimous heart" could deal "properly with the wickedest traitors that the world has ever seen. " The ex-prisoner wished to break completely the power of the South's old leaders. [25]

Besides his prison-stimulated hatred, Dow had other reasons for favoring a harsh and thorough reconstruction of the South. As an abolitionist, he believed that if "the Rebel states should be readmitted to the Union" without security for "the rights and liberties of the blacks, the sin, shame and infamy to the North will be very great. . . ." He feared that ex-Confederates might reduce the Negroes to near-slavery and regain national dominance. Later in the Reconstruction Period, the Portland tanner worried that congressmen from a resurgent South might eliminate the protective tariff and load their section's war losses upon the Northern taxpayers. As a bank director, he expressed particular concern lest a Southern-supported Democratic administration decide to repay United States bonds in greenbacks instead of gold. Dow wished to safeguard the antislavery, political and economic fruits of Northern victory. [26]

The Republican politician believed with an intensity heightened by his imprisonment that only the Radical Republican policy of stern reconstruction would protect the results of the war. When President Andrew Johnson broke with the Radicals, he growled, "Hang Johnson up by the heels like a dead crow in a cornfield, to frighten all his tribe. " To help elect Republicans, Dow exploited his reputation as a leading prisoner of war. In speeches, he used the story of Libby's atrocities to turn Northern voters against "democratic-copperhead-rebel" candidates. [27] During the bitter Civil War, he had completed in his own mind the identification between partisanship and patriotism. In peacetime, he would eventually face the problem of distinguishing between the interests of his victorious party and those of his own prohibition crusade.

Chapter XIII

A VOICE CRYING IN THE WILDERNESS

In the period after the Civil War, Neal Dow found his prohibition crusade in a sorry state. The decline of the movement from its high point of the mid-1850's had continued. Dow had noticed during his army career how other teetotalers in uniform had abandoned their interest in the cause and had taken to drink. Behind the lines, officials had reacted to the decreasing pressure for prohibition by repealing or ceasing to enforce their Maine Laws. Dow wrathfully watched 300 illegal dealers in his own small city of Portland pour forth an almost unchecked flow of beer, wine and spirits. From the viewpoint of the Maine Law leader, his prohibitory paradise had become a wilderness wet with the Demon Rum. Overcoming indecision induced by fear of hurting his party, Dow would again call upon voters to use his political tactics to dry up the land. He would raise the loudest of the voices preparing the way for prohibition.

Dow first helped to revive the moribund temperance organizations. From August 1 to 3, 1865, at Saratoga Springs, New York, he attended the Fifth National Temperance Convention. There he met such veteran supporters of the movement as New York philanthropist Edward C. Delavan and also younger prohibitionists. When James H. Black of Pennsylvania, a lawyer and Methodist leader, pushed for the establishment of a publishing organization to provide a solid financial base for temperance propaganda, Dow and the other delegates agreed to replace the dying American Temperance Union with a National Temperance Society and Publishing House. The prohibitionist leader himself took the floor to silence a few dissidents who favored the shelving of the Maine Law agitation and a return to moral suasion. In rebuttal, he proclaimed that the annihilation of liquor-selling was the only final cure for intemperance. Admitting that during the war Maine's prohibitionists had permitted the election of anti-prohibitionist officials, Dow promised to resume his appeals to the voters to elect loyal enforcers of his law.

But, when the Republican prohibitionist sought to recoup his crusade's wartime losses, he soon discovered that the Civil War period had not similarly weakened his opponents. By imposing new taxes on beer and whiskey, his own party's national administration had begun the process of discouraging small brewers and distillers and hurrying centralization in the manufacture of those beverages. To lobby against additional taxes, the growing beer and whiskey companies had for the first time formed powerful trade associations. The united liquor interest also rallied the increasing number of foreign-born voters against the prohibitionists and their political friends. As Dow had once thrown the balance of power against Maine's dominant Democracy, so his enemies threatened recently-entrenched Republicanism. In the decade after the Civil War, worried Republican politicians in Connecticut, Massachusetts and Michigan repealed their state's Maine Laws and even in Maine, New Hampshire and Vermont, the remaining prohibitory states, Dow and his friends could not secure adequate enforcement. To overcome the political power of the anti-prohibitionists, Dow faced the problem of recruiting a huge army of voters. [1]

Meeting the challenge, he prepared to devote even more of his time to prohibitionist propaganda. Since the early 1850's, he had put most of the responsibility for the day-to-day conduct of his tannery and other business first upon the shoulders of his father and then upon those of his older son. The latter, whom he had made a partner in 1861, was becoming an increasingly able businessman. In the winter of 1868-69, when for the second time the tannery burned down, the elder Dow blessed his foresighted Frederick for insisting upon the insurance which enabled them to rebuild. Five years later, however, learning that his frail son was not well enough to continue managing the tannery, Neal Dow closed their plant and thus ended his family's long connection with the trade. Soon afterward, he also concluded his forty-one year career as a bank director. He retained his earlier investments in stock and in Portland real estate. With an ample income from dividends and rents, the successful capitalist was more free than ever to work for the temperance cause. [2]

In the years following the Civil War, Dow became a professional publicist for prohibition. He wrote both paid and unpaid articles for religious and reform journals. For the paid essays, on which he sometimes spent no more than an hour, he collected $10 or $15. "I think ever so much of money earned that way, ten times more than of rents or dividends. . . ," exclaimed the studious writer. Any "blockhead," he proudly explained, "may have ever so much" in the latter way "--and ever so many do!" Dow also began to ask payment of his expenses for delivering temperance lectures. Since, however, he often travelled free through railroad passes, he was using the term "expenses" as a euphemism for "fees." He varied his price for a speech from $20 to $50 according to the meeting's size, distance from Portland and proximity to others. Feeling a need to justify the payments to posterity, he explained through his diary that he had suffered heavy losses in the Peck embezzlement, the two tannery fires and the liquidation of his business. "Do not like to speak of pecuniary matters," alleged the tightfisted old Yankee, "--So many others vastly more important."

No matter what the size of his fee, Dow gave each sponsoring group an effective, expert address. To reassure himself before beginning, he developed the habit of pausing for a silent prayer for divine assistance. "Often from being very anxious--I become quiet and calm--with no nervousness, " he remarked. Guiding himself with brief outlines written on cards, he would then speak from one to two hours. He supported his arguments for prohibition with cardboard-mounted newspaper articles on the costliness of the liquor traffic and on the success of the Maine Law. Dow, raising his firm baritone voice to an emotional pitch, particularly liked to quote Senator Lot M. Morrill's arraignment of liquor-selling as "'the gigantic crime of crimes.'" For twenty years after the Civil War, Dow made frequent lecture tours in the region from Maine to Iowa and from Canada to the upper South. No one man did more to propagate the gospel of prohibition. [3]

During the postwar period, Dow also devoted his attention to Great Britain. There, in contrast to the demoralization of his American associates, the prohibitionists had gained in numbers and influence. Through correspondence with Secretary Thomas H. Barker of the United Kingdom Alliance, Dow had counseled his British disciples and had learned of their progress. The well-financed Alliance, despite the continued opposition of some teetotalers to its concentration on legal measures, had become the nation's leading anti-alcohol group. Using tactics similar to Dow's, it had introduced a "vote for vote" plan of endorsing parliamentary candidates pledged to support the Alliance's Permissive Bill for a "Local Veto" on liquor licenses. The Alliance had made local option prohibition at least a minor British election issue. In 1865, Dow received an invitation from his friend Barker to come over in the fall to lend the authority of the Maine Law's author to the Alliance's propaganda. [4]

Because of illness in his family, Dow postponed his second British tour until the following year. Since the fall of 1864, he had worried over his younger son, Frank's, consumptive cough and loss of weight. Late in 1865, he sent his wife and Frank to Minnesota to seek a more favorable climate. He received from them letters telling of the eighteen-year-old's improving health. Then, on December 14, he learned to his shock that his son had died on the previous day. Dow was distraught at the first death among his grown children, but, on his trip to the west to escort back his wife, he struggled to keep his usual composure. On December 27 at Portland, he buried Frank. Turning away from the grave, he vowed to preserve his son's memory and to busy himself with his remaining work. [5]

Dow soon carried out his intention. On May 19, 1866, he sailed from Quebec for a "Temperance Missionary Tour" of Great Britain. He left behind his wife. A stout, grey-haired woman, Cornelia Dow had aged more quickly than her husband. Though she no longer had young children to keep her at home, she was subject to attacks of nervous tremors and other illnesses. Neal Dow never took her as a companion on his lecture tours. Instead, he again criss-crossed the United Kingdom in the company of Dr. Frederic R. Lees, the master of medical arguments against alcohol. In his speeches, Dow hammered constantly at the license system as the fountainhead of British drunkenness.

To justify his violent attacks on the "gin palaces, " he pointed to the admission of Thomas Hughes that the hardhitting Dow had first offended and then converted the author of TOM BROWN'S SCHOOLDAYS. On November 23, 1867, Dow left for home confident that his disciples would soon conquer Great Britain. [6]

Through letters and newspapers, the American prohibitionist leader continued to follow closely the Alliance's fight for its Permissive Bill. After the 1868 parliamentary election, the new Liberal ministry of William E. Gladstone promised a License Bill to satisfy the temperance men. In the spring of 1871, Home Secretary Henry Bruce proposed a measure to reduce the number of liquor licenses and generally restrict the trade. Dow immediately attacked Bruce's Bill. He advised Thomas H. Barker that, "It is not really for the interest of the country, certainly not for the interest of the agitation, that any poultice, any emollient should be applied to the hideous cancer of British drunkenness." Following its ideological leader's advice to demand "the knife as the only possible remedy, " the Alliance refused to endorse anything but its Permissive Bill. The combined antagonism of the prohibitionists and liquorsellers forced the ministry to withdraw Bruce's Bill. Though the House of Commons also rejected the Permissive Bill, Dow was sure that the prohibitionists controlled the future. [7]

In April of 1873, the prohibitionist lecturer once more crossed the Atlantic to help his British disciples. Three weeks after his arrival, he watched the Liberal-dominated House of Commons again vote down the Permissive Bill. He decided that the defeat of the Liberals, whom most temperance men had supported, was a necessity for the prohibitionists. "The party had opposed us violently and insolently, " he later reasoned, "--and if they should not suffer from it--we could not win." Through 1873 on the platforms and in the press of Great Britain, he attacked the Liberal leaders' conduct. Taking note of increasing newspaper criticism of his violent political prohibitionism, he asked his Alliance friends whether he should not "be mild and tame--as the English fashion is?" He boasted to his wife, "They said no. I'd better be nobody but--Neal Dow!" Dow continued to urge the British prohibitionists to rule or ruin their party.

Dow hoped that in the 1874 general election the Liberals would lose control of Parliament by a small margin. He did not anticipate the organized wrath of the liquor interests at Bruce's Bill and at a milder Licensing Act of 1872. Incongruously, the publicans joined the Alliance-men to sweep in a large Conservative majority. Prime Minister Gladstone complained of being "borne down in a torrent of gin and beer." But Dow, as he resumed his incessant rounds of lecturing, rejoiced that the Liberals were "down and cannot rise again without our help." He was sure that his prohibitionist friends, despite their inexperience in "political management, " were strong enough to be "masters of the situation." As in his earlier political battles, he expected by throwing the balance of power to force the enactment of prohibition. [8]

Eventually, however, even energetic Neal Dow began to flag in his drive to close Britain's legion of pubs. Despite occasional vacations in Great Britain and on the continent, he began to feel that intensive lecturing was sapping his strength. In late February and early March, 1875, he contracted a hoarse cough and became so tired that he could hardly write in his diary. On March 19, the day before his seventy-first birthday, he began a long rest at the home of a Herefordshire physician. Thenceforth, he was acutely aware of his on-rushing years. "Am no longer lithe and quick and active . . . ," he later explained. "I cannot walk fast--nor far . . . . I do not like noise and bustle--but do like quiet and repose--<u>growing old</u>!!" In May, 25 months and 289 speeches after his arrival in Great Britain, the white-haired old man was glad to sail for home. 9

At triumphant receptions in Portland, Boston and New York, Dow boasted of the Alliance's political prohibition agitation. He cried that "the sturdy English will has decreed that the rum traffic shall cease." He did not mention that the Alliance's attempts to control the Liberals were leading to an informal alliance between the liquor interests and the powerful Conservative party. He and the Alliance, through their extreme demands, had encouraged the organization of opposition to any new restriction of liquor-selling. Not for generations would Parliament pass a law as strict as Bruce's Bill. And, even with eventual Liberal aid, Dow's friends would never win enactment of their Permissive Bill. Demanding all or nothing in the treatment of "the most drunken nation in the world," Dow would lose both the poultice and the knife. 10

But, being still hopeful that his tactics would succeed, Dow resumed his agitation for prohibition in his own country and thereby took advantage of a general revival of the American temperance movement. After 1872, Reform Clubs originated by a group of ex-drinkers at Gardiner, Maine, had spread across the northern half of the country. Dow and other prohibitionists had quickly seen that, as in the earlier Washingtonian revival, they could use the new teetotaling groups to strengthen their cause. Then, in the winter of 1873-74, bands of praying, singing women had begun invading Midwestern saloons. The leaders of this "Woman's Crusade" had organized a permanent Woman's Christian Temperance Union dedicated to war on the Demon Rum. Besides replacing its Civil War casualties, the temperance army had begun to develop new strength in the Midwest and even in the South. Dow had a favorable opportunity to recruit active prohibitionists. 11

Dow took his Maine Law message to the temperance camp meetings of the new teetotalers. These meetings, patterned on the outdoor religious services for which the Methodists were especially noted, indicated that denomination's growing importance in the anti-alcohol movement. Almost every August from the mid-1870's to the mid-1890's, Dow commuted from Portland to the nearby National and Maine State Temperance Camp Meetings. At more distant gatherings, he actually "camped." In September, 1876, for example, he stayed in a very simple cottage on a beautiful campground by the shore of Lake Winnepesaukee, New Hampshire. Excursion trains and boats brought thousands of other people for daytime visits. In the grove or in the "tabernacle" tent, Dow and his fellow speakers preached prohibition and total abstinence to the vast crowds. He saw that, through the new system of combining an outing with an oration, "great good must be done" for his cause. [12]

While talking prohibition, Dow did not neglect to set a positive example. He believed that the enforcement of the Maine Law in his home city was "of incalculable importance to the temperance cause--the world over . . . ." After his return from his third trip to Great Britain, he pressed the Portland authorities to make their first sustained drive against liquor-selling since before the Civil War. In numerous articles, he boasted that in Maine all but "the worst class of our foreign population," who operated small secret shops in the larger towns, had abandoned liquor-selling. According to Washington Gladden, noted preacher of the "Social Gospel," Dow continued to pursue anyone who disagreed with him with "vulgar and violent abuse." Yet Dow was under almost constant counterattack. Critics pointed to the many Maine citizens who paid the United States tax on liquor-dealers and especially to the open disregard for the Maine Law in Portland's hotels. Dow had not yet proved that prohibition really prohibited in his native city. [13]

As in earlier years, Dow believed that the way to stop the persistent liquor-sellers was to give "more jail to the rascals." Beginning in the fall of 1875, he resumed his annual petition campaigns and appearances before legislative committees. In January, 1877, he and extremist members of the Reform Clubs and the Woman's Christian Temperance Union drove the lawmakers to make the seizure of liquor easier and to punish its owners with mandatory three month jail sentences. As the act also forbade distilling in Maine, Dow had finally regained most of the ground lost through the weak and compromising Maine Law of 1858. "All except the lowest Irish dens will be cleaned out by this law," he happily predicted, "and these must be smoked out by brimstone. . . . " A hostile Boston editor thereupon offered "a small bet that more legislation will be called for next winter, as well as an appropriation for brimstone." Sure enough, Dow returned to seek another law "to give the coup de grace to the secret grogshops."[14]

By his demands for strict and well-enforced prohibitory laws, the Republican temperance man drew himself into conflict with his own party. While he had found the Maine Republicans willing to grant only part of his wishes, he had previously been patient with them. Desiring a stern Reconstruction of the South, he had even voted for anti-prohibitionists to insure his party's continued control. He had, moreover, felt a strong family interest in the Republicans because his son Frederick was slowly becoming an important local leader of the party. Therefore, though the elder Dow had sometimes threatened Republican officials in his quest for effective prohibition, he had not actually used his bolting tactics against them. In 1877, however, when Republican President Rutherford B. Hayes began to conciliate the South, Neal Dow privately condemned the President for failing to protect the rights of Southern Negroes and thereby permitting the return to power of the section's old leaders. He would no longer give unswerving loyalty to his party. [15]

A VOICE CRYING IN THE WILDERNESS

Early in 1880, Dow came to a breaking point with the Maine Republicans. In February, he and a delegation from the State Temperance Convention hopefully presented another "'Act Additional'" to the Republican-controlled legislature. But the Republicans, just back in power after an interlude of Democratic rule, were unwilling to risk antagonizing voters with Dow's extreme legislation. As the British Liberals had done, they sought to satisfy the prohibitionists with a milder substitute law. Dow raged that the "Republican wire-pullers" had become the "special friend and protector of the liquor-traffic. . . ." Since the previous two state elections had been close, the practical politician saw a promising opportunity to punish his party. In March, he declared, "I shall be very much disappointed if the temperance voters in the State do not . . . accept the issue at the ballot-box."[16]

The bolting Republican took refuge in the Prohibition Reform party. Eleven years earlier, other temperance Republicans disgusted with their party's compromising course toward prohibition had founded this independent political group. They had believed that the history of the Liberty and Free Soil parties, predecessors to Republicanism, proved the possibility of overturning existing parties and forcing a realignment on their own moral issue. But James H. Black of Pennsylvania, a leader of the National Temperance Society and Publishing House and the party's first presidential nominee, had polled only a few thousand votes. On the state level, the Prohibitionists had done little better. In May, 1880, the Prophet of Prohibition received a request from Black to permit the Prohibition party to strengthen its presidential ticket with his name. Dow replied that, if the nomination were "'spontaneous and unanimous,'" he would accept.

Dow himself planned to attend the Prohibition party's National Convention at Cleveland but, when his daughter Cornelia or "Cornie" went to Massachusetts to attend a funeral, he did not wish to leave his aging wife alone. On June 17, 1880, he learned by telegram that 142 fervent delegates from twelve states had that day unanimously nominated him "with cheer upon cheer, and the doxology." He was to stand upon a platform denouncing the other political parties and calling for nationwide prohibition and women's suffrage. Nearly a month later, Dow formally accepted the nomination. Appealing to history, he stated, "There was never a time before the final victory, when the anti-slavery movement had so large a following as Prohibition now has. . . ." Yet the experienced politician did not share the hope of his Irish servant that she would cook for him in the White House. Instead, he merely wished that his candidacy would "prove to be the humble beginning of a triumphant end."[17]

Through the summer of 1880, Dow ignored his presidential nomination to concentrate on the Maine political campaign. He and other extreme prohibitionists were angry at the refusal of the Republican candidate for re-election, Governor Daniel F. Davis, to appoint special constables to enforce their law in the nullifying city of Bangor. On July 22 at Augusta, when Dow tried to get a State Temperance Convention to adopt an anti-Republican address to the people, Republican prohibitionists and officeholders blocked his proposal and, after he had returned home, broke up the meeting. The frustrated Maine Law leader fought back savagely. At subsequent meetings, he wildly alleged that "a Republican mob of one thousand, led by ex-Gov. Anson P. Morrill" had wrecked the convention. He advised prohibitionists to punish his old party. In the September gubernatorial election, 433 votes for two Prohibitionist candidates weakened the Republicans enough to give a small plurality to the fusion Democratic-Greenback nominee. Dow exulted that his tiny bolt had rebuked the Republican attempt to "cater for rum-votes."[18]

The Prohibitionist presidential candidate soon demonstrated, however, that, while he might use third party action to coerce the Republicans, he still identified himself with his old party. General Dow did no active campaigning and did not even put an electoral ticket in the field in his own state. Nevertheless, some Maine Republicans still feared that a repetition of the September Prohibitionist bolt might take enough votes from the Republican General James A. Garfield to give the state to General Winfield Scott Hancock, the Democratic nominee. In late October, 1880, Dow received a note from Chairman James G. Blaine of the Republican State Committee urging him to write a public letter of withdrawal from the electoral campaign of the generals. Though Dow declined, he said, according to Blaine's newspaper organ, "I was never a more stalwart Republican than I am now, and do most earnestly wish success to Gen. Garfield." On October 29, Dow publicly denied reports of his withdrawal and subsequently voted for himself. But he rejoiced that the 10,304 Americans who did likewise had not prevented Garfield from beating "the ex-slavedriving-rebel element." Candidate Dow had not been a convinced member of the Prohibition party.[19]

Dow continued to wave the Prohibition party like a club at the Maine Republicans. Beginning in 1881, he began to threaten to strike a new blow with it unless the Republicans supported a constitutional amendment, similar to one previously adopted in Kansas, which would make prohibition part of the state's fundamental law. Prior to the election of 1882, the Republicans sought to appease him and his friends by endorsing a referendum on constitutional prohibition and by making his son, Frederick, chairman of the party's State Committee. In addition, Republican gubernatorial nominee Frederick Robie visited Neal Dow and promised to back enforced prohibition. On election day, while a Prohibition party candidate got a handful of votes, Robie with the support of the two Dows swept to victory. While Frederick Dow received the important post of Collector of the Port of Portland, his father gained from the legislature an order to hold the desired referendum at the 1884 election--but failed to get more stringent amendments to the Maine Law itself. By the fall of 1883, Dow was attacking the Governor for not assisting his personal prosecutions of Portland liquor-sellers and was declaring, "We have fully made up our minds now to break with the Republican party in Maine. . . ."[20]

As the 1884 presidential campaign opened, however, the Prohibition party candidate of 1880 silenced his threats and once more responded to his strong personal and family interest in the Republican party. On June 17, 1884, while passing through Augusta, he called on Republican presidential candidate James G. Blaine. Though Dow denied the immediate Democratic charge that he had made a "bargain" to back Blaine, he later made statements favorable to the "Plumed Knight." On June 26, according to Portland's Republican organ, he declared that in Maine, Iowa and Kansas, where the Republicans had agreed to support prohibition with constitutional amendments and laws, "temperance men feel themselves bound in honor to be loyal to party." By embracing the chieftain of the Republican "bosses" whom he had attacked intermittently, Dow embittered Maine's third party Prohibitionists. Nathan Franklin Woodbury, Secretary of the Prohibition party's State Committee, publicly commented that, unless Dow had previously falsified against the Republicans, he was proposing "treachery and disloyalty to his own convictions."[21]

Dow later admitted that, since many Republican prohibitionists favored Blaine, he thought it "wise and expedient, under all circumstances," to devote himself wholly to seeking their support in the referendum on his constitutional amendment. He believed that a heavy vote for prohibition would provide a popular reaffirmation of his policy and strengthen his appeal for more laws to enforce it. In late July and August, 1884, he spoke at camp meetings around the state, wrote articles and mailed out campaign literature. In the election on September 8, against little organized opposition, Dow carried the state for his proposition by a majority of 70,783 to 23,811. The larger cities, however, which enforced the Maine Law the least, turned out majorities or strong minorities against it. And James G. Blaine declined to vote at all on the prohibition issue.[22]

Accepting the explanation that Blaine had not wished to "obtrude" a state issue into the national contest, Dow remained true to the Republican presidential candidate. But resentful Prohibitionist voters nevertheless helped to unhorse the Plumed Knight. In the November presidential election, 25,000 votes for Prohibition party nominee John P. St. John were one of several reasons for Blaine's fatal loss of New York to Democrat Grover Cleveland "The men in power who through the Rebellion, sought the life of the Nation!" Dow sorrowfully exclaimed. Because of the change in administrations, he would soon see his son lose the Portland Collectorship. More serious to the elder Dow, he found the Republicans resentful of the Prohibitionists' role in their defeat and unwilling to grant promised amendments to the Maine Law. Once more he had failed to gain enforced prohibition through a political bargain.[23]

The Maine Law leader turned from his strategy of threatening the Republicans to serious third party action. For the first time, because of the Republican defeat, he began to believe that the Prohibition party could duplicate the success of the early antislavery groups in replacing one of the country's dominant parties. He decided that the loss of another presidential election would close the Republicans' "glorious record" and lead to the formation of a victorious anti-alcohol party. On February 28, 1885, Neal Dow announced his break with his old party. Thereafter he often denounced the Republicans for refusing to strengthen the Maine Law. He once charged that the legislature had treated the prohibitionists "in a way that would be proper and suitable, if we had been a lot of cranks asking for a large appropriation" to build "a flying machine." On February 11, 1886, at a Prohibition party rally at Portland, he said of the Republicans, "They have spit in our faces and kicked us out. I, for one, am out."[24]

In 1886 in Maine's biennial election, the new convert to the Prohibition party had his first major opportunity to strike back at the Republicans. Taking the stump to help in a relatively intensive canvass of the state, Dow attacked Maine's Republican leaders and received in return charges that he was a fanatic who spoke only for himself. On September 13, he was one of less than 4,000 voters for the Prohibitionist gubernatorial candidate. "The Prohibitionists have cast their ballots," gloated one of the victorious Republicans, "and the Republican party survives." From temperance men in other states, Dow received warnings that the small Prohibitionist vote had made the Maine Law appear unpopular. He saw anti-prohibitionists compare his earlier claims of the Maine Law's effectiveness with his campaign charges that in every Republican city except Portland prohibition "has been and is absolutely ignored." Still the old man had no doubt of his political wisdom. He self-righteously replied that "we have not yet made any false move, nor have we failed in any. . . ."[25]

Continuing to back third party action to enforce the Maine Law in Portland, Dow himself became once more a candidate for office. On February 12, 1888, he accepted the Prohibition party's mayoralty nomination. The Democrats, who were deadlocked over their own nomination, saw that by backing the "Father of the Maine Law" they could embarrass temperance Republicans in Portland and throughout the nation. On February 20, while the skies rained down cold water, a laughing, cheering rally of what Dow had called the "'rum Democracy'" recommended that "all good citizens" support "our able and distinguished fellow citizen, the Hon. Neal Dow for Mayor." Though Dow knew that most of the Democrats were still against prohibition, he expressed gratification at their endorsement. He had long criticized the incumbent Republican mayor, whom his own son was backing, and rejoiced at the opportunity to punish "the ring."

In the mayoralty campaign, Dow demonstrated his complete break with his policy of cooperating with the Republicans. He drew his chief newspaper support from Editor John M. Adams of the Democratic EASTERN ARGUS, once one of his bitterest enemies, and was a target for the abuse of the Republican PRESS. While in the past he had often sneered at "low Irish rum-holes," he thought it a "very dirty trick" for the Republicans to distribute at the Catholic cathedral handbills quoting his former remarks. He believed with President Frances E. Willard of the National Woman's Christian Temperance Union, who came to Portland to support him, that the question dividing him and his Republican opponent was one of "law and order" versus "the saloons." Dow persuaded a few of the prohibitionist Republicans to vote for him but he lost many regular Democrats. On March 6, 1888, he received only 1934 votes compared to 3504 for the Republican mayor. Dow informed temperance men in other states that his defeat was a rejection of enforced prohibition. He thereby also provided anti-prohibitionists with another proof of the Maine Law's unpopularity. [26]

Despite setbacks, the old man hoped against hope that in the 1888 presidential election the prohibition party would again cause a Republican defeat. He believed that the Prohibitionists, unlike the Republicans, could gain the backing of the temperance Democrats of the South. Indeed, the former advocate of harsh Reconstruction proclaimed that there was "no more solid South, no more solid North, and no more waving of the bloody shirt." On May 30 and 31, 1888, at Indianapolis, Dow joined delegates similarly imbued with the mood of sectional reconciliation in attending the Prohibition party's National Convention. He made one brief and unsuccessful speech against the political expediency of backing women's suffrage. While he personally favored letting women vote, he privately confessed that the debate on it "gave me grave doubts as to the benefits any way--of woman and the ballot." During the subsequent campaign, he spoke for the Prohibitionists at several Maine meetings. But, in contrast to the previous election, the Republicans won the presidency. Dow began to realize that he was running out of time to see the fulfillment of his dream of an anti-alcohol victory. [27]

Since the Civil War, as he had for most of his adult life, Neal Dow had attempted by manipulation of political parties to gain enforced prohibition. In Great Britain and the United States, he had first tried to work through existing parties and had then advocated bolting. In both areas, he had eventually demonstrated that he and his disciplined army could gain lip-service to prohibition. But he could not induce the politicians to antagonize the sizable groups of voters opposed to his policy. Instead, he and the United Kingdom Alliance had actually delayed the enactment of less extreme British restrictions on liquor-selling. And in his own city, as Dow himself admitted, he had not by twenty years of effort reduced the number of illegal "rum-sellers." Yet, despite his failures, the Maine Law leader had helped to keep alive the theory of prohibition. More than any other man, he had spoken out to insure that the reviving temperance movement of the late 19th century would remain true to his policy. Amid the deepening shadows of his eighty-four years, he would rightly become his crusade's symbol.

Chapter XIV

SAINTLY SYMBOL

"General, I was [damned] glad to hear yesterday that you were dead, " remarked a wealthy drinking-man in Neal Dow's later years. "I am [damned] sorry to see to-day that you are yet living. "[1] To such anti-prohibitionists, Dow had made himself the hated epitome of the crusade to ban the Demon Rum. But he was also a symbol in the eyes of his co-believers to whom the old man had become a living legend--the Prophet of Prohibition. As the oil of Dow's life ran low, his followers puffed the light of his reputation into a final brilliant burst.

Both Dow himself and his followers viewed him as an embodied testimonial to the virtues of prolonged total abstinence. In appearance, the octogenarian belied his age. True, his long hair and bushy sideburns were white as snow. But he still had a youthful spark in his bright blue eyes and color in his slightly wrinkled cheeks. While he had become somewhat stooped, he maintained his lifelong pride in his physical strength. To keep his short body robust, Dow devoted part of each day to such exercise as lifting dumbbells and walking downtown. On the increasing number of days which he considered too inclement to venture outside, he marched back and forth on a "home parade ground" in his back hallway. To a hero-worshipping New York temperance woman, the spry old man appeared to be "as alert and active as a boy. "

Neal Dow continued to enjoy generally good health. He occasionally complained of such minor ailments as over-strained eyes, colds, rheumatism and bronchitis. The latter he attributed to his stay in Libby Prison. Because of his youthful reading of medical books and his disagreement with many doctors' prescriptions of alcoholic drinks, he had less than average faith in physicians and often attempted self-medication. As a preventive for rheumatism, he sometimes carried a bag of "Salt Peter. " On his last trip to Great Britain, he had acquired a "galvanic metallic belt" in which he had, for a time, "unlimited faith" as "a cure for almost all nervous diseases. " To guard against headaches and upset stomach, he gave constant attention to his diet. But, despite minor failings, he knew that he suffered "from very few, if any, of the infirmities of old age. "[2]

SAINTLY SYMBOL

Dow outlived his partner in almost fifty-three years of happy marriage. In the winter of 1882-83, he helplessly watched seventy-four-year-old Cornelia Dow's life slip away. On January 13, 1883, after a heart attack and a paralytic stroke, his wife died. With the stoicism of his Quaker upbringing, her husband concealed from the world his sorrow and privately poured his emotion over many pages of his diary. "I can hardly realize that the remains of my dear wife are up in her chamber, all alone . . . ," he mourned. "For these many nights, she has been watched and cared for tenderly . . . and now no one present . . . to respond to and anticipate every want and to minister to every need. There is no want, no more need forever." To Dow, the big old house seemed strange and empty. He felt "that we are waiting for the coming of somebody. May the Great King come," he implored, "and bless us and comfort us and prepare us for the great day, now so rapidly approaching."[3]

Dow replaced his wife as mistress of his household with his unmarried youngest daughter. Cornelia or "Cornie," as he called her, was a stout, determined woman of forty. Her equally stubborn father sometimes clashed with her over such matters as his increasing insistence upon eating lightly. When Cornie offered him food, the old man often snapped, "Half of that!" and then sometimes received considerably less than half from his annoyed daughter. To Cornie's irritation, Dow also walked around the neighborhood in a shawl long after other men had stopped wearing them. He further displeased her through invitations to his white-bearded temperance associate, George H. Shirley, to pay regular visits. Under Republican administrations, his old friend had long filled a sinecure in the New York Custom House. Dow was far more willing than Cornie to tolerate Shirley's general lack of social grace. But the elder Dow and his daughter, an active officer of the Woman's Christian Temperance Union, fully shared a common interest in prohibition and other reforms. In the 1890's, when Cornelia attended W. C. T. U. conventions, her father missed his companion.[4]

In the late 1880's, Dow lost close contact with Emma, his second-oldest daughter. A cheerful, optimistic woman in her forties, Emma was the wife of Cashier William Edward Gould of Portland's First National Bank. Her husband, a man of holy appearance, was a public pillar of the Congregational Church and a secret stock speculator. In September, 1886, Dow and the rest of Portland learned that Gould had embezzled over $167,000 of the bank's funds. Emma took bravely her husband's ten year prison sentence and the loss of all their property. Dow shared with Gould's father the cost of supporting his daughter and their two granddaughters. Since, as in the case of pious State Treasurer Benjamin D. Peck, Dow was also one of Gould's bondsmen, he paid because of the embezzlement a total of $22,000. "I make no comment on this," he sorrowfully wrote about Gould's crime, "--the sin--shame & horror of it--cannot be put into words." After four years in prison, Gould obtained a presidential pardon and moved with his family to New Hampshire. While Dow occasionally met Emma thereafter, he never again saw his sanctimonious son-in-law.[5]

119

Once or twice a year, Dow went to Lancaster, New Hampshire to visit the oldest of his daughters. In 1860, after careful investigation, he had permitted Louisa to marry prosperous Jacob Benton. Since then, his childless daughter had lived in Washington during the period when Benton was a Republican congressman and had travelled widely in search of health. Increasingly crippled by rheumatism, she had finally become unable to leave her fine New Hampshire home. There Dow usually found her cheerfully occupied with books. Her father took pride in Louisa's ability to read several foreign tongues. He himself, since his European tours, regularly read French works. With their common interest in books, Dow felt particularly close to studious Louisa.

Both father and daughter had read BLACK BEAUTY and appreciated its lesson of kindness to animals. Indeed, to advance the cause, Louisa translated the book into an international language called Volapük. As further testimony of her love for horses, she had a granite drinking-fountain built for her town. On September 29, 1892, two days before the dedication of her gift to the beasts, a runaway horse killed her husband. After the funeral, Dow helped to unveil the fountain which became an ironic memorial to his late son-in-law. On December 7, 1895, after Louisa had undergone an operation for cancer, the sorrowing father also lost his sixty-four-year-old daughter. [6]

In his later years, Dow was most intimate with Frederick, his one remaining son. Since the death in 1869 of Neal Dow's sister, Harriet, "Fred" had lived with his wife and two children in the old family homestead across Congress Street from his father's mansion. In 1891, the elder Dow had his son and family move in with him. The two men shared many interests and were often together. As Neal Dow had planned, his boy had inherited and then enlarged an important place in Portland's political, economic and social life. Frederick Neal Dow, a leading Republican politician, became in the late 1880's the publisher of a major newspaper, the PORTLAND EVENING EXPRESS, and also the Speaker of the Maine House of Representatives. But, though Neal Dow had trained his son to be a firm temperance man, he could not lead conservative Fred into the forlorn hope of the Prohibition party. Instead, while the two men never openly clashed, the father often found himself denouncing his own son's political associates as saloon-protecting "bosses." [7]

Even in politics, however, Dow finally drew back close to his son and to his own early principles. In 1892, he cast his third ballot for the unsuccessful national candidates of the Prohibition party and declared that the Republicans' alleged alliance with the liquor-sellers would eventually kill his old party. But he admitted, "I am the same Republican now that I ever was, all but the rum." As when he had voted for protectionist President John Quincy Adams, he favored a high tariff and blamed the hard times of the mid-1890's upon the Democratic national administration's policy of sending "our money abroad to hire foreigners to do all our own work, leaving our own countrymen at home without employment." In 1896, when the Democrats and part of the Prohibitionists called for the coinage of silver at an artificially high ratio to gold, bondholder Neal Dow denounced the inflationary scheme as "a lie, a cheat, a

fraud. " He refrained from voting in the presidential contest and approved of
the Republican victory "over the ignorant. " Raised a Federalist, he retained his original preference for rule by "the intelligent, the virtuous and the
learned. "[8]

With his son's increasing aid, wealthy Neal Dow continued to attend to his
investments and to reap the financial benefits of Portland's growth. In the
sixty years since he had bought the first of his sixteen pieces of real estate,
he had seen the village on the peninsula triple its population to become by 1890
a city of over 36, 000 people. Pushing ahead the better-quality residential area,
the city's commercial district was shifting westward along Congress Street
toward Dow's once-rural neighborhood. Between the late 1870's and the early
1890's, Dow built three business blocks on property which he owned within the
new shopping area. Near his own home, he demolished old buildings and even
gave up his beloved garden to make room for seven multiple dwellings. The
ex-banker also managed large holdings of stock belonging to himself and to
George H. Shirley. Still eager for maximum gain, he supplemented his comfortable income from rents and dividends with a $90 pension for his Civil
War leg-wound and conducted a long but unsuccessful battle for an increase.
As always, however, Dow could well afford to live as he pleased. [9]

He particularly enjoyed the luxury of a good stable. Despite his family's
fears, the old man still often drove his spirited horses. Once, after trying
one of his son's animals, he complained, "I don't see why Fred keeps such a
dull horse. " But on August 29, 1890, while Dow was riding in the suburbs
behind "Duke, " "a furious horse, " an axle broke and overturned his chaise.
Crazed with fear, "Duke" broke his harness and ran away. The eighty-six-
year-old driver, only slightly bruised, crawled from the wreckage and later
regarded his narrow escape as "an interposition of Providence. " Thereafter,
he began permitting Flannagan, his man-of-all-work, to take the reins. Whether in his chaise or huddled in his coupe sleigh against winter's blast, General
Dow continued to be a familiar figure on Portland's cobbled streets. [10]

As he had since adolescence, Dow spent considerable time with his books,
magazines and newspapers. Immediately after rising at five o'clock on summer mornings and at six in winter, he began his day's reading. He subscribed
to local newspapers, reform and religious journals and the New York TRIBUNE.
Still interested in mechanics, he regularly read the SCIENTIFIC AMERICAN.
He enjoyed, besides books in English, French historical works and the novels
of Jules Verne. Except in winter, when he found the library too cold, he made
the northern room his headquarters. He ran shelving up to its ceiling to house
his growing collection of books, sat in his favorite high-backed rocker beneath
the elaborate gas chandelier and read "as much as my eyes will bear. "[11]

The abstemious Dow continued to give his major attention to encouraging the
negative virtues. He disapproved of playing cards and gambling. Cornie knew
better than to tell him that she played bezique with Fred's family. Neal Dow,
as he had since boyhood, also often expressed his disgust for the "tobacco
slave" and his weed. In 1885, when Phillips Brooks visited Dow, amused

neighbors observed the popular preacher leaning out a bedroom window to smoke a cigar. Three years later, when ninety-one-year-old John T. Walton went blind, Dow attributed the affliction of his dying Washingtonian friend to the tobacco habit. Besides opposing gaming and smoking, Neal Dow remained a staunch Sabbatarian. He almost never travelled on Sunday and, in the 1890's, held a nominal position as a vice-president of the New England Sabbath Protective League. He was a true son of Portland's puritanical "Sixty-Nine."[12]

Above all, Dow opposed the Demon Rum. While he ceased his extensive canvasses for prohibition, he delivered an occasional speech at meetings in Portland and in other northeastern cities. In the spring of 1889, he received an invitation from his British friends, with whom he had remained in contact, to make a fourth trip overseas. After booking passage, the octogenarian yielded to his children's arguments against exposing himself to such fatigues. According to a reporter, a Portland liquor-dealer who had rejoiced at Dow's proposed departure moaned, "He found out that I wanted him to go, and that made him stay here." Dow increasingly deferred to his feebleness. In 1891, when he did not attend a National Temperance Convention, he explained, "My family think I ought not to draw unnecessary drafts on a future where possibly the margin is not large enough to honor them." But, even in semi-retirement, he maintained his constant flow of prohibitionist articles.[13]

Recalling how the churches had founded the original temperance movement, Dow began to appeal more and more to religious-minded people to aid his crusade. He believed that, if ministers and church members would act upon their professed opposition to liquor-selling, he could win his long-sought victory. Since the Civil War, disgusted with many ministers' timid stands on the slavery and prohibition questions, he had abandoned his former practice of attending Congregational services. Neither early nor late in life did the ex-Quaker have much regard for formal creeds or liturgy. He continued to believe in a personal God and in His "special providence" in human affairs. In Dow's later years, he repeatedly read and reread the Bible. As for churchgoing, however, he declared that, until the ministers "do their duty, . . . I will silently and quietly protest by staying away."[14]

Almost singlehanded, Dow continued on a lesser scale his battle to make Portland's Republican officials enforce the Maine Law. He published in his old Democratic foe, the EASTERN ARGUS, biting but ineffectual open letters to the mayor. In 1891, he rejoiced at an enforcement drive led by Sheriff Leander E. Cram and a year later, he and the Prohibitionists helped to re-elect the Republican sheriff. But, as Cram's efforts flagged, a rhymster commented:

> "Leander Cram once bravely swam
> The Hellespont of rum;
> But like Sheriff Webb, by the flood and ebb,
> He at last was overcome.
> So Hero Dow, in sadness now,

SAINTLY SYMBOL

> Thus from his Cram divorced,
> Sits by the sea with the law that he
> Will never see enforced."

Dow himself charged that the sheriff had begun to manufacture cigars and was selling them to the barrooms. On July 7, 1895, in the last of five annual open air addresses on Portland's Munjoy Hill, the ninety-one-year-old spoke out, as he put it, "plainer than ever before about the corruption of our Authorities."[15]

To make his state a better example to the world's prohibitionists, the old man carried on his effort to punish violators of the Maine Law with spectacularly increased fines and imprisonment. Harking back to his youth, he even suggested informally that the restoration of the whipping post for "rumsellers" would be "a remedy that would have beneficial results." From the legislative session of 1891, he and his friends finally obtained a ban on selling imported liquor in the original packages and also secured sharply increased penalties for transporting liquor into the state for illegal sale. Two years later, however, opponents got an opinion from Maine Chief Justice John A. Peters that the transportation penalties were disproportionate to the offense. Dow, who had visited Augusta to request new restrictions, then saw the Republican-controlled 1893 legislature instead reduce the punishment for importing and transporting liquor. He had lost most of his gains.[16]

In one of his last controversies, the frustrated Maine Law leader turned on the Chief Justice. Attacking Peters, he also expressed a longstanding resentment of the anti-prohibitionist judge's nullification of the Maine Law through imposing low fines and simply ignoring its mandatory provisions. On July 30, 1893, before a Portland meeting, Dow repeated his familiar claim that no man could claim constitutional rights "inconsistent with the general good." Then, using the device of pretending that Peters was sitting on an empty stool beside him, he harangued the Chief Justice on the ruin wrought by rum. "And yet this man, taking advantage of his high position," Dow cried, raising the stool, "says that a year in jail is too much for a man engaged in working such misery. The Chief Justice lives in Bang-o-r." With this reference to the state's center of illegal liquor-selling, the octogenarian orator showed that he could still draw laughter from a friendly audience. In a series of newspaper articles, he continued his assault on the hostile judge.[17]

In preparation for the 1895 legislative session, Dow for the last time circulated at his own expense petitions for more amendments to the Maine Law. On January 17, 1895, in a seventy-five minute speech before a committee of lawmakers, he hit at the Chief Justice for misinterpreting the State Constitution and at the 1893 legislature for reducing the penalties for violators of prohibition. Besides additional imprisonment for those bringing liquor into Maine, he called for stripping the courts of almost all discretion in handling Maine Law cases. After four more trips to Augusta, the old man finally got the respectful committee to report a milder form of his bill. But, almost without debate, the House of Representatives indefinitely postponed it. The advocate of pains and penalties had suffered his ultimate rebuff. [18]

Dow could cheer himself with the knowledge that the world's prohibitionists did not share the politicians' attitude toward him and his ideas. Instead, he was becoming the increasingly revered symbol of the anti-alcohol crusade. His big brick house was a Mecca to travelling temperance people and especially to members of the powerful Woman's Christian Temperance Union. From one female visitor, the occupant of the shrine of prohibition drew the worshipful comment that his "abundant silken snow-white hair" was "a veritable crown of glory." In 1888 and 1892, Dow also briefly entertained the W. C. T. U.'s harder-headed President and prime mover, Frances E. Willard. Born of transplanted New England stock, the prim ex-teacher had played an important part in arousing American women to demand the vote and social reform. Dow enjoyed making the acquaintance of Frances Willard, who was thirty-five years his junior, and admired her "zeal and devotion." Wise in the techniques of publicity needed to appeal to her sentimental followers, the prohibitionist spinster in turn helped to transform aged Neal Dow from a warlike leader into an heroic relic. [19]

In the early 1890's, by invitation of Frances E. Willard, Dow appeared at several national W. C. T. U. meetings. Unable to walk far or well, he often travelled to his engagements with the aid of his temperance-minded daughter, Cornelia. On the platform, he no longer wore the bright clothes of his young manhood. Instead, as if in reversion to the sober dress of the Quakers, he wore a black, almost ministerial suit with a white stock. For the subject-matter of his speeches, Dow liked to draw upon his memory of the "old rum time" before the Maine Law and then assure his co-believers that prohibition had wrought a wondrous improvement. When pleased with his own oration, he later referred like a preacher to his unusual "'freedom'" and "'liberty.'" The old man usually felt that the interminable handshaking with admirers from the audience tired him more than the speeches themselves. He attracted crowds anxious to meet and have their children see the Prophet of Prohibition. [20]

During the fall of 1893, Dow learned that Frances E. Willard, who was then in Great Britain, was planning a worldwide celebration of his ninetieth birthday. As she told him, she intended to make March 20, 1894, a "'high day in Zion'" both to honor Dow and to build up "prohibition sentiment which you were the first to embody in law." At her suggestion, the United Kingdom Alliance, the Good Templars and other anti-alcohol groups joined her many local unions in calling meetings and distributing literature. The National Temperance Society and Publishing House took advantage of the occasion to advise local groups to purchase stocks of its two thousand publications including a "Neal Dow Prohibition Song Leaflet." As the great day approached, Dow received hundreds of congratulatory letters and telegrams from temperance leaders, old friends, clergymen and Maine politicians. He optimistically hoped that the excitement would produce a temperance revival.

On Dow's birthday, aided by Fred and Cornelia, he greeted a large crowd of callers and accepted many flowers and gifts. That evening, he went to a commemorative meeting at the Portland City Hall. In the women on the platform, on which a portrait of Frances Willard flanked his own, he might have seen indications of the increasing importance of the opposite sex in his movement. He listened to the mayor, the governor and temperance people eulogize the Father of the Maine Law. Dramatically he replied, "I who am about to die, salute you." While his voice had a touch of huskiness, he spoke and gestured with strength and enthusiasm. At his moment of recognition as the Prophet of Prohibition, Dow appropriately reiterated his belief that heavier penalties would end illegal liquor-selling. A critic had already sourly suggested that Portland's "rumsellers" might close voluntarily to attend his meeting. But, despite Dow's failure to wipe out his city's liquor traffic, the old master of publicity could count the birthday celebration as a great personal success.[21]

To insure that posterity would remember his fame as the symbol of his cause, Dow left several reminders. He preserved the many letters written by him which his wife had saved during their over fifty years of married life. In addition, Dow kept a diary for about his last twenty-five years. Instead of making it an intimate document, he filled its pages with descriptions of faraway places for his family circle and autobiographical items for future scholars. From 1853 until his death, he pasted clippings relating to himself and prohibition into twenty-eight large scrapbooks which he often used as a valuable reference tool in preparing articles. But, in 1866, he had also observed, "Fifty years hence, these Vols. will have great interest for the student of the history of the Maine Law and even the general reader."[22]

On December 18, 1879, Dow had noted his intention to begin writing the most ambitious device for perpetuating his memory--his reminiscences. He had explained that he had not previously prepared his memoirs "as it seemed to me to savor of vanity, in supposing that such a matter could be of public interest or importance--and the attempt would seem to me to look like obtrusiveness." He had usually accompanied his strong publicity of himself and his work with such professions of modesty. Even in referring to the reminiscences in his dairy, he minimized the personal element and referred to them as his "History of the Maine Law." Between 1886 and the closing months of his life, Dow wrote and dictated the bulk of a weighty manuscript.

Despite his announced intention of effacing himself from his memoirs, Dow produced a conventional autobiography complete with genealogy and childhood recollections. He also included much temperance history and his familiar arguments for prohibition. By research among his old letters and scrapbooks, Dow avoided most misstatements of fact but, as in his description of the Portland Riot, he often inadequately treated incidents unflattering to himself and his cause. In the last week of his life, he also instructed his family to remove any reference likely "to wound the feelings of the closest friend of any with whom I have been in controversy. . . ." After his death, his son, Frederick edited and published THE REMINISCENSES OF NEAL DOW: RECOLLECTIONS OF EIGHTY YEARS. The Dow who walked its 769 pages was not the ambitious warrior who had fought to impose his views on the world. Instead, with his armor and weapons removed, he was the soft, saintly symbol of prohibition. [23]

While completing his legacy to posterity, General Dow began to weaken more rapidly. By the fall of 1895, when he received a letter from Frances E. Willard "urging--begging me to come" to the W. C. T. U.'s annual meeting, he felt that he could not make the journey to Baltimore. On June 4, 1896, with a brief speech at a Boston banquet, he closed his successful career as a public speaker. In January, 1897, the old man had an attack of upset stomach which further enfeebled him. To avoid wearisome climbing, he began sleeping downstairs on a little iron and brass bedstead. Frances Willard set in motion plans to celebrate his ninety-third birthday and hoped that the day would "some day be a National and International holiday." Unable to attend the meeting on March 20, 1897, at the Portland City Hall, Dow sent a message of hope for the eventual victory of prohibition. He had finally realized that he would not live to see the triumph. [24]

In the spring of 1897, Dow was still able to spend hours in reading and writing. Accompanied by his daughter, Cornelia, he rode out to watch new construction in the city and to enjoy the budding countryside. Soon after, he became much more feeble. On July 23 in a caricature of his once fine hand, he scrawled a final entry in his dairy. On September 25, exhausted by the effort to dress, the old man fainted. He rallied but two days later found himself unable to rise. Commenting, "This is the beginning of the end," he gave Cornelia instructions for his funeral service. He remained conscious almost until death. According to his son, his last reference to himself was, "I am so weary; I long to be free." On October 2, 1897, at 2:30 p.m., Neal Dow quietly expired. [25]

Three days later, Dow's body lay in state in the Payson Memorial Church, the successor to the old Second Parish Congregational Meetinghouse. George H. Shirley was the only contemporary of his youth among the throng attending the funeral. The dead man whose life had spanned the century had outlived almost all the rest. The names of the organizations which sent delegations roughly summarized Dow's varied career. Members of the Veteran Firemen's Association, the Maine Charitable Mechanic Association, the city government, the state legislature, the 13th Maine Regiment, the National Temperance Society, the Woman's Christian Temperance Union and the New England Sabbath Protective League had gathered to hear Portland's leading Protestant clergymen eulogize the reformer. Then the mayor, the governor and many of the politicians whom Dow had so bitterly attacked carried the large casket containing his small body to the black-plumed hearse. The horses pulled Dow's cortege slowly westward to the family plot in Evergreen Cemetery where, far short of his arid Canaan, the Prophet of Prohibition rested. [26]

The principal newspapers of the United States and Great Britain mourned the passing of the "Apostle of Temperance" and "Father of Prohibition." They bore witness to Dow's success in making himself the internationally-known symbol of the war against the liquor traffic. Flying the banner of humanitarianism, he had violently assailed his opponents. He had once helped to revolutionize state and national politics and had unsuccessfully campaigned to repeat the feat. More than any other man of the 19th century, he had propagated prohibition throughout the English-speaking world. Yet he had not been able to stop liquor-selling in his own small city. With unconscious irony, his friends praised most strongly the educational and persuasive side-effects of the prohibitionist's agitation. His oldest enemy, the Portland EASTERN ARGUS, believed that he had at least proved the failure of "compulsion" as an agent of reform. "This is something gained," the Democratic organ wryly commented, "and we have chiefly to thank Neal Dow for it."[27]

But the men and women whom Dow had converted to prohibition shared his vision of its future. The evangelical religious leaders and well-financed temperance organizations carried on his crusade against the Demon Rum. Within a few decades, American prohibitionists who remembered their dead champion's political methods and objective induced first many states and then the nation to adopt his theory of compulsion. As in Neal Dow's more limited war on the liquor traffic, apathetic support, urban opposition, lax enforcement and other problems crippled national prohibition and brought about its repeal. A generation later, however, many Americans still professed the faith of the Prophet of Prohibition.

NOTES

CHAPTER I

[1]Neal Dow, THE REMINISCENCES OF NEAL DOW, RECOLLECTIONS OF EIGHTY YEARS (Portland, Maine, 1898), 217-20; Alonzo A. Miner, "Neal Dow and His Life Work" in NEW ENGLAND MAGAZINE, 10:397-412 (June, 1894); interview with Dow in New York WORLD, August 25, 1886, reprinted in Manchester (England) ALLIANCE NEWS, September 11, 1886, clipping in the Neal Dow Scrapbook, 20:440. All Dow Scrapbooks cited in this chapter are on deposit in the library of Drew University.

[2]Dow, REMINISCENCES, 1-3, 28, 37; Robert Piercy Dow, THE BOOK OF DOW, GENEALOGICAL MEMOIRS OF THE DESCENDANTS OF HENRY DOW 1637, THOMAS DOW 1639 AND OTHERS OF THE NAME, IMMIGRANTS TO AMERICA DURING COLONIAL TIMES, ALSO THE ALLIED FAMILY OF NUDD ([Rutland, Vermont], 1929), 27-34, 89-96, 302.

[3]Dow, REMINISCENCES, 3-19, 25, picture opposite 28; Robert P. Dow, BOOK OF DOW, 302, 320, 328-30; Louis C. Hatch, MAINE, A HISTORY (3 vols., New York, 1919), 3:671; Federal Writers' Project, MAINE, A GUIDE 'DOWN EAST' (Boston, 1937), 37, 39, 40-41, 55, and PORTLAND CITY GUIDE (Portland, 1940), 3-5, 19-38; William Willis, THE HISTORY OF PORT-LAND FROM ITS FIRST SETTLEMENT, WITH NOTICES OF THE NEIGHBOR-ING TOWNS AND OF THE CHANGES OF GOVERNMENT IN MAINE, part 2: 153-57, 176-85 (Portland, 1883); deed from Dorcas, James D. and Mary Deering to Josiah Dow, June 30, 1796, acknowledged and recorded, December 3, 1798, in Dow Scrapbook, 19:98.

[4]Dow, REMINISCENCES, picture facing 12, 20, 25, 28-29; notes of an interview by the author with Dow's granddaughter, Mrs. William C. Eaton of Portland, Maine; note by Frederick N. Dow on Neal Dow to wife, January 24, 1862. Unless otherwise indicated, all manuscript items cited in this chapter are in the Dow Collection in Mrs. Eaton's possession.

[5]Dow, REMINISCENCES, 35-37; Dow to wife, March 23, 1863.

[6]Dow, REMINISCENCES, 29-30.

[7]Ibid., 25-26, 38-39, 204-05.

[8]Clifford S. Griffin, THEIR BROTHERS' KEEPERS, MORAL STEWARDSHIP IN THE UNITED STATES, 1800-1865 (New Brunswick, New Jersey, c. 1960), 3-13.

[9]Dow, REMINISCENCES, 22, 39-40, 44-46, 121, 124-26, 130, 158-59, 166-70; Willis, HISTORY OF PORTLAND, part 2: 187-88, 282-84; Moses Green-leaf, A SURVEY OF THE STATE OF MAINE IN REFERENCE TO ITS GEO-GRAPHICAL FEATURES, STATISTICS AND POLITICAL ECONOMY (Portland, 1829), 274, 451, 452; Neal Dow, AN ORATION DELIVERED BEFORE THE MAINE CHARITABLE MECHANIC ASSOCIATION AT THEIR TRIENNIAL CEL-EBRATION, JULY 4, 1829 (Portland, 1829), 10-11, 24. In 1820, Portland's

rum distilleries were the most important manufacturing industry in Cumberland County. The census ennumerator commented on their product, "The article, generally speaking, in good demand." DIGEST OF ACCOUNTS OF MANUFACTURING ESTABLISHMENTS IN THE UNITED STATES AND OF THEIR MANUFACTURES, MADE UNDER DIRECTION OF THE SECRETARY OF STATE IN PURSUANCE OF A RESOLUTION OF 30TH MARCH, 1822 (Washington, 1823), 2; Federal Writers' Project, MAINE, 60; Samuel Freeman, ed., EXTRACTS FROM THE JOURNALS KEPT BY THE REV. THOMAS SMITH, LATE PASTOR OF THE FIRST CHURCH OF CHRIST IN FALMOUTH IN THE COUNTY OF YORK (NOW CUMBERLAND) FROM THE YEAR 1720 TO THE YEAR 1788, WITH AN APPENDIX CONTAINING A VARIETY OF OTHER MATTERS (Portland, 1821), 105; reports of election results in Portland EASTERN ARGUS, November 8, 30, 1804, April 5, 1815, April 20, 1819, April 9, 1822.

[10]Griffin, THEIR BROTHERS' KEEPERS, 10-16, 37; Charles I. Foster, AN ERRAND OF MERCY, THE EVANGELICAL UNITED FRONT, 1790-1837 (Chapel Hill, c. 1960), 133-135; Bernard A. Weisberger, THEY GATHERED AT THE RIVER, THE STORY OF THE GREAT REVIVALISTS AND THEIR IMPACT UPON RELIGION IN AMERICA (Boston, c. 1958), 5-10, 76-77.

[11]Dow, REMINISCENCES, 103, 157-61, 184-92; records of the Sixty-Nine reprinted in Portland WASHINGTONIAN JOURNAL, February 10, 17, 24, 1847; letter of "W." in Portland MAINE TEMPERANCE GAZETTE AND WASHINGTONIAN HERALD, September 15, 1842; ARGUS, news report, July 12, letter of "Equity," December 5, letter of "A Friend to Order," December 27, 1815, letter of "Fair Play," February 13, letters of "The Baptist," March 19 and 26, news report, June 19, 1816, notice of Overseers of the Poor, May 28, 1818; Willis, HISTORY OF PORTLAND, 231, 234-35, 286-87; Harris E. Starr, "Edward Payson" in Dumas Malone, ed., DICTIONARY OF AMERICAN BIOGRAPHY (20 vols., New York, 1928-36), 14: 333-34; Griffin, THEIR BROTHERS' KEEPERS, 13, 37-38.

[12]Dow, REMINISCENCES, 31-34, 47-58; Leonard Bolles Ellis, HISTORY OF NEW BEDFORD AND ITS VICINITY, 1602-1892 (Syracuse, New York, 1892), 626-30; Daniel Ricketson, THE HISTORY OF NEW BEDFORD, BRISTOL COUNTY, MASSACHUSETTS, INCLUDING A HISTORY OF THE OLD TOWNSHIP OF DARTMOUTH AND THE PRESENT TOWNSHIPS OF WESTPORT, DARTMOUTH AND FAIRHAVEN FROM THEIR EARLIEST SETTLEMENTS TO THE PRESENT TIME (New Bedford, 1858), 325-27; Dow to wife, May 16, 1863; notes of an interview by the author with Mrs. William C. Eaton; Dow, ORATION BEFORE THE MECHANIC ASSOCIATION, 10-11, 13.

[13]Dow, REMINISCENCES, 68-73.

[14]Ibid., 102-04; Hatch, MAINE HISTORY, 3:733-34.

[15]Dow, REMINISCENCES, 59, 101-02, 126, 618-19.

CHAPTER II

[1]Neal Dow, THE REMINISCENCES OF NEAL DOW, RECOLLECTIONS OF EIGHTY YEARS (Portland, 1898), 61, 65-66, 192-93, 195; "Select Tunes for the Flute," a book of music compiled by Dow. Unless otherwise indicated, all manuscript items cited in this chapter are in the Dow Collection in the possession of Mrs. William C. Eaton of Portland.

[2]Dow, REMINISCENCES, 57, 66, picture opposite 332; notes of an interview by the author with Mrs. William C. Eaton; reminiscence by the Reverend Cyrus Hamlin of Dow's young manhood in Portland EXPRESS, March 21, 1894, clipping in Neal Dow Scrapbook, 26:68. All Dow Scrapbooks cited in this chapter are on deposit in the library of Drew University.

[3]Dow, REMINISCENCES, 73-81.

[4]Ibid., 78, 81, 86; legal notice of partnership in PORTLAND ADVERTISER, April 4, 1826; Dow's Ledger Number 1, p. 8; /Charles Holden7, CONSTITUTION OF THE MAINE CHARITABLE MECHANIC ASSOCIATION, INSTITUTED JANUARY 16, 1815, AND INCORPORATED JUNE 14, 1815, WITH A HISTORICAL SKETCH (Portland, 1875), 61; Neal Dow, AN ORATION DELIVERED BEFORE THE MAINE CHARITABLE MECHANIC ASSOCIATION AT THEIR TRIENNIAL CELEBRATION, JULY 4, 1829 (Portland, 1829); reminiscence by Hamlin, EXPRESS, March 21, 1894, in Dow Scrapbook, 26:68.

[5]PORTLAND ADVERTISER, June 13, 27, 1826, April 3, 1827; Dow, REMINISCENCES, 60, 104-06; specimen of Dow's minutes of the Deluge Company in Alonzo A. Miner, "Neal Dow and His Life Work" in NEW ENGLAND MAGAZINE, 10:400 (June, 1894).

[6]Dow, REMINISCENCES, 60-61, 92-94, 125-29; ADVERTISER, March 7, 17, 1826, September 5, October 17, 24, 1828; William A. Robinson, "William Pitt Fessenden" in Dumas Malone, ed., DICTIONARY OF AMERICAN BIOGRAPHY (20 vols., New York, 1928-36), 6:348-50; Carleton Mabee, THE AMERICAN LEONARDO, A LIFE OF SAMUEL F. B. MORSE (New York, 1943), 208-09; Neal Dow to wife, August 11, 1830; notes of an interview by the author with Mrs. William C. Eaton.

[7]Dow, REMINISCENCES, 66-68, picture facing 332; John Neal, PORTLAND ILLUSTRATED (Portland, 1874), frontispiece, and WANDERING RECOLLECTIONS OF A SOMEWHAT BUSY LIFE, AN AUTOBIOGRAPHY (Boston, 1869), 333-34; Milton Ellis, "John Neal" in Malone, ed., DICTIONARY OF AMERICAN BIOGRAPHY, 13:398-99.

[8]Letter of "Auguste," mistakenly printed "Augusta," and Neal's strictures thereon in Portland YANKEE AND BOSTON LITERARY GAZETTE, August 27, September 3, 1828; Neal, WANDERING RECOLLECTIONS, 347.

[9]Clifford S. Griffin, THEIR BROTHERS' KEEPERS, MORAL STEWARDSHIP IN THE UNITED STATES, 1800-1865 (New Brunswick, New Jersey, c. 1960), 5-7, 23-49; Charles I. Foster, AN ERRAND OF MERCY, THE EVANGELICAL UNITED FRONT, 1790-1837 (Chapel Hill, North Carolina, c. 1960), 47-57, 121-32. For the quotation, see Lyman Beecher, THE MEMORY OF

OUR FATHERS, A SERMON DELIVERED AT PLYMOUTH ON THE TWENTY-SECOND OF DECEMBER, 1827 (Boston, 1828), 18.

[10]Dow's Private Expense Account Book indicates that his personal spending for what he considered charitable purposes rose from $3.25 in 1830 to $204.63 in 1850. His individual donations were rarely over $5. He spent increasing amounts on temperance tracts and on his expenses to attend temperance meetings. For his views on slavery, see Dow, REMINISCENCES, 22-23, 125, and Neal, WANDERING RECOLLECTIONS, 334-35.

[11]Lyman Beecher, SIX SERMONS ON THE NATURE, OCCASIONS, SIGNS, EVILS AND REMEDY OF INTEMPERANCE (6th ed., Boston, 1828), 62-66, 89-101; Dow, REMINISCENCES, 196-98; John A. Krout, THE ORIGINS OF PROHIBITION (New York, 1925), 101-18; Foster, ERRAND OF MERCY, 171-73; ADVERTISER, October 16, 1827.

[12]Dow, REMINISCENCES, 109-10, 206-07. On December 31, 1835, the Deluge Company held one of Portland's first wineless public suppers. ADVERTISER, January 5, 1836.

[13]ADVERTISER, December 25, 1827, February 28, 1828; Portland CHRISTIAN MIRROR, February 24, 1831; PORTLAND ADVERTISER AND GAZETTE, February 12, 1830; John Neal, ADDRESS DELIVERED BEFORE THE PORTLAND ASSOCIATION FOR THE PROMOTION OF TEMPERANCE, FEBRUARY 11, 1829 (Portland, 1829); Portland EASTERN ARGUS, October 23, 1827.

[14]Dow, REMINISCENCES, 205-10; ARGUS, February 3, 1829; Holden, CONSTITUTION OF THE MECHANIC ASSOCIATION, 16; ADVERTISER AND GAZETTE, February 6, 1829; William Hutchinson Rowe, THE MARITIME HISTORY OF MAINE, THREE CENTURIES OF SHIPBUILDING & SEAFARING (New York, c. 1948), 112-15, 127-28.

[15]Dow, ORATION BEFORE THE MECHANIC ASSOCIATION, and REMINISCENCES, 210-11.

[16]Ibid., 20, 193-95; Krout, ORIGINS OF PROHIBITION, 106; Augusta MAINE TEMPERANCE GAZETTE, October 14, 1841. Dow continued for about fifteen years to approve of the use of wine for medicinal purposes and to permit it in his home. Portland MAINE TEMPERANCE JOURNAL, February 18, 1860; Private Expense Account Book, July 11, 1837; Neal, WANDERING RECOLLECTIONS, 370.

CHAPTER III

[1]Neal Dow, THE REMINISCENCES OF NEAL DOW, RECOLLECTIONS OF EIGHTY YEARS (Portland, 1898), 82-88.

[2]Dow spent $552 for his large lot and $4,766.18 for his house, making a total of $5,318.18. Dow's Ledger Number 1 and Private Expense Account Book. Unless otherwise stated, all manuscript items cited in this chapter are in the Dow Collection in the possession of Mrs. William C. Eaton of Portland. See also the author's notes of an interview with Mrs. Eaton; Frederick N. Dow,

"Reminiscences, " ch. 2, a typed manuscript; Dow, REMINISCENCES, 82-83; reminiscence by George H. Shirley in PORTLAND HERALD, February 22, 1894, clipping in the Neal Dow Scrapbook, 25:136. Unless otherwise noted, all Dow Scrapbooks cited in this chapter are on deposit in the library of Drew University.

[3]As his own parents had done, Dow sent his children to private schools. In the 1840's, he owned an elementary schoolhouse and paid his children's tuition through a reduction in rent. Dow, REMINISCENCES, 73, 86; record pages of the family BIBLE in the Dow Collection; Neal Dow to wife, May 19, 1835; Frederick N. Dow, "Reminiscences, " ch. 3. pp. 1-4, ch. 4, pp. 1-9; a ledger covering 1840-48 hereafter cited as Ledger Number 2, pp. 23, 77; Lillian M. N. Stevens, "Glimpses of Neal Dow at Home" in UNION SIGNAL, February 25, 1897, clipping in the Neal Dow Scrapbook, 28:3, in the New York State Library; Frederick N. Dow, PROHIBITION, WHY, HOW, THEN, NOW (n. p., 1931), 5-6.

[4]Dow's Ledgers Number 1 and Number 2 give a complete picture of his early business activities. See also his REMINISCENCES, 90-91. The quotation is from Dow to Thomas Drew, January 1, 1837, copied in the back of Ledger Number 1.

[5]Dow, REMINISCENCES, 90, 214-15; Portland PRESS, August 9, 1871; PORTLAND SUNDAY TIMES, February 3, 1901, clipping in the Portland Scrapbook, Vol. 1, of the Maine Historical Society; BIOGRAPHICAL REVIEW, CUMBERLAND COUNTY, MAINE (Boston, 1896), 193-95.

[6]A year before his speculation, Dow opined that he was "satisfied that nothing can be done in the land way, by persons unacquainted with particular tracts, and the qualities etc. " Dow to wife, "(Winter of 1833-34), " May 14, 16, 19, 1835, Ledger Number 1, pp. 5, 13, 42, 54, 55, 58, 72, 83, 85, Ledger Number 2, pp. 12, 29, 32, 33, 40, 43; Dow, REMINISCENCES, 89-90.

[7]THE PORTLAND DIRECTORY, CONTAINING THE NAMES OF THE INHABITANTS, THEIR OCCUPATIONS, PLACES OF BUSINESS AND DWELLING HOUSES AND THE CITY REGISTER WITH LISTS OF THE STREETS, COURTS AND WHARVES, THE CITY OFFICERS, PUBLIC OFFICES, BANKS AND SOCIETIES, TOGETHER WITH OTHER USEFUL INFORMATION (Portland, 1834), map in front and 9-10. For Dow's investments in Portland real estate, see the "Schedules of Property" in his Ledgers Number 1 and Number 2 and Dow to John Hodgdon, April 16, 1831, copied in the back of the former.

[8]Dow's Private Expense Account Book, May, October, 1834; Ledger Number 1, pp. 52, 80, 87; Dow to wife, August 27, 1832, August 11, 1839.

[9]Dow mistakenly gives 1837 as the date on which he became Chief Engineer. Dow, REMINISCENCES, 51, 58, 66, 106-07, 109, 128-33; PORTLAND ADVERTISER, October 15, 1831, May 18, 1832, April 2, 1833, January 16, September 17, 1834, April 7, 9, 1835, October 18, 1838, April 18, 1839, August 7, 1840, January 6, 1847. The last issue announces Dow's election as one of the Atheneum's directors. See also, Ledger Number 1, p. 107, Ledger Number 2, p. 10; PORTLAND EXPRESS, March 20, 1894, clipping

in Dow Scrapbook, 25:200; PORTLAND PRESS, October 9, 1897; Dow to Thomas C. Amory, March 8, 1830, in the Boston Public Library. For an account of the political background of Dow's appointment as Chief Engineer, see a letter of John Neal in Portland MAINE EXPOSITOR, October 19, 1853.

[10]Dow's Private Expense Account Book, February 4, 1830; Ledger Number 1, p. 17; Dow, REMINISCENSES, 87; Dow to wife, August 11, 1830, August 27, 1832, May 16, 1835, October 16, 1840, November 7, 1852, October 30, 1853; Frances E. Willard, "Neal Dow at Home, " clipping in Dow Scrapbook, 22:174.

[11]Dow, REMINISCENCES, 125-26, 131-32; William B. Hesseltine, THE RISE AND FALL OF THIRD PARTIES FROM ANTI-MASONRY TO WALLACE (Washington, c. 1948), 10-11; Charles McCarthy, THE ANTIMASONIC PARTY, A STUDY OF POLITICAL ANTIMASONRY IN THE UNITED STATES, 1827-1840 (ANNUAL REPORT OF THE AMERICAN HISTORICAL ASSOCIATION, 1902), 1:371, 537-50; anti-Jackson address and circular to Anti-Masons in the ADVERTISER, October 29, November 2, 1832; Dow to Ralph R. Gurley, January 18, 1835, Letters Received 60, pt. 1, Papers of the American Colonization Society, Library of Congress.

[12]In 1833, a violent debate between colonizationists and abolitionists, the latter of whom had already organized, preceded the formation of a Portland branch of the American Colonization Society. Ex-Governor Albion K. Parris was the new group's president and Josiah Dow was on its committee to solicit members. Portland CHRISTIAN MIRROR, July 18, 25, 31, 1833; ADVERTISER, July 26, 1833. The ADVERTISER for August 31, 1835, contains a notice appointing Neal Dow to a committee of the Colonization Society's auxiliary. See also, Dow to Gerrit Smith, April 21, 1836, in the Gerrit Smith Papers, Syracuse University. A photostat is in the author's possession. For the anti-abolitionist mob, see Dow, REMINISCENCES, 107-09; John Neal, WANDERING RECOLLECTIONS OF A SOMEWHAT BUSY LIFE, AN AUTO-BIOGRAPHY (Boston, 1869), 401, 403-04, 406; CHRISTIAN MIRROR, December 8, 1836, and Portland JOURNAL OF REFORM, November 2, 1836.

[13]ANNUAL REPORT OF THE CUMBERLAND COUNTY TEMPERANCE SOCIETY, 1831, p. 1, 1835, p. 12; notice of meeting in the PORTLAND ADVERTISER AND GAZETTE, March 22, 1830; ANNUAL REPORT OF THE MAINE TEMPERANCE SOCIETY, 1833, pp. 8-70, 1834, pp. 21-24, 28; "Minute Book of the Portland Young Men's Temperance Society, 1833-34," with list of members; Dow, REMINISCENCES, 211-14; CHRISTIAN MIRROR, February 24, 1831, January 23, 1834.

[14]Dow, REMINISCENCES, 215-16; Cumberland County Temperance Society, REPORT, 1835, pp. 13-14; Maine Temperance Society, REPORT, 1835, p. 28.

[15]Dow, REMINISCENCES, 96-97.

[16]Ibid. , 232; John A. Krout, THE ORIGINS OF PROHIBITION (New York, 1925), 155-58, 162-68; CHRISTIAN MIRROR, February 12, 1835, January 21, March 3, 17, 24, 31, April 7, 1836; Neal, WANDERING RECOLLECTIONS,

363-70.

[17]Krout, ORIGINS OF PROHIBITION, 153-67; Clifford S. Griffin, THEIR BROTHERS' KEEPERS, MORAL STEWARDSHIP IN THE UNITED STATES, 1800-1865 (New Brunswick, New Jersey, c. 1960), 71-72.

[18]Dow, REMINISCENCES, 165-66, 232-34, 240; ANNUAL REPORT OF THE MAINE TEMPERANCE SOCIETY, 1833, p. 3; Augusta JOURNAL, February 5, 7, 1835; CHRISTIAN MIRROR, February 18, 25, 1836, March 2, 9, 1837. For Adams, see Edwin C. Whittemore, ed., THE CENTENNIAL HISTORY OF WATERVILLE, KENNEBEC COUNTY, MAINE, INCLUDING THE HISTORICAL ADDRESS AND THE POEM PRESENTED AT THE CELEBRATION OF THE CENTENNIAL ANNIVERSARY OF THE INCORPORATION OF THE TOWN, JUNE 23D, 1902 (Waterville, 1902), 441-42; Freeman Yates, "The Maine Law, A Complete History of Its Origin, Operation & Progress," ch. 4, in the Detroit TEMPERANCE ADVOCATE, 1853 or 1854, clipping in Dow Scrapbook, 1:36. For King, see Louis C. Hatch, MAINE, A HISTORY (3 vols., New York, 1919), 1:118-20.

[19]Dow, REMINISCENCES, 197, 214, 234-35, 243-47, 265-66; ADVERTISER, September 14, 1836, February 27, 1837; manuscript "Journal of the Maine House of Representatives," 1837, pp. 143, 228, 299, microfilm copy in the library of the Wisconsin Historical Society; CHRISTIAN MIRROR, March 30, 1837. For Appleton, see also John J. Babson, HISTORY OF THE TOWN OF GLOUCESTER, CAPE ANN, INCLUDING THE TOWN OF ROCKPORT (Gloucester, Massachusetts, 1860), 363; Thomas F. Waters, IPSWICH IN THE MASSACHUSETTS BAY COLONY, A HISTORY OF THE TOWN FROM 1700 TO 1917 (2 vols., Ipswich, 1917), 2:716, and THE OLD BAY ROAD FROM SALTONSTALL'S BROOK AND SAMUEL APPLETON'S FARM AND A GENEALOGY OF THE IPSWICH DESCENDENTS OF SAMUEL APPLETON. PUBLICATIONS OF THE IPSWICH HISTORICAL SOCIETY, NO. 15 (Salem, Massachusetts, 1907), 39.

[20]CHRISTIAN MIRROR, April 27, May 11, 1837; Neal, WANDERING RECOLLECTIONS, 376-77; Dow, REMINISCENCES, 268.

[21]CHRISTIAN MIRROR, Statement of the Executive Committee of the Maine Temperance Society, February 23, editorial, March 23, 1837, Report of the Executive Committee of the Maine Temperance Union, March 15, 1838; Augusta GOSPEL BANNER AND MAINE CHRISTIAN PILOT, February 11, 1837, February 17, March 10, 1838; Dow, REMINISCENCES, 253; Krout, ORIGINS OF PROHIBITION, 160-62.

[22]CHRISTIAN MIRROR, December 28, 1837; Portland EASTERN ARGUS, January 19, February 24, March 2, 3, 7, 12, 13, 15, 22, 23, 1838; Augusta KENNEBEC JOURNAL, March 28, 1838; GOSPEL BANNER, February 16, 1839; ADVERTISER, February 25, March 7, 12, 15, 16, October 1, 1839; Augusta MAINE TEMPERANCE GAZETTE, February 28, March 21, August 1, December 5, 1839, February 13, 1840; Dow, REMINISCENCES, 251-54, 269-70. While the proponents of statewide prohibition had suffered a setback, a temperance lecturer passing through Maine in the spring of 1840 ex-

pressed surprise at the large number of towns in which little or no liquor was sold. Excerpt from a letter of S. Chipman in the JOURNAL OF THE AMERICAN TEMPERANCE UNION, April, 1840.

CHAPTER IV

[1]Neal Dow, THE REMINISCENCES OF NEAL DOW, RECOLLECTIONS OF EIGHTY YEARS (Portland, 1898), 271-72; John A. Krout, THE ORIGINS OF PROHIBITION (New York, 1925), 182-88.

[2]Letters of "N. D." in the Augusta MAINE TEMPERANCE GAZETTE, March 12, April 16, 1840. Dow frequently signed newspaper letters "N. D." or "D." See also, Portland CHRISTIAN MIRROR, March 4, 11, 1841. A Congregational minister, Lovejoy was the brother of abolitionist martyr Elijah Lovejoy, an editor killed in 1837 at Alton, Illinois. Nehemiah Cleveland, HISTORY OF BOWDOIN COLLEGE WITH BIOGRAPHICAL SKETCHES OF ITS GRADUATES FROM 1806 TO 1879 INCLUSIVE (Boston, 1882), 396.

[3]Dow, REMINISCENCES, 272-74, picture opposite 276, 291-92; Freeman Yates, "The Maine Law, A Complete History of Its Origin, Operation and Progress," ch. 3, in the Detroit TEMPERANCE ADVOCATE, 1853 or 1854, clipping in the Dow Scrapbook, 1:32-34; letters of "N. D." and "T. O. L." in the TEMPERANCE GAZETTE for, respectively, May 13, 27, 1841; letter of "D." in the PORTLAND ADVERTISER, May 20, 1841. For Walton, see [W. Woodford Clayton], HISTORY OF CUMBERLAND CO., MAINE, WITH ILLUSTRATIONS AND BIOGRAPHICAL SKETCHES OF ITS PROMINENT MEN AND PIONEERS (Philadelphia, 1880), 129, and the Neal Dow Diary, April 15, 1888. Unless otherwise indicated, all Dow Scrapbooks cited in this chapter are on deposit in the library of Drew University and all manuscript items are in the Dow Collection in the possession of Mrs. William C. Eaton of Portland, Maine.

[4]Dow, REMINISCENCES, 274-75, 277-78, 284-85; ADVERTISER, July 6, 12, August 6, 19, 1841; May 19, 1842; TEMPERANCE GAZETTE, May 27, June 3, July 15, 1841. For one of Jedediah Dow's advertisements for rum and groceries, see ADVERTISER, December 18, 1824. With characteristic enthusiasm, John Neal berated his fellow lawyers for refusing to join the temperance movement and for continuing to serve wine. Portland MAINE WASHINGTONIAN JOURNAL AND TEMPERANCE HERALD, March 8, 1843.

[5]Letters of "N. D." to the TEMPERANCE GAZETTE, June 3, 10, 24, July 1, August 12, October 14, 21, 28, 1841. Throughout this correspondence, Dow deprecates the effectiveness of using only "moral suasion" and calls for legal repression of liquor-sellers. Dow justifies his tactics in his REMINISCENCES, 93-94, 230, 255-56. For Cummings, see the CHRISTIAN MIRROR, July 22, 1841.

[6]Krout, ORIGINS OF PROHIBITION, 200-07; TEMPERANCE GAZETTE, September 30, October 28, 1841. Yates, "The Maine Law," ch. 3, in the

Detroit TEMPERANCE ADVOCATE, 1853 or 1854, clipping in the Dow Scrapbook, 1:32-34; MAINE TEMPERANCE GAZETTE AND WASHINGTONIAN HERALD, November 11, December 9, 1841. At its 1841 meeting, the Maine Temperance Union had districted the state. Its Western District included York, Cumberland and Oxford Counties. CHRISTIAN MIRROR, February 17, 1841. On October 12, 1842, at a meeting at Portland, Dow became chairman of the Executive Committee of the whole Maine Temperance Union. JOURNAL OF THE AMERICAN TEMPERANCE UNION, 6:172 (November, 1842).

[7]Letter of "N. D." and editorial comment in the TEMPERANCE GAZETTE AND W. H., for, respectively, January 6, 13, 1842; Augusta GOSPEL BANNER, February 12, 1842.

[8]The license law did not apply to wholesale transactions of over 28 gallons. Letters of "N. D.," TEMPERANCE GAZETTE AND W. H., March 31, April 21, 28, May 12, 1842. See also letters signed as indicated in the following issues of the ADVERTISER, "Many" and "H.," June 28, "D.," July 2, August 17, 23, 24, "Augustine Haines," August 19, 1842.

[9]ADVERTISER, August 1, 1842; Dow, REMINISCENCES, 278-80; letter of "N. D." and editorial material in the TEMPERANCE GAZETTE AND W. H., July 28, August 4, 11, September 1, 29, October 6, 13, 27, 1842; Portland MAINE WASHINGTONIAN JOURNAL AND TEMPERANCE HERALD, November 9, 16, 23, 1842. The title of the last source represents a second change of name for the Reverend Thomas Adams' MAINE TEMPERANCE GAZETTE.

[10]Dow, REMINISCENCES, 109-18; WASHINGTONIAN JOURNAL AND T. H., December 14, 1842, February 8, 15, 22, March 8, 29, April 5, 19, 1843; ADVERTISER, January 28, February 28, March 3, 7, 9, 14, 15, 24, 25, April 3, 4, 1843. For Codman and Smith, see, respectively, Cleveland, HISTORY OF BOWDOIN, 187, and Carleton Mabee, THE AMERICAN LEONARDO, A LIFE OF SAMUEL F. B. MORSE (New York, 1943), 208-11.

[11]WASHINGTONIAN JOURNAL AND T. H., May 10, June 7, July 19, August 2, 23, 1843, and the following items in the indicated issues of the ADVERTISER, report on the meeting, July 14, letter of Neal Dow, August 5, letter of Eliphalet Case, August 7, letter of Dow, August 16, letter of Case, August 23, 1843.

[12]Dow, REMINISCENCES, 298-99; ADVERTISER, February 14, March 20, 1844.

[13]Dow, REMINISCENCES, 301-02. In the fall of 1843, Judge Daniel Goodenow of the District Court had pressed County Attorney Augustine Haines to prosecute and convict unlicensed liquor-sellers. Encouraged by this temporary victory, Dow crowed that no more cases would be "HUNG UP TO DRY." Letters of "Franklin" and "N. D." in the WASHINGTONIAN JOURNAL AND T. H., October 25, 1843.

[14]WASHINGTONIAN JOURNAL AND T. H., October 4, 1843; Portland TRUE WASHINGTONIAN AND MARTHA WASHINGTON ADVOCATE, October 4, 1843, January 10, 17, February 7, June 26, July 3, 10, 1844; Augusta

GOSPEL BANNER, February 17, 24, 1844; CHRISTIAN MIRROR, February 22, 1844; ADVERTISER, March 18, 21, 25, 1844. In a letter in the JOURNAL OF THE AMERICAN TEMPERANCE UNION, 8:87 (June, 1844), Dow denied the moral suasionists' status as "friends of Temperance." He spoke of "a small clique, the members of which claim to be temperance men, but whose chief object it is to uphold and countenance the 'Rum Traffic,' and to prevent its entire and speedy suppression."

[15]In June, 1844, the Portland authorities introduced a plan of licensing four merchants, "who have the cause of temperance at heart," to sell liquor for medicinal and industrial purposes and warned all other sellers to stop. ADVERTISER, June 12, October 25, 1844; CHRISTIAN MIRROR, February 13, 1845; Neal Dow, Private Expense Account Book, January 31, 1845.

CHAPTER V

[1]Neal Dow to the editor of the WORCESTER CATARACT, quoted in the JOURNAL OF THE AMERICAN TEMPERANCE UNION, 9:189 (December, 1845).

[2]On July 4, 1840, at Gorham, Maine, as part of the furious Whig campaign to elect General William H. "Old Tippecanoe" Harrison to the presidency, Dow had delivered a "non-partisan" address designed to aid the Whigs "without irritating such Democrats as might favor me with their presence." Neal Dow, THE REMINISCENCES OF NEAL DOW, RECOLLECTIONS OF EIGHTY YEARS (Portland, 1898), 136-37. For Dow's commission, see General Order Number 1 of Governor Edward Kent, in the PORTLAND ADVERTISER, January 27, 1841, and John Neal, WANDERING RECOLLECTIONS OF A SOMEWHAT BUSY LIFE, AN AUTOBIOGRAPHY (Boston, 1869), 407-09. The letters, signed "D.," are in the ADVERTISER, January 13, 21, 27, February 3, March 1, 4, 11, 19, 30, May 7, 11, 1841.

[3]Dow, REMINISCENCES, 120-21, 280-83, 306; Frederick N. Dow, "Reminiscences," a typed manuscript, ch. 8, pp. 1-5. Unless otherwise indicated, all manuscript items cited in this chapter are in the Dow Collection in the possession of Mrs. William C. Eaton of Portland, Maine. For Dow's activity in city politics, see page 32 above; ADVERTISER, March 24, 1844, April 15, 1845, April 4, 1846; L. L. Sadler to Francis O. J. Smith, April 20, 1845, in the F. O. J. Smith Correspondence, New York Public Library; Portland WASHINGTONIAN JOURNAL, April 22, 1846, April 7, 1847. In April, 1846, because of bolting of the Whig ticket, Dow lost his $100 a year job as Chief Engineer. More interested by then in temperance than in fire-fighting, he declined the invitation of the Deluge Company to return to his old post as its Captain. ADVERTISER, April 7, 1846; Dow, REMINISCENCES, 118. By abolishing the compulsory militia muster, the legislature had eliminated his original reason for becoming a fireman. Louis C. Hatch, MAINE, A HISTORY (3 vols., New York, 1919), 3:734-35.

4WASHINGTONIAN JOURNAL, November 29, 1843, March 5, 1845; Portland CHRISTIAN MIRROR, February 13, 1845; ADVERTISER, February 14, 20, 1845; Augusta GOSPEL BANNER, April 5, 1845.

5ADVERTISER, September 5, 8, October 3, 1845, November 6, 17, 20, 1847. Nehemiah Cleveland, HISTORY OF BOWDOIN COLLEGE WITH BIOGRAPHICAL SKETCHES OF ITS GRADUATES FROM 1806 TO 1879 INCLUSIVE (Boston, 1882), 390; Portland MAINE TEMPERANCE GAZETTE AND WASHINGTONIAN HERALD, November 18, 1841. In recalling his controversy with Barnes, Dow later confused incidents of the legislative campaigns of 1845 and 1847. Dow, REMINISCENCES, 315-18.

6ADVERTISER, September 9, 18, 30, October 1, 3, 4, 6, 7, 9, 1845; Portland EASTERN ARGUS, October 2, 1845.

7Shirley shortened the name of Adams' former newspaper to the WASHINGTONIAN JOURNAL, March 5, December 3, 1845, January 7, 21, 28, February 4, 11, 25, 1846, and letter of "N. D." in the latter issue; Neal Dow to wife, January 7, 12, February 19, 1845, February 11, 1846; Dow, REMINISCENCES, 290-98. For Shirley's replacement of Adams, see the MAINE WASHINGTONIAN JOURNAL AND TEMPERANCE HERALD, September 13, 1843. Dow, who was ever conscious of the need for a publicity organ, twice in 1846 contributed $10 to Shirley's newspaper. Neal Dow, Private Expense Account Book, March 14, June 29, 1846. For Shirley, see Dow to wife, October 16, 1859, November 29, 1868; notes of an interview of the author with Mrs. William C. Eaton, clipping from a Bethel, Maine, newspaper in the Neal Dow Scrapbook, 27:336. All Dow Scrapbooks cited in this chapter are on deposit in the library of Drew University.

8See the following items in the indicated issues of the WASHINGTONIAN JOURNAL, letter of "N. D., " February 25, letter of "Amicus, " April 22, call for the meeting of the Maine Temperance Union, June 3, proceedings of the meeting, July 8, 1846; Dow, REMINISCENCES, 260-61; Henry S. Clubb, THE MAINE LIQUOR LAW, ITS ORIGIN, HISTORY AND RESULTS, INCLUDING A LIFE OF HON. NEAL DOW (New York, 1856), 18-19.

9Correspondents for the East Thomaston LIME ROCK GAZETTE, Hallowell LIBERTY STANDARD and NORWAY ADVERTISER quoted in the WASHINGTONIAN JOURNAL, July 8, 1846; Dow, REMINISCENCES, 261.

10Dow, REMINISCENCES, 313-15; William Pitt Fessenden to Ellen M. Fessenden, July 23, 1846, in the Fessenden Papers, Bowdoin College. A microfilm copy is in the library of the University of Virginia. See also, WASHINGTONIAN JOURNAL, July 22, 29, August 5, 1846, and ACTS AND RESOLVES PASSED BY THE TWENTY-SIXTH LEGISLATURE OF THE STATE OF MAINE, A. D. 1846, pp. 189-95.

11Circular letter of Neal Dow, September 18, 1846, in the Dow Scrapbook, 12:145; Clubb, THE MAINE LAW, 19; letter of Neal Dow in the JOURNAL OF THE AMERICAN TEMPERANCE UNION, 10:150 (October, 1846). On September 30, 1846, the WASHINGTONIAN JOURNAL reported that it was receiving letters raising the question of abandoning the use of tobacco. Subsequent prohibitionist victories would produce the same proposal for additional reform.

[12]WASHINGTONIAN JOURNAL, October 7, 28, November 4, December 2, 23, 30, 1846; January 20, March 24, July 14, 1847. Dow, REMINISCENCES, 299-300.

[13]Among the licensees was Royal Williams, owner of Portland's last distillery. WASHINGTONIAN JOURNAL, October 14, November 4, 11, December 30, 1846, January 20, 27, February 3, May 3, 12, July 7, 21, August 4, September 15, 1847.

[14]ADVERTISER, September 13, 14, 23, 27, 28, October 12, 23, 26 30, November 4-6, 9, 15, 18, 20, 22, 23, December 1, 3, 14, 28, 1847; the following items in the indicated issues of the WASHINGTONIAN JOURNAL, editorial, November 3, letter of Neal Dow reprinted on November 17 from the EASTERN ARGUS, editorial and letter of Dow, November 24, 1847, letter of Dow, January 19, 1848. At the general election in September, 1847, Maine's voters approved a constitutional amendment requiring only a plurality in future elections of representatives. ARGUS, September 25, 1847. Soon after the contest, Dow paid $43 to Temperance editor George H. Shirley. Dow, Private Expense Account Book, March, 1848.

[15]Letters of "N. D." in the WASHINGTONIAN JOURNAL, July 26, August 2, September 27, October 11, November 1, 1848. Dow held stock in the Atlantic and St. Lawrence and Androscoggin and Kennebec Railroads. Dow, Ledger Number 2, pp. 43, 89. On July 3, 1849, he defeated his old enemy, Phineas Barnes, for a place on the Board of Directors of the latter line and served until 1851. ARGUS, July 6, 1849; ADVERTISER, July 17, 1850, July 2, 1851. For the quotations on Dow's policy, see Freeman Yates, "The Maine Law, A Complete History of Its Origin, Operation & Progress" in the Detroit TEMPERANCE ADVOCATE, 1853 or 1854, clipping in the Dow Scrapbook, 1:40, and Clubb, THE MAINE LAW, 21-22. In May, 1848, the American Temperance Union selected Dow to replace Edward Kent as its Vice-President for Maine. ANNUAL REPORT OF THE AMERICAN TEMPERANCE UNION, 1848, p. 3.

CHAPTER VI

[1]Henry S. Clubb, THE MAINE LIQUOR LAW, ITS ORIGIN, HISTORY AND RESULTS, INCLUDING A LIFE OF HON. NEAL DOW (New York, 1856), 22; PORTLAND ADVERTISER, February 26, March 17, 19, July 2, 1849. In April, 1849, after a lapse of a year, a few temperance voters again bolted the regular tickets in the Portland municipal election. In two trials, 27 and 61 votes cast for Dow blocked the Whig mayoralty candidate from getting a popular majority. Portland EASTERN ARGUS, April 5, 1849.

[2]Neal Dow, THE REMINISCENCES OF NEAL DOW, RECOLLECTIONS OF EIGHTY YEARS (Portland, 1898), 288, 318-19; Portland WASHINGTONIAN JOURNAL, March 22, 1848; Portland CHRISTIAN MIRROR, June 28, 1849;

Dow, Private Expense Account Book, June, 1849. Unless otherwise indicated, all manuscript items cited in this chapter are in the Dow Collection in the possession of Mrs. William C. Eaton of Portland. For the text of Dow's proposed law, see the Augusta KENNEBEC JOURNAL, August 23, 1849. In the opinion of one editor, the cowhiding at Augusta of a pro-temperance trial justice helped to excite the lawmakers to grant Dow's request. Augusta GOSPEL BANNER, August 18, 1849.

3In the 1844 presidential election, because Dow objected to Whig candidate Henry Clay's reputation as a duelist and slaveholder, he had voted for James G. Birney, the unsuccessful Liberty party nominee. Dow, REMINISCENCES, 138. In joining the Free Soilers, Dow declared that "he would have his nose held to the grindstone by Southerners no longer." ADVERTISER, July 29, 1848. For the split in the Democracy, see Ibid., May 24 and June 27, 1849, and Lewis C. Hatch, MAINE, A HISTORY (3 vols., New York, 1919), 2:335-36, 341-46.

4Dow, REMINISCENCES, 122-23, 133-34; Charles E. Hamlin, THE LIFE AND TIMES OF HANNIBAL HAMLIN (Cambridge, Massachusetts, 1899), 42-43, picture facing 178, 196-214; CHRISTIAN MIRROR, February 14, 1850; Washington NATIONAL INTELLIGENCER, March 11, 1850; Dow, Private Expense Account Book, March 11, 1850; letter of "D.," ADVERTISER, March 8, 1850. Dow later sent some boxes of honey produced by bees in his garden to some congressmen's wives whom he had met. One of them wrote him that ". . . we all pronounce it FIRST RATE--'and no mistake'--'FREE soil or no free soil.'" Roxy Smith to Neal Dow, March 15, 1850, in the Neal Dow Scrapbook, 2:231. All Dow scrapbooks cited in this chapter are on deposit in the library of Drew University.

5ADVERTISER, May 22, 1850; Hamlin, HAMLIN, 236-49; Neal Dow to Hannibal Hamlin, July 25, [1850], December 23, 1850, George F. Emery to Hamlin, July 27, 1850, in the Hannibal Hamlin Papers, Maine Historical Society; Augusta KENNEBEC JOURNAL, September 5, 1850. As a minimum concession to the prohibitionists, the legislature amended the Prohibitory Law of 1846 to provide punishment for being a "common seller" of liquor. ADVERTISER, September 3, and, Extra, October, 1850; Dow, REMINISCENCES, 263, 319-21.

6This was the last meeting of the Maine Temperance Union. Dow, REMINISCENCES, 263-64, 309, 321-22; Clubb, THE MAINE LAW, 23; Gardiner FOUNTAIN AND JOURNAL, September 6, 1850. In 1848, just after Dow had delivered three temperance lectures at Durham, residents had organized the first of the Watchman Clubs. Everett S. Stackpole, HISTORY OF DURHAM, MAINE, WITH GENEALOGICAL NOTES (Lewiston, Maine, 1899), 131.

7Dow, REMINISCENCES, 322, 329-30, 362, 381; Clubb, THE MAINE LAW, 25-26. In 1850, Portland's one distillery was the last in Maine. MESSAGE OF THE PRESIDENT OF THE UNITED STATES COMMUNICATING A DIGEST OF MANUFACTURES ACCORDING TO THE THE RETURNS OF THE SEVENTH CENSUS (35 Congress, 2 session, Senate Executive Document no. 39), 47.

8Dow, REMINISCENCES, 322-27; ADVERTISER, April 8, 9, 17, 21, 22, June 28, 1851; ARGUS, April 9, 1851. An anonymous temperance writer later recalled that one of Dow's Temperance Watchman election workers, who was a reformed drinking-man, celebrated his chief's triumph by getting dead drunk. Clipping from the Portland EXPRESS, Dow Scrapbook, 24:34.

9Dow, REMINISCENCES, 332, 334-53, 433-34; Clubb, THE MAINE LAW, 28; ADVERTISER, May 15, 1851; Emma H. Nason, OLD HALLOWELL ON THE KENNEBEC (Augusta, Maine, 1909), 307-09.

10Dow, REMINISCENCES, 309, 362-81; ADVERTISER, June 23, July 14, September 30, 1851; ARGUS, August 18, 1851, quoted in the Portland MAINE EXPOSITOR, March 17, 1852; Portland MAINE TEMPERANCE WATCHMAN, November 29, December 6, 1851, January 24, 1852; John Neal, WANDERING RECOLLECTIONS OF A SOMEWHAT BUSY LIFE, AN AUTOBIOGRAPHY (Boston, 1869), 381.

11Report of Neal Dow in the TEMPERANCE WATCHMAN, October 4, 1851; Dow, REMINISCENCES, 401-10.

12Neal Dow to "Mr. Manchester," August 4, 1851, in the Essex Institute, Salem, Massachusetts. A photostatic copy is in the author's possession. TEMPERANCE WATCHMAN, August 30, October 25, 1851, January 17, 1852. Dow unsuccessfully invited two antislavery senators to lend their prestige to Portland's 1851 celebration of Independence Day. Neal Dow to Charles Sumner, May 20, 1851, in the Charles Sumner Papers, Harvard University, and Dow to William H. Seward, June 6, 1851, in the William H. Seward Collection, University of Rochester. A photostatic copy of the latter is in the author's possession.

13John Marsh, TEMPERANCE RECOLLECTIONS, LABORS, DEFEATS, TRIUMPHS, AN AUTOBIOGRAPHY (New York, 1866), 242-48; PROCEEDINGS OF THE FOURTH NATIONAL TEMPERANCE CONVENTION, 1851, pp. 1-33. Dow also drew the enthusiastic endorsements of the Reverend Lyman Beecher, whose writings had helped inspire his temperance work, and of the Reverend Thomas Adams, his associate of the early 1840's who was then living in Ohio. TEMPERANCE WATCHMAN, August 23, September 27, 1851.

14Clifford S. Griffin, THEIR BROTHERS' KEEPERS, MORAL STEWARD-SHIP IN THE UNITED STATES, 1800-1865 (New Brunswick, New Jersey, 1960), 149-51; ANNUAL REPORT OF THE AMERICAN TEMPERANCE UNION, 1852, pp. 7-14, 33; John Marsh, THE NAPOLEON OF TEMPERANCE, SKETCHES OF THE LIFE AND CHARACTER OF THE HON. NEAL DOW, MAYOR OF PORTLAND AND AUTHOR OF THE MAINE LIQUOR LAW (New York, 1852), 4; SIX REASONS WHY THE STATE OF NEW YORK SHOULD ADOPT THE MAINE LIQUOR LAW, PRESENTED BY THE STATE TEMPERANCE SOCIETY TO THE PEOPLE OF THE STATE, WITH THE MAINE LAW (New York, 1852); "A Massachusetts Clergyman," THE LAW OF MAINE AND THE LAW OF GOD, ALSO A REVIEW OF LOVEJOY'S LECTURE ON PROHIBITORY LAWS IN REGARD TO THE USE OF INTOXICATING DRINKS (Boston, 1852); TEMPERANCE WATCHMAN, December 13, 1851.

[15]Mary T. Mann, LIFE OF HORACE MANN (2d ed. , Boston, 1865), 348; Llerena Friend, SAM HOUSTON, THE GREAT DESIGNER (Austin, 1954), 280-81; TEMPERANCE WATCHMAN, February 28, 1852; Dow, REMINIS-CENCES, 415-16.

[16]Neal, WANDERING RECOLLECTIONS, 363-76. As late as December, 1851, John Neal was an active prohibitionist. TEMPERANCE WATCHMAN, December 20, 27, 1851, January 17, 1852. For "Kitty's" previous convictions, see the Portland WASHINGTONIAN JOURNAL, January 12, 1848, and the ADVERTISER, December 16, 1850, August 25, October 14, 1851. For the subsequent controversy, see a letter of Neal Dow and John Neal's comments on it reprinted from the Portland STATE OF MAINE in the EXPOSITOR, September 14, 1853.

[17]AMERICAN TEMPERANCE MAGAZINE AND SONS OF TEMPERANCE OFFERING (July, 1851), 1:237-43; Neal, WANDERING RECOLLECTIONS, 378-80, 385-86; EXPOSITOR, March 24, 1852, September 14, 1853. In an 1847 speech before the Portland aldermen, Dow had used many of the same instances of intemperance later recounted in the "True Tale" but had not involved Neal's family. Portland WASHINGTONIAN JOURNAL, February 3, March 3, 1847. Also in 1847, when John Neal had prosecuted a dealer under the Prohibitory Law of 1846 for selling liquor to Neal's heavy-drinking son, the lawyer had then admitted that, because of his opposition to extreme temperance measures, "it might, perhaps, now be charged upon him, that the judgement of God were, in consequence, visited upon him. " Ibid. , September 1, 1847.

[18]In August, 1851, Dow had had one seizure made on an arriving steamboat. ADVERTISER, August 2, 4, 1851, January 15, 1852; Dow, REMINISCENCES, 367-76, 381-83, 395-96, 403, 422-23; TEMPERANCE WATCHMAN, February 14, March 20, April 3, 1852; EXPOSITOR, March 2, April 5, 1852. After the election, Frederick W. Nichols and Company, one of Dow's old enemies and the sometime publishers of the TRUE WASHINGTONIAN, announced that it would continue publication of the EXPOSITOR as a statewide anti-Maine Law organ. Ibid. , April 14, 1852.

[19]ADVERTISER, March 22, 23, April 2, 5, 6, 1852; ARGUS, April 2, 1852; Dow, REMINISCENCES, 418-22. William Pitt Fessenden, the Whig who referred to the "Neal Dow party, " was Dow's City Solicitor and thus prosecuted liquor-sellers. He informed his cousin, however, that, "You need not conclude that I am either ultra-temperance, or 'teetotaller' [sic]--only 'Maine law'. . . . " Like Fessenden, many of Dow's political backers opposed "tippling shops" but themselves drank in their homes. William Pitt Fessenden to Elizabeth C. Warriner, May 9, 1852, in the William Pitt Fessenden Papers, Bowdoin College. A microfilm copy is at the University of Virginia.

[20]TEMPERANCE WATCHMAN, April 3, 1852; ARGUS, March 30, 1852; CHRISTIAN MIRROR, July 24, August 7, 1851, March 30, 1852.

[21]ADVERTISER, April 7, 13, 1852; Dow, REMINISCENCES, 423-27; TEMPERANCE WATCHMAN, April 10, 1852; THE MAINE LAW ILLUSTRATED,

BEING THE RESULT OF AN INVESTIGATION MADE IN THE MAINE LAW STATES BY A. FAREWELL AND G. P. URE, PRESIDENT AND SECRETARY OF THE CANADIAN PROHIBITORY LAW LEAGUE DURING THE MONTH OF FEBRUARY, 1855 (Toronto, Canada, n. d.), 50, 70-71; letter of John Neal in the EXPOSITOR, September 28, 1853.

CHAPTER VII

[1]ANNUAL REPORT OF THE AMERICAN TEMPERANCE UNION, 1855, p. 5.

[2]In 1851, Dow's older sister, Emma, who had married Neal D. Shaw of Baring, Maine, also died. Neal Dow, THE REMINISCENCES OF NEAL DOW, RECOLLECTIONS OF EIGHTY YEARS (Portland, 1898), 20-22, 26, 87-89, 91-92; Neal Dow to Cornelia Dow, September 17, October 3, 1853, January 17, March 1, 1854. Unless otherwise noted, all manuscript items cited in this chapter are in the Dow Collection in the possession of Mrs. William C. Eaton of Portland.

[3]Going on a speaking tour after Russell's death, Dow left his wife to nurse another sickly son, five-year-old Frank. Dow to wife, September 4, 1852, June 8, 14, 18, 30, July 1, 2, 1853, and the record page in the family Bible, in the Dow Collection, Portland.

[4]Dow, REMINISCENCES, 431-32, 453-59, 463-74, 496-97, 501. All of the Dow Collection's scores of letters written by Dow from 1852 through 1855 relate to his tours. The quoted words are in Dow to wife, January 19, 1853. Specimens of Dow's railroad and steamboat passes are pasted inside the front cover of the first volume of the Dow Scrapbook. All Dow Scrapbooks cited in this chapter are on deposit in Drew University. For a listener's reaction to Dow, see the SYRACUSE CHRONICLE quoted in the Portland MAINE TEMPERANCE WATCHMAN, June 25, 1853.

[5]Dow to wife, September 18, 1853; American Temperance Union, ANNUAL REPORT, 1853, pp. 39-43; Neal Dow to Edward C. Delavan in a clipping from the Albany DAILY STATE REGISTER, August 15, 1854, in the Dow Scrapbook, 3:62.

[6]Dow, REMINISCENCES, 433-47; Louis C. Hatch, MAINE, A HISTORY (3 vols., New York, 1919), 2:359-62; Neal Dow to James M. Wilson, August 11, 1852, in the Miscellaneous Manuscripts, New York Historical Society; Dow to wife, September 4, 1852; PORTLAND ADVERTISER, September 14, 16, 1852. For a discussion of the situation of the Maine Democracy with a prophecy of its disruption, see John Hubbard to Hannibal Hamlin, January 12, 1852. Hubbard subsequently pleased Dow by presiding over a State Temperance Convention and publicly espousing the Maine Law. Dow to Hamlin, January 23, 1852. Both these letters are in the Hannibal Hamlin Papers, Maine Historical Society.

[7]Dow, REMINISCENCES, 138-39; Neal Dow to William H. Seward, June 24, September 25, October 1, 1852, in the Seward Collection, University of Roch-

ester; Dow to Gerrit Smith, November 15, 1852, in the Smith Manuscripts, Syracuse University.

8Dow, REMINISCENCES, 447-52; text of the amended Maine Law in the Portland MAINE EXPOSITOR, April 13, 1853; American Temperance Union, ANNUAL REPORT, 1852, pp. 15-38, 1853, pp. 6-31, 39-43; Albert Bushnell Hart, ed., COMMONWEALTH HISTORY OF MASSACHUSETTS (5 vols., New York, 1930), 4:481; Walter Hill Crockett, VERMONT, THE GREEN MOUNTAIN STATE (5 vols., New York, 1921), 3:400-01, 405-08; Floyd B. Streeter, "History of Prohibitory Legislation in Michigan" in MICHIGAN HISTORY MAGAZINE, 2:294-98 (April, 1918); Logan Esarey, FROM 1850 TO THE PRESENT (A HISTORY OF INDIANA, Vol. 2, Indianapolis, 1918), 615-17; New York HERALD quoted in the EXPOSITOR, May 25, 1853.

9Dow, REMINISCENCES, 463-71, 473-95. As part of an incisive analysis of the effect of the Maine Law on the Democracy, a Maine Democratic politician friendly to prohibition remarked that Dow's act had "been a curse to the democratic party and produced a schism which puzzles the wisest heads to get rid of." George F. Emery to Cyrus Woodman, August 16, 1853, in the Cyrus Woodman Papers, Wisconsin Historical Society. For Dow's tours and the progress of prohibition in other states, see Dow to wife, May 26, June 8, 23, 25, 28, August 14, 23, September 28, 1853; letter of "D." in the Portland MAINE TEMPERANCE JOURNAL, February 4, 1854; Eugene H. Roseboom and Frances P. Weisenburger, A HISTORY OF OHIO (New York, 1934), 238-39; Asa Earl Martin, "The Temperance Movement in Pennsylvania prior to the Civil War" in the PENNSYLVANIA MAGAZINE OF HISTORY AND BIOGRAPHY, 49:218-19, 226-27 (April, 1925); American Temperance Union, ANNUAL REPORT, 1854, pp. 7-31, 52. Frank L. Byrne, "Cold Water Crusade, The Wisconsin Temperance Movement, 1832-60," an M. S. thesis in the University of Wisconsin Library, contains a detailed discussion of the political elements in one state which in 1853 allied themselves on the Maine Law issue.

10Dow's friends circulated a story that Portland boys regularly teased John Neal by shouting "shingles" at him. The cry signified that Neal's "upper story" needed "shingling." Clipping from an unknown newspaper in the Dow Scrapbook, 1:81. In October, 1853, after publishing several letters on the ineffectiveness of the Maine Law, Neal greatly weakened his case by prosecuting under that statute a liquor-seller who was in turn prosecuting Neal's reckless son for felonious assault. ADVERTISER, October 28, 1853; Portland EASTERN ARGUS reprinted in EXPOSITOR, December 21, 1853. See also, TEMPERANCE WATCHMAN, February 12, 26, letters of John Neal and Neal Dow on September 3 reprinted from the Portland STATE OF MAINE, 1853; EXPOSITOR, letter of Neal reprinted on September 7 from S. OF M., letter of Dow with Neal's comments reprinted on September 14 from S. OF M., letter of Neal in the issue of November 2, 1853; STATE OF MAINE, October 31, 1853; ADVERTISER, November 3, 1853; American Temperance Union, AN APPEAL TO THE PUBLIC FROM WELL AUTHENTICATED RESULTS OF THE MAINE LAW (New York, 1853); Dow to wife, September 6, 17, 18, 26,

October 3, 30, to Louisa Dow, September 11, 13, 1853. Dow was also continuing his personal feud with the Reverend Asa Cummings, editor of the Congregationalist Portland CHRISTIAN MIRROR. Letter of Dow reprinted from the ADVERTISER in the TEMPERANCE WATCHMAN, March 26, 1853.

11The World's Temperance Convention was held in conjunction with New York's Crystal Palace Exposition. In a letter to the separate meeting held by the feminists before the World's Convention, Dow said, "I see neither the wisdom or expediency of excluding women from Temperance Conventions; their earnest, equal and powerful co-operation I earnestly desire." PROCEEDINGS OF THE WHOLE WORLD'S TEMPERANCE CONVENTION, 1853, p. 25. For Dow's meeting, see Dow to wife, September 6, 9, 1853; PROCEEDINGS OF THE WORLD'S TEMPERANCE CONVENTION, 1853; proceedings of the convention in the New York DAILY TRIBUNE, September 7-9, 1853; letter of James M'Cune Smith in the New York SEMI-WEEKLY TRIBUNE, September 13, 1853; New York SPIRITUAL TELEGRAPH, September 17, 1853; Dow, REMINISCENCES, 472-73.

12Ibid., 494-95, 501-03; Hatch, MAINE HISTORY, 2:377-78; Neal Dow to Hannibal Hamlin, April 7, 1854, in the Hamlin Papers, Maine Historical Society; Dow to wife, March 26, 29, 1854; Carroll John Noonan, NATIVISM IN CONNECTICUT, 1829-1860 (Washington, 1938), 178-90. For a significant discussion of the possibility of creating "a strong independent party essentially whig" to control Maine, see a copy of William Pitt Fessenden to William G. Crosby, February 11, 1854, in the William Pitt Fessenden Papers, Library of Congress.

13By June, 1854, rumors were circulating in Portland that the local Catholics had guns stored in their church and that the priest had poison ready to distribute to Irish servant girls in preparation for the mass murder of the Protestant majority. Letter of John O'Donnell reprinted from the STATE OF MAINE in the EXPOSITOR, June 28, 1854; Portland MAINE TEMPERANCE JOURNAL, quotation in the issue of April 15 from the Boston TRAVELLER, editorials in the issues of September 30, November 25, December 30, 1854; Dow, REMINISCENCES, 497-500, 514; Hatch, MAINE HISTORY, 1:303-04; "I Don't Know," KNOW-NOTHINGISM: ILLUSTRATED WITH "CUTS", THE PORTRAITS DRAWN FROM LIFE (n. p., 1855), 4-5; ARGUS, editorial reprinted in the issue of September 6 from the BANGOR JOURNAL, and editorial in the issue of September 8, 1854. One Portland Know-Nothing lodge began its financial records on July 20, 1854. Dow's name did not appear among its members but the roster included both liquor-sellers and such prohibitionists as Mayor James B. Cahoon. John M. Gould, "Notes on a Ledger of a Portland Lodge of the Order of United Americans," a manuscript in the Maine Historical Society.

14Dow, REMINISCENCES, 501-18; Hatch, MAINE HISTORY, 2:381-82; TEMPERANCE JOURNAL, proceedings of the State Temperance Convention reprinted on July 8 from the ADVERTISER, schedule of Dow's speeches, August 5, account of a Dow speech reprinted on August 26 from the BIDDEFORD

UNION, 1854; Dow to wife, August 16, 1854; Dow to T. R. Trimby, August 29, 1854, in the author's possession.

15Andrew W. Crandall, THE EARLY HISTORY OF THE REPUBLICAN PARTY, 1854-1856 (Boston, c. 1930), 14-26; Proceedings of the Maine Republican State Convention in the TEMPERANCE JOURNAL, March 3, 1855; American Temperance Union, ANNUAL REPORT, 1855, pp. 5-37, 42-43; telegrams to Neal Dow from B. W. Williams, March 14, S. L. Tilley, March 29, April 13, J. F. Becket, April 27, 1855, in the Dow Scrapbook, 4:113, 162-63, 180. For a full account of the spread of the Maine Law as of 1855, see Henry S. Clubb, THE MAINE LIQUOR LAW, ITS ORIGIN, HISTORY AND RESULTS, INCLUDING A LIFE OF HON. NEAL DOW (New York, 1856), 71-98.

16Attacking the judge of Portland's Municipal Court for failing to enforce the Maine Law, Dow also persuaded the legislature to replace that court with a Police Court. EXPOSITOR, February 22, 1854; editorial from the TEMPERANCE JOURNAL, September 23, 1854, initialed "N. D." in pencil, in the Dow Scrapbook, 3:79; ADVERTISER, text of Dow's bill, January 23, letters of "C.," January 26 and February 6, 1855; TEMPERANCE JOURNAL, account of Dow's speech to the lawmakers reprinted on February 3 from the KENNEBEC JOURNAL, editorial, March 24, text of the "Intensified Maine Law," April 7, 1855; American Temperance Union, ANNUAL REPORT, 1855, p. 37.

17Dow to wife, October 14, 19, 27, 1852, January 26, 29, 1853, January 20, 22, 1854, to Louisa Dow, January 25, 1854; Clubb, THE MAINE LAW, 31-32, 37-39; Portland MAINE TEMPERANCE WATCHMAN, February 19, 1853. In 1854, Dow learned that a British shipowner had named a brigantine for him. In the summer of the same year, he received an honorary L. L. D. degree from Indiana Asbury University and also a good deal of editorial gibes on the subject. One letter writer asked if the initials stood for "Large Leather Dealer" while another humorist suggested "Liquor Law Doctor." Advertisement from the LIVERPOOL (England) MERCURY, May 5, 1854, clipping from the BUNKER HILL AURORA, in the Dow Scrapbook, 2:248, 3:10; letter of "Publicola" in the EXPOSITOR, August 23, 1854; Dow, REMINISCENCES, 501.

18Dow, REMINISCENCES, 459-63, 497-500, 522-28; Clubb, THE MAINE LAW, 41-47; ARGUS, March 14, 24, 27, 29, April 3, 4, 6, 1855; ADVERTISER, March 26, 30, April 6, 17, 1855; BOSTON TRANSCRIPT, March 30, 1855; Dow to wife, March 31, 1855. The typed copy in the Dow Collection is misdated March 31, 1852. Another indication of the personal bitterness lingering after the election was Elder Peck's statement that the "moral character" of John A. Poor, publisher of the STATE OF MAINE, was "rotteness itself." TEMPERANCE JOURNAL, March 10, 31, April 7, 14, 21, 28, 1855.

19Dow, REMINISCENCES, 528; Clubb, THE MAINE LAW, 67.

CHAPTER VIII

[1]"I Don't Know," KNOW NOTHINGISM, ILLUSTRATED WITH "CUTS," THE PORTRAITS DRAWN FROM LIFE (n. p., 1855), 5-6. A copy of this unusual item is in the Portland Public Library. For the references to the Irish, see the Portland MAINE TEMPERANCE JOURNAL, March 31, 1855; letter of "One of the Irish Cattle" in the Portland EASTERN ARGUS, April 5, 1855.

[2]Dow's salary for the year was $1200. PORTLAND ADVERTISER, April 20, May 3, 1855; TEMPERANCE JOURNAL, April 28, May 19, 1855; ARGUS, May 9, 1855.

[3]REPORT OF THE COMMITTEE APPOINTED BY THE BOARD OF ALDERMEN OF THE CITY OF PORTLAND TO INVESTIGATE THE CAUSES AND CONSEQUENCES OF THE RIOT ON THE EVENING OF JUNE 2, 1855 (Portland, 1855), 6-10, 42-43; THE DEATH OF JOHN ROBBINS OF DEER ISLE WHO WAS SHOT IN THE STREETS OF PORTLAND BY ORDER OF NEAL DOW, MAYOR, JUNE 2d, 1855, A FULL REPORT OF THE TESTIMONY TAKEN BEFORE THE CORONER'S INQUEST, AS PUBLISHED IN THE "STATE OF MAINE" NEWSPAPER (Portland, 1855), 98-101; account of Dow's trial as reprinted from the ADVERTISER in the TEMPERANCE JOURNAL, June 9, 1855; Neal Dow, THE REMINISCENCES OF NEAL DOW, RECOLLECTIONS OF EIGHTY YEARS (Portland, 1898), 536-37.

[4]Aldermen's Committee, REPORT, 11-14; Dow, REMINISCENCES, 531-32; Coroner's Inquest, TESTIMONY, 50-51; TEMPERANCE JOURNAL, June 9, 1855.

[5]Coroner's Inquest, TESTIMONY, 92, 100.

[6]Aldermen's Committee, REPORT, 11-24; Coroner's Inquest, TESTIMONY, 15-16, 22-25, 50-51, 78-80. For a drawing of Market Square at night, see Edward H. Elwell, PORTLAND AND VICINITY, WITH A SKETCH OF OLD ORCHARD BEACH AND OTHER MAINE RESORTS (Revised ed., Portland, 1881), 39.

[7]Dow, REMINISCENCES, 95, 530, 534; Coroner's Inquest, TESTIMONY, 10-12, 15, 22-24, 28-35, 37, 43-57, 67-69, 78-80, 92, 99, 101-02, 104-05; Aldermen's Committee, REPORT, 17-21, 24-26. For a contemporary description of the Portland Police, see Frederick N. Dow, "Reminiscences," ch. 2, p. 12. Unless otherwise indicated, all manuscript items cited in this chapter are in the Dow Collection in the possession of Mrs. William C. Eaton of Portland.

[8]Aldermen's Committee, REPORT, 26-28; Coroner's Inquest, TESTIMONY, 7-12, 15, 24-25, 57, 59-60, 95-96, 103.

[9]Aldermen's Committee, REPORT, 28-41; Coroner's Inquest, TESTIMONY, 7-15, 20-22, 25, 27, 30-35, 41-43, 51-56, 58-59, 78-79, 93-94, 97-98.

[10]Coroner's Inquest, TESTIMONY, 4-5, 39-40, 79, 105.

[11]Ibid., 69, 96, 98, 103, 111-12; ADVERTISER, June 4, 1855; John Neal,

WANDERING RECOLLECTIONS OF A SOMEWHAT BUSY LIFE, AN AUTO-
BIOGRAPHY (Boston, 1869), 409; TEMPERANCE JOURNAL, June 16, 1855;
ARGUS, June 12, 1855.

[12]Ibid., editorials June 4, 5, quotations in the issue of June 8 from the
BOSTON POST and HARTFORD TIMES: 1855; Henry S. Clubb, THE MAINE
LIQUOR LAW, ITS ORIGIN, HISTORY AND RESULTS, INCLUDING A LIFE
OF HON. NEAL DOW(New York, 1856), 63; ADVERTISER, June 5, 6, 1855;
BUFFALO COMMERCIAL ADVERTISER quoted in the Portland MAINE EX-
POSITOR, July 11, 1855; lithograph in the Dow Scrapbook, 4:305. All Dow
Scrapbooks cited in this chapter are on deposit in Drew University.

[13]ADVERTISER, June 4-6, 9, 1855; Coroner's Inquest, TESTIMONY, 74-
75, 81, 88; ARGUS, June 5, 8, 1855; EXPOSITOR, July 18, 1855.

[14]Account of the trial reprinted from the ADVERTISER in the TEMPER-
ANCE JOURNAL, June 9, 1855; ARGUS, June 6, 11, 1855; Dow, REMINIS-
CENCES, 542.

[15]Coroner's Inquest, TESTIMONY, 3-6, 104; ADVERTISER, ARGUS,
June 13, 1855; Aldermen's Committee, REPORT, 3-6; Dow, REMINISCEN-
CES, 538.

[16]Dow's report as reprinted in Coroner's Inquest, TESTIMONY, 109-11;
Clubb, THE MAINE LAW, 64-65. The Reverend Asa Cummings' Portland
CHRISTIAN MIRROR was skeptical of the Dowites' account of the liquor purchase. TEMPERANCE JOURNAL, June 9, 16, 23, 1855. Democratic Editor
John M. Adams alleged that the contrast between Dow's report of a ferocious
mob and the frail door that had withstood attack for two and a half hours indicated that the mayor was "crazy." ARGUS, June 14, 1855.

[17]Among the speakers at the Democratic Convention was former Governor
John Hubbard. The politician whom Dow had backed in 1853 said that he had
only signed the Maine Law because of its great legislative majority and denied ever favoring an "ultra-prohibitory law." EXPOSITOR, June 27, July 4,
11, 1855; TEMPERANCE JOURNAL, July 7, 21, 1855; ARGUS, September 10,
1855; Dow, REMINISCENCES, 549-52.

[18]Coroner's Inquest, TESTIMONY, 106-08; Aldermen's Committee, RE-
PORT, 34, 48-49; ADVERTISER, July 11, 13, 1855; Portland INQUIRER
quoted in the EXPOSITOR, July 18, 1855; ARGUS, July 17, 1855, April 8,
1856. The Dowites finally rested their justification of their leader's actions
on the law of riot. For a discussion, see /Charles Stewart Daveis7, "The
Law of Riot, The Portland Riot," in THE MONTHLY LAW REPORTER, 8:361-
86 (November, 1855). For an analysis by an Anti-Dow lawyer, see Joseph A.
Ware, REVIEW OF THE TESTIMONY TAKEN BEFORE THE SECOND IN-
QUEST ON THE BODY OF JOHN ROBBINS, WHO WAS SHOT AT PORTLAND,
JUNE 2D, 1855, TOGETHER WITH REMARKS ON THE REPORT OF THE
INVESTIGATING COMMITTEE APPOINTED BY MAYOR DOW AND THE AL-
DERMEN, JUNE 9, 1855 (Portland, 1855).

[19]ARGUS, August 15, 25, 29, 1855; TEMPERANCE JOURNAL, editorial,
September 15, editorial reprinted on September 29 from the BANGOR MER-

CURY, 1855; Dow, REMINISCENCES, 552-55. On September 11, 1855, the
ADVERTISER wryly headlined its account of the Republican defeat as follows:

"The Election.

Singular Freak of the People

- - - - - - - - - - -

The City Fails Us!

- - - - - - - - - -

Ditto the Rural Districts!!

Ditto the Rest of the State!!!"

[20]Letter of Neal Dow in the ANNUAL REPORT OF THE AMERICAN TEM-
PERANCE UNION, 1856, p. 8; Neal Dow to [?], September 27, 1855, in
the Gratz Collection, Pennsylvania Historical Society. A photostat is in the
author's possession. TEMPERANCE JOURNAL, September 29, 1855; Neal
Dow to the editor of the Albany (New York) PROHIBITIONIST, clipping in the
Dow Scrapbook, 5:12; Portland MAINE TEMPERANCE JOURNAL AND IN-
QUIRER, December 8, 1855.

[21]Ibid., letter of "Steam," March 20, editorial, April 17, 1856; clippings
of editorials from Ibid., March 13, 20, 1856, initialed "N. D." in pencil, in
the Dow Scrapbook, 6:181, 202; letter of "A Citizen," ADVERTISER, March
17, 1856; Dow, REMINISCENCES, 555-58. The legislature also repealed the
Republicans' Naturalization Law. Louis C. Hatch, MAINE, A HISTORY (3
vols., New York, 1919), 2:392.

[22]The new city government immediately granted licenses under the Barnes
Law. Dow, REMINISCENCES, 528, 543; ARGUS, April 1, 2, 8, 1856; AD-
VERTISER, April 5, 7, 9, May 7, 1856; JOURNAL AND INQUIRER, April 10,
17, 1856.

[23]Dow, REMINISCENCES, 558-61; Hatch, MAINE HISTORY, 2:398-99, 402;
ADVERTISER, April 28, July 9, August 8, letter of Neal Dow in the issue of
August 28, November 4, 1856; ARGUS, August 12, 27, November 5, 6, 1856,
February 17, 1857; Neal Dow to Louisa Dow, November 2, 9, 1856.

[24]JOURNAL AND INQUIRER, January 17, February 7, 14, 21, 26, March
12, 1857; Dow, REMINISCENCES, 561; ARGUS, January 14, 17, 1857.

[25]Correspondence of the AMERICAN reprinted in the ADVERTISER, July
11, 1855; American Temperance Union, ANNUAL REPORT, 1856, pp. 5-44,
1857, pp. 5-20; Dow, REMINISCENCES, 548-49; John Allen Krout, "The Maine
Law in New York Politics" in NEW YORK HISTORY, 34:270-72 (July, 1936);
Asa Earl Martin, "The Temperance Movement in Pennsylvania prior to the
Civil War" in the PENNSYLVANIA MAGAZINE OF HISTORY AND BIOGRA-
PHY, 49:229-30 (April, 1925); J. Thomas Scharf, HISTORY OF DELAWARE,
1609-1888 (2 vols., Philadelphia, 1888), 1:327-28; Logan Esarey, FROM 1850
TO THE PRESENT (A HISTORY OF INDIANA, Vol. 2, Indianapolis, 1918),

615-21; Arthur C. Cole, THE ERA OF THE CIVIL WAR, 1848-1870 (THE CENTENNIAL HISTORY OF ILLINOIS, Vol. 3, Springfield, 1919), 207-11; Frank L. Byrne, "Maine Law Versus Lager Beer, A Dilemma of Wisconsin's Young Republican Party"in the WISCONSIN MAGAZINE OF HISTORY, 42:118-20 (Winter, 1958-59).

CHAPTER IX

[1]Neal Dow to wife, October 15, 1852; Birmingham (England) DAILY PRESS, May 22, 1857, clipping in the Neal Dow Scrapbook, 8:89. Unless otherwise indicated, all manuscript items cited in this chapter are in the Dow Collection in the possession of Mrs. William C. Eaton of Portland and all Dow Scrapbooks are on deposit in the library of Drew University.

[2]Peter T. Winskill, THE TEMPERANCE MOVEMENT AND ITS WORKERS, A RECORD OF SOCIAL, MORAL, RELIGIOUS AND POLITICAL PROGRESS (4 vols., London, England, 1892), 1:32, 33, 49-50, 57-59, 104, 2:221, 223, 3:13-17; Henry Carter, THE ENGLISH TEMPERANCE MOVEMENT, A STUDY IN OBJECTIVES, Vol. 1, THE FORMATIVE PERIOD, 1830-1899 (London, England, 1933), 33-35; Dow to John Marsh, September 7, 1846, in the JOURNAL OF THE AMERICAN TEMPERANCE UNION, October, 1846.

[3]Winskill, THE TEMPERANCE MOVEMENT, 1:250-51, 2:278-81; Neal Dow, THE REMINISCENCES OF NEAL DOW, RECOLLECTIONS OF EIGHTY YEARS (Portland, 1898), 570, 578-79; Dow to Louisa Dow, August 9, 1857; Dow to the Secretaries of the United Kingdom Alliance, April 3, 1853, March 13, 1854, in, respectively, London (England) NEWS AND CHRONICLE reprinted in Portland MAINE TEMPERANCE WATCHMAN, May 21, 1853, and London (England) ATLAS reprinted in Portland MAINE TEMPERANCE JOURNAL, May 27, 1854; letters of Thomas H. Barker in TEMPERANCE JOURNAL, May 26, 1855, and in Portland JOURNAL AND INQUIRER, January 10, 1857.

[4]Frederick N. Dow, "Reminiscences," ch. 5, pp. 1-18, ch. 7, pp. 1-4, ch. 8, pp. 5-6, ch. 9, p. 1, a typed manuscript; MAINE TEMPERANCE JOURNAL, November 8, 1859; Dow, REMINISCENCES, 235-36; PORTLAND ADVERTISER, January 11, 1850; Daniel C. Colesworthy, SCHOOL IS OUT (Boston, 1876), 370-71.

[5]Dow, REMINISCENCES, 572-73; Portland MAINE TEMPERANCE JOURNAL AND INQUIRER, March 19, 26, April 9, 1857.

[6]Dow to wife, April 8, 11, 1857; Neal Dow Diary, April 7-20, 1857, and an account of the 1857 voyage written at the beginning of Dow's diary for 1866; Dow, REMINISCENCES, 574-77, 602.

[7]Extracts from the Liverpool DAILY POST, Manchester EXAMINER and Manchester TIMES, in the MAINE TEMPERANCE JOURNAL AND INQUIRER, May 14, 1857; John B. Gough, AUTOBIOGRAPHY AND PERSONAL RECOLLECTIONS OF JOHN B. GOUGH WITH TWENTY-SIX YEARS' EXPERIENCE

AS A PUBLIC SPEAKER (Springfield, Massachusetts, 1870), 392-94; Winskill, THE TEMPERANCE MOVEMENT, 2:282, 3:89-95, 100-06; Dow to Secretary of the United Kingdom Alliance, April 22, 1857, in MISCELLANEOUS ALLIANCE PAPERS, NO. 20 (Manchester, England, n. d.); printed circular letter of Dow, April 27, 1857, in the Dow Scrapbook, 12:165; Dow to Louisa Dow, April 21, 1857.

[8]Dow, REMINISCENCES, 582-86; entry for April 23, 1857, in the pages at the front of Dow's diary for 1866; GLASGOW (Scotland) COMMONWEALTH AND BRITISH TEMPERANCE ADVOCATE, reprinted in MAINE TEMPERANCE JOURNAL AND INQUIRER, May 21, 1857; "The Great Welcome Meeting" in ALLIANCE MISCELLANEOUS PAPERS, NO. 21, pp. 2-8; photograph of Dow in England in the front of volume 8 of the Dow Scrapbook.

[9]Dow, REMINISCENCES, 587-89; account of the Manchester Soirée in ALLIANCE MISCELLANEOUS PAPERS, NO. 21, pp. 8-15.

[10]Dow Diary, April 27-October 23, 1857; Dow to wife, April 11, May 15, 1857, to Louisa, April 21, June 2, 19, October 11, 17, 1857, to Frederick, May 13, 1857; Dow, REMINISCENCES, 580-81, 599-605; Winskill, THE TEMPERANCE MOVEMENT, 1:165-66.

[11]Dow to Edward C. Delavan and an account of a reception for Dow in MAINE TEMPERANCE JOURNAL AND INQUIRER for, respectively, August 27 and November 19, 1857; Dow, REMINISCENCES, 610-11; clippings from London TIMES, May 26, 1857, and London SATURDAY REVIEW, May 30, 1857, in the Dow Scrapbook, 8:17.

[12]Dow, REMINISCENCES, 611-13; Dow Diary, October 12, 1857; letter of "N. D. " in the London TIMES, October 15, 1857; MAINE TEMPERANCE JOURNAL AND INQUIRER, November 12, 1857.

[13]Dow Diary, October 14, 24-November 5, 1857; Dow to Louisa, September 17, 1857; letter of Theodore L. Cuyler in a clipping from the London (England) WEEKLY RECORD, November 21, 1857, in the Dow Scrapbook, 7:161; Carter, THE ENGLISH TEMPERANCE MOVEMENT, 86-93.

[14]Clippings initialed in pencil "N. D. " from JOURNAL AND INQUIRER, January 10, 31, February 14, 1857, in Dow Scrapbook, 6:234, 247, 276; JOURNAL AND INQUIRER, July 2, December 17, 24, 1857, January 7, 21, 1858; Dow Diary, December 25, 28, 30, 1857, January 11-14, 18, 1858.

[15]Dow, REMINISCENCES, 562-63; JOURNAL AND INQUIRER, January 21, February 4, 25, March 4, 11, April 8, 1858; editorial from Ibid. initialed "N. D. "and letter of Dow to John Marsh in a clipping from Glasgow (Scotland) WEEKLY JOURNAL OF THE SCOTTISH TEMPERANCE LEAGUE, April 17, 1858, in Dow Scrapbook, 7:202, 231. William Willis, Republican mayor of Portland and a Maine Law man, felt that, despite the opposition of "the ultras Dow & Stackpole & their adherents, "the "strongest temperance men" endorsed the Thomas Maine Law. "The fools who oppose will not only injure themselves & their cause, " he believed, "but I fear will damage our party some. " William Willis to William Pitt Fessenden, March 2, 1858, in the William Pitt Fessenden Papers, Bowdoin College. A microfilm copy is at the University

of Virginia.

16JOURNAL AND INQUIRER, April 1, 8, 29, May 6, 27, June 3, 10, July 1, 8, September 9, letter of "D." in September 23, 1858; Dow, REMINISCENCES, 563; Dow Diary, April 14-15, 19, 27, 29, May 3, 10-15, 18-20, 24, 25-28, June 2-4, 1858; PORTLAND ADVERTISER, June 7, 1858; Portland EASTERN ARGUS, June 4, 9, 1858.

17Letter of Dow clipped from an unknown newspaper in Dow Scrapbook, 9:107; Portland MAINE TEMPERANCE JOURNAL, June 17, August 5, 19, 26, September 2, 16, October 14, November 4, 11, 25, 1858.

18TEMPERANCE JOURNAL, December 23, 30, 1858, January 6, 1859; Dow to John Marsh, December 20, 1858, in American Temperance Union, ANNUAL REPORT, 1859, pp. 17-18; Theodore L. Cuyler, RECOLLECTIONS OF A LONG LIFE, AN AUTOBIOGRAPHY (New York, c. 1902), 51-54. Insensitive as usual to the effects upon others of his attacks, Dow could not understand why Cuyler failed to answer a subsequent personal letter. Dow to wife, April 19, 1860. He later remarked that his acquaintance with Cuyler "latterly . . . has lacked somewhat of its early intimacy. . . ." Dow, REMINISCENCES, 454-55, 457.

CHAPTER X

1PORTLAND ADVERTISER, November 16-19, 1858; Neal Dow, THE REMINISCENCES OF NEAL DOW, RECOLLECTIONS OF EIGHTY YEARS (Portland, 1898), 544; Portland EASTERN ARGUS, November 18, 1858; Portland MAINE TEMPERANCE JOURNAL, November 25, December 2, 1858; Neal Dow to Thomas H. Barker in a clipping from the Manchester (England) ALLIANCE WEEKLY NEWS in the Neal Dow Scrapbook, 7:250. All Dow Scrapbooks cited in this chapter are on deposit at Drew University.

2ADVERTISER, January 6, 7, 14, 15, 25, 27, February 1, 3, 5, 14, 16, 22, March 8, 22, 26, 1859; article from BANGOR DAILY EVENING TIMES, reprinted in a clipping from the ARGUS, and a clipping from the Boston ATLAS AND DAILY BEE in Dow Scrapbook, 7:79-80, 9:230, respectively; Neal Dow to wife, January 7, 21, 27, February 17, 28, March 15, 20, 1859. Unless otherwise noted, all manuscript items cited in this chapter are in the Dow Collection in the possession of Mrs. William C. Eaton of Portland.

3Dow to Louisa Dow, September 17, 1857, to wife, January 7, 1859; [Maine Legislature], REPORT OF THE JOINT SELECT COMMITTEE ON THE DEFALCATION OF BENJ. D. PECK, LATE TREASURER OF THE STATE OF MAINE (Augusta, 1860), 5, 6, 25-30; Louis C. Hatch, MAINE, A HISTORY (3 vols., New York, 1919), 2:417; Neal Dow Diary, October 25, 27, 29, November 2, 5, 1858.

4Maine Legislature, PECK COMMITTEE REPORT, 9-24, 29-30, 38-40; Dow to the editor of ARGUS, January 11, 1860.

5Maine Legislature, PECK COMMITTEE REPORT, 29-31, 49-50; ADVER-

TISER, December 28, 30, 1859; January 3, 1860; ARGUS, Decmeber 31, 1859.

[6]Dow to wife, January 4, 1860 /misdated August 4, 1860/; ADVERTISER, September 12-14, 1859, January 9, 1860; Morrill's message to the legislature in TEMPERANCE JOURNAL, January 14, 1860.

[7]Maine Legislature, PECK COMMITTEE REPORT, 31-37; letters of "A Portland Inquirer" and "Another Inquirer" in ARGUS, February 27, 28, 1860, respectively. The receivers of the Norombega Bank had temporarily jailed Peck. He avoided imprisonment for his embezzlement from the State Treasury. ADVERTISER, January 5, 1860.

[8]Dow, REMINISCENCES, 680-82; ADVERTISER, December 31, 1859; TEMPERANCE JOURNAL, January 28, 1860; ARGUS, February 16, 24, 27, 28, 1860.

[9]Maine Legislature, PECK COMMITTEE REPORT, 3, 24, 30-31, 35-37, 51-52, 57, 63-64; Maine Attorney General, ANNUAL REPORT, 1861, p. 4, 1866, p. 6, 1871, pp. 7-8, 1872, pp. 5-6; ADVERTISER, May 3, September 3, 1860; Dow to wife, March 15, 21, April 9, 16, 17, 19, 1860.

[10]Dow to wife, April 9, 1860; ARGUS, March 10, August 31, 1860. The TEMPERANCE JOURNAL, March 17, 1860, termed the committee's report "candid, fair, and at the same time frank and outspoken. . . . "

[11]Dow to wife, January 11, April 3, 9, 16, 1860.

[12]Ibid., January 11, February 22, March 5, 25, April 3, 9, 19, 25, May 6, 10, 14, 1860; Family Bible in the Dow Collection; A. N. Somers, HISTORY OF LANCASTER, NEW HAMPSHIRE (Concord, New Hampshire, 1898), 468-69.

[13]See the following items in the indicated issues of the TEMPERANCE JOURNAL, editorial, October 25, 1859, proceedings of the annual meeting of the State Temperance Association, January 21, letter of "S.," January 28, letter of "C.," June 4, Dow's circular calling meeting of State Temperance Association, December 15, 1860, Association's proceedings, January 26, editorial, March 23, 1861.

[14]The Democrats later sold part of the municipal stock in the Gas Company, eliminating the city's dominant interest and thereby consummating their bargain with the leading stockholders. ADVERTISER, July 21, 1855, March 21, April 3, 4, 10, July 11, 19, 20, September 1, October 29, 1860; ARGUS, July 23, 1855, March 5, 12, 14, letters of "Citizen" and "Jefferson" in the issues for March 17 and 27, respectively, 1860; TEMPERANCE JOURNAL, July 28, 1859; Dow to wife, April 3, May 10, 16, 18, to Louisa, May 14, 20, 1860; Dow Diary, May 11- June 2, 23-28, 1860.

[15]ARGUS, March 8, 16, 1860; TEMPERANCE JOURNAL, September 10, 1860.

CHAPTER XI

[1]Neal Dow to Charles Sumner, June 24, 1860, in the Sumner Papers, Harvard University; Neal Dow, THE REMINISCENCES OF NEAL DOW, RECOLLECTIONS OF EIGHTY YEARS (Portland, 1898), 140; letter of Dow in a clipping from the Manchester (England) GUARDIAN, January 31, 1861, in the Neal Dow Scrapbook, 10:113. Unless otherwise indicated, all Dow Scrapbooks cited in this chapter are on deposit in the library of Drew University.

[2]Dow to John A. Andrew, January 19, May 20, 1861, in the Andrew Papers, Massachusetts Historical Society; editorial initialed in pencil "N. D." in a clipping from the Portland MAINE JOURNAL, January 26, 1861, in the Dow Scrapbook, 10:124; letter of "Plain Truth" in MAINE JOURNAL, February 2, 1861; Dow, REMINISCENCES, 620, 622.

[3]Ibid., 89, 618-21, 624-28; Dow to Frederick Dow, May 20, June 15, August 7, 1862. Unless otherwise noted, all manuscript items cited in this chapter are in the Dow Collection in the possession of Mrs. William C. Eaton of Portland. For Dow's raising of money for the state, see his undated letter in Israel Washburn Papers, vol. 3, Library of Congress.

[4]Dow, REMINISCENCES, 628-32; Lewiston EVANGELIST, October 16, 1861, in Dow Scrapbook, 10:41; advertisement and "Correspondence" in Portland MAINE TEMPERANCE JOURNAL, November 9, 16, 1861. Dow received monthly pay and allowances of $211 which his later promotion to brigadier-general raised to $299.50. J. H. Eaton, THE ARMY PAYMASTER'S MANUAL OR COLLECTION OF OFFICIAL RULES FOR THE INFORMATION AND GUIDANCE OF OFFICERS OF THE PAY DEPARTMENT OF THE UNITED STATES ARMY WITH TABLES OF THE MONTHLY PAY, SUBSISTENCE & C. AND OF THE DAILY PAY OF THE ARMY, REVISED TO INCLUDE JUNE 30, 1864 (Washington, 1864), 123, 127. Dow sent home almost all his pay. By the winter of 1862-63, by applying his pay and the receipts of property sold at war-inflated prices, he had paid his debts. Dow to Frederick Dow, July 8, December 1, 1862, January 26, 1863.

[5]Dow, REMINISCENCES, 631, 634-38; Edwin B. Lufkin, HISTORY OF THE THIRTEENTH MAINE REGIMENT FROM ITS ORGANIZATION IN 1861 TO ITS MUSTER-OUT IN 1865 (Bridgton, Maine, 1898), 1-9; Portland TRANSCRIPT, December 21, 1861; Dow to Frederick Dow, February 5, 1862.

[6]Hans L. Trefousse, BEN BUTLER, THE SOUTH CALLED HIM BEAST! (New York, c. 1957), 53-97; Dow, REMINISCENCES, 640-43; Dow to John A. Andrew, May 20, 1861, in the Andrew Papers, Massachusetts Historical Society; Dow to Frederick Dow, February 5, September 11, 1862.

[7]Lufkin, THIRTEENTH MAINE, 10-13; Dow, REMINISCENCES, 638-47; Portland TRANSCRIPT, December 21, 1861; Dow to Cornelia Dow, January 24, to wife, January 30, February 17, April 6, December 7, 1862.

[8]Dow to wife, February 26, March 13, to Cornelia Dow, March 5, 1862; Dow, REMINISCENCES, 643; David Donald, ed., DIVIDED WE FOUGHT, A

PICTORIAL HISTORY OF THE WAR, 1861-1865 (New York, 1952), 95.

[9]Dow, REMINISCENCES, 647-62; Dow to wife, March 2, 11, 17, to Frederick Dow, March 29, 1862; Benjamin F. Butler, BUTLER'S BOOK, AUTO-BIOGRAPHY AND PERSONAL REMINISCENCES OF MAJOR-GENERAL BENJAMIN F. BUTLER (Boston, 1892), 344-47.

[10]Dow to wife, March 23, April 6, May 17, July 2, to Frank Dow, March 25, to Frederick Dow, May 15, June 27, 1862; Neal Dow Diary, April 5, May 20, 1862; Lufkin, THIRTEENTH MAINE, 23-28; Dow, REMINISCENCES, 663-68.

[11]Dow to wife, March 11, May 15, June 5, 24, to Frederick Dow, March 24, April 29, May 15, November 4, 1862; Dow, REMINISCENCES, 668-72.

[12]Dow to wife, July 2, 9, 12, to Frederick Dow, July 4, 1862; Dow Diary, July 11, 12, 1862. After Dow left the 13th Maine, according to his successor in command, the unit began to lose "the cognomen of 'Neal Dow Regt'" and received from Butler's headquarters assurance of being reunited. Colonel Henry Rust, Jr. to Governor Israel Washburn, December 9, 1862, in Israel Washburn Papers, Library of Congress.

[13]Dow to wife, July 12, September 1, 1862; Dow, REMINISCENCES, 678-80.

[14]Dow Diary, July 14, 15, 18, August 16-27, September 17-20, 1862; Dow to Frederick Dow, March 29, July 16, 19, 1862, January 20, 1863, to wife, May 29, July 16, 22, August 9, September 16, 1862; Lufkin, THIRTEENTH MAINE, 35-46; Dow to R. S. Davis, July 18, 1862, in United States War Department, THE WAR OF THE REBELLION, A COMPILATION OF THE OFFICIAL RECORDS OF THE UNION AND CONFEDERATE ARMIES (70 vols., Washington, 1880-1901), Series 1, 15:522-25, hereafter cited as "O. R."; Dow, REMINISCENCES, 672, 675-76, 684.

[15]Dow to Frederick Dow, July 16, August 7, September 19, to wife July 22, August 14, September 1, 1862.

[16]Dow to wife, August 9, 14, 30, September 1, 7, 30, 1862; Dow to Butler, August 18, 1862, in PRIVATE AND OFFICIAL CORRESPONDENCE OF GEN. BENJAMIN F. BUTLER DURING THE PERIOD OF THE CIVIL WAR (5 vols., n. p., 1917), 2:199-200.

[17]Dow to wife, August 14, September 16, 21, 30, October 19, to Frederick Dow, September 11, 19, 28, 1862; Dow to George C. Strong, October 10, 1862, Fred Martin to Dow, October 10, 1862, Butler to Edwin M. Stanton, October 25, 1862, in BUTLER CORRESPONDENCE, 2:411-12.

[18]Dow to wife, September 30, October 4, 7, 10, to Frederick Dow, October 8, November 4, 1862; Dow Diary, October 6-9, 1862; Henry W. Closson to Lewis G. Arnold, September 13, 1862, in O. R., Ser. 1, 15:569-70; Gouverneur Morris, THE HISTORY OF A VOLUNTEER REGIMENT, BEING A SUCCINT ACCOUNT OF THE ORGANIZATION, SERVICES AND ADVENTURES OF THE SIXTH REGIMENT NEW YORK VOLUNTEERS INFANTRY KNOWN AS WILSON ZOUAVES: WHERE THEY WENT, WHAT THEY DID AND WHAT THEY SAW IN THE WAR OF THE REBELLION, 1861 TO 1865 (New York,

1891), 20, 25, 78-83; Dow, REMINISCENCES, 676-77; General Order 24 of the District of Pensacola, Department of the Gulf, October 22, 1862, in Adjutant General's Office, Department of Florida, 10:153-54, National Archives.

[19]Dow to wife, October 10, 19, 30, to Frederick Dow, November 4, 1862; Statements of Thomas B. and Henry P. Smith and Victor Reand, O. R., Ser. 2, 6:270-73; Circular Order of Dist. of Pensacola, Dept. of the Gulf, October 17, 1862, in A. G. O., Dept. of Florida, 28:345-46, and Dow to Nathaniel P. Banks, January 23, 1863, Letter D-114, Box 4, Letters Received, 1863, Dept. of the Gulf, in U. S. Army Commands, R. G. 98, National Archives.

[20]Dow to George C. Strong, October 16, 1862, Letter 23, Box 4, Letters Rec., 1863, and November 21, 1862, Letter D-20, Box 1, Letters Rec., 1862, in U. S. Army Commands, R. G. 98, National Archives; Butler to Dow, October 25, 1862, A. N. Shipley to J. W. Shaffer, November 15, 1862, George C. Strong to Dow, November 17, 1862, in BUTLER CORRESPONDENCE, 2:404, 483-85; Dow to Frederick Dow, December 1, 10, 1862, March 2, 1863, to wife, December 7, 21, 1862.

[21]Dow to wife, December 12, 1862, January 18, 26, May 11, 1863, to Frederick Dow, January 30, February 14, 1863; Fred Harvey Harrington, FIGHTING POLITICIAN, MAJOR GENERAL N. P. BANKS (Philadelphia, 1948), 3-4, 8-9, 15, 18-20, 45, 62; General Order 111, December 17, 1862, and Special Order 13, January 13, 1863, of the Dept. of the Gulf, Dow to Nathaniel P. Banks, January 1, 1863, in O. R., Ser. 1, 15:611, 628-29, 646.

[22]Dow, REMINISCENCES, 684-85; Dow to Frederick Dow, January 30, February 23, to wife, February 5, 24, April 4, 1863; a statement of facts in the Johnson case, written by Dow but undated and unsigned, Letter D-231, Box 4, Letters Rec., 1863, Dept. of the Gulf, in U. S. Army Commands, R. G. 98, National Archives; 100 U. S. REPORTS S. C., 158-95.

[23]Dow to Frederick Dow, January 30, March 2, 17, to wife, February 8, 23, 24, 26, March 6, 8, 14, 1863; Dow, REMINISCENCES, 676-77, 683. Dow was most popular with the New Englanders in his brigade. One thought him "very pleasant" in contrast with Sherman, a Regular Army officer and "a stern looking old fellow." Charles McGregor, HISTORY OF THE FIFTEENTH REGIMENT, NEW HAMPSHIRE VOLUNTEERS, 1862-1863 (n. p., 1900), 258-59. On the other hand, a soldier of the 128th New York declared that Dow was "unpopular with the boys." Lawrence Van Alstyne, DIARY OF AN ENLISTED MAN (New Haven, 1910), April 10, 1863. A captain in the same regiment found it "the greatest of all the many wonders we have how so thoroughly incompetent & unofficerlike a man" as Dow "should retain so high a position." Robert F. Wilkinson to /William and Mary E. Wilkinson7, April 24, 1863, in Miscellaneous Mss.-Robert F. Wilkinson, New York Historical Society.

[24]Dow to wife, May 11, 19, 21, 1863; Harrington, BANKS, 117-20; McGregor, FIFTEENTH NEW HAMPSHIRE, 295-300.

[25]Dow to wife, May 23, 1863; Richard B. Irwin to Rear-Admiral Farragut, May 26, 1863, Brigadier-General T. W. Sherman to Brigadier-General Andrews, May 23, 24, 25, 1863, in O. R., Ser. 1, vol. 26, pt. 1, pp. 84-85

501, 503, 505.

[26]Dow to wife, May 26, 1863; McGregor, FIFTEENTH NEW HAMPSHIRE, 315-16.

[27]Dow to wife, May 26, to Frederick Dow, May 27, 29, 1863; Dow, REMINISCENCES, 691-95; Col. T. G. Kingsley to Adj.-Gen., U. S., June 3, 1863, Lt. Col. Joseph Selden to Gen. J. D. Williams, May 31, 1863, Capt. Francis S. Keese to Brig. Gen. Neal Dow, May 31, 1863, Special Order 123 of the 19th Corps, May 27, 1863, Maj.-Gen. N. P. Banks to Gen. Weitzel, 1:45 p. m. and 2:15 p. m., May 27, 1863, Richard B. Irwin to Gen. Weitzel, 4:30 p. m., May 27, 1863, and to Col. S. B. Holabird, 7:00 p. m., May 27, 1863, in O. R., Ser. 1, vol. 26, pt. 1, pp. 123-25, 508-10; Harrington, BANKS, 121; McGregor, FIFTEENTH NEW HAMPSHIRE, 328-39, 375; PORT HUDSON, ITS HISTORY FROM AN INTERIOR POINT OF VIEW AS SKETCHED FROM THE DIARY OF AN OFFICER (n. p., 1937), 33. According to a hostile member of Dow's brigade, "One of the boys said the Rebs began at the wrong end of the general." Van Alstyne, DIARY OF AN ENLISTED MAN, May 28, 1863.

[28]Dow to wife, May 27, 30, June 12, 25, 26, 29, to Frederick Dow, May 29, June 15, to Cornelia Dow, June 6, 1863; Dow, REMINISCENCES, 696-702; Dow to R. D. Irwin, June 10, 1863, with an indorsement by Maj. Gen. N. P. Banks, July 13, 1863, copy in Neal Dow Pension File, Certificate 147693, Can 2765, Bundle 15, National Archives; Dow to Capt. Hoffman, June 30, 1863, in Miscellaneous Mss.-D, New York Historical Society.

CHAPTER XII

[1]Neal Dow to Frederick Dow, September 6, 1863. Unless otherwise noted, all manuscript items cited in this chapter are in the Dow Collection in the possession of Mrs. William C. Eaton of Portland.

[2]Dow to wife, July 1, 1863, February 26, 1864; Neal Dow, THE REMINISCENCES OF NEAL DOW, RECOLLECTIONS OF EIGHTY YEARS (Portland, 1898), 699-703; James H. Berry to Henry W. Blair, April 6, 1899, in Charles McGregor, HISTORY OF THE FIFTEENTH REGIMENT, NEW HAMPSHIRE VOLUNTEERS, 1862-1863 (n. p., 1900), 455.

[3]Dow to wife, July 12, 1863; Dow, REMINISCENCES, 704-11; Francis Trevelyan Miller, THE PHOTOGRAPHIC HISTORY OF THE CIVIL WAR (10 vols., New York, 1911), 7:57.

[4]Joint Resolutions of the Confederate Congress, May 1, 1863, E. J. Fitzpatrick to G. G. Garner, August 22, 1863, and Statement of Victor Reand, in United States War Department, THE WAR OF THE REBELLION, A COMPILATION OF THE OFFICIAL RECORDS OF THE UNION AND CONFEDERATE ARMIES (70 vols., Washington, 1880-1901), Series 2, 5:940, 6:270, 272-73, hereafter cited as "O. R."; Dow to wife, July 29, October 16, 1863; Richmond ENQUIRER, August 1, 1863, quoted in New York WORLD, August 5, 1863.

[5]Dow, REMINISCENCES, 712-16; Dow to wife, August 16, 23, September

6, 13, 30, October 4, November 11, to Frederick Dow, September 6, October 6, 1863. Stanton did not inform the Confederates that he had made Morgan a hostage for Dow. Letters of E. B. French, Lot M. Morrill and Darius Forbes to Abraham Lincoln, August 10, 15, 17, 1863, respectively, E. A. Hitchcock to S. A. Meredith, August 18, 1863, S. A. Meredith to E. A. Hitchcock, August 25, 1863, letters of Edwin M. Stanton and H. W. Halleck to E. A. Hitchcock, August 27, 1863, two letters of W. Hoffman to S. A. Meredith, August 28, 1863, W. Hoffman to John S. Mason, August 28, 1863, and Robert Ould to S. A. Meredith, August 28, 1863, in O. R., Ser. 2, 6:192, 206, 211-14, 226, 229, 335-37.

6Dabney S. Maury to S. Cooper, September 8, 1863, with inclosures, Cooper to Maury, September 22, 1863, in O. R., Ser. 2, 6:269-73, 312; Dow to Frederick Dow, October 6, to wife, October 12, 14, 16, 1863.

7Dow, REMINISCENCES, 718-19; James M. Wells, "WITH TOUCH OF ELBOW" OR DEATH BEFORE DISHONOR, A THRILLING NARRATIVE OF ADVENTURE ON LAND AND SEA (Philadelphia, 1909), 140-41; Frederic F. Cavada, LIBBY LIFE, EXPERIENCE OF A PRISONER OF WAR IN RICHMOND, VA., 1863-64 (Philadelphia, 1865), 41-49; Lt. Col. E. Szabad, "Diary in Libby Prison" in EVERY SATURDAY, 5:424, 426 (April 4, 1868); H. Clay Trumbull, WAR MEMORIES OF AN ARMY CHAPLAIN (New York, 1898), 291-92. For further material on Libby, see Frank L. Byrne, "Libby Prison: A Study in Emotions" in JOURNAL OF SOUTHERN HISTORY, 24:430-44 (November, 1958).

8Dow, REMINISCENCES, 717-19; Trumbull, WAR MEMORIES, 293-95; Dow to wife, November 2, 29, 1863, January 21, 1864, to Frederick Dow, November 12, 21, 1863; Dow Diary, December 11, 31, 1863, February 4, 16, 1864; Samuel H. M. Byers, WHAT I SAW IN DIXIE OR SIXTEEN MONTHS IN REBEL PRISONS (Danville, New York, 1868), 13.

9James M. Sanderson, MY RECORD IN REBELDOM AS WRITTEN BY FRIEND AND FOE, COMPRISING THE OFFICIAL CHARGES AND EVIDENCE BEFORE THE MILITARY COMMISSION IN WASHINGTON, BRIG. GEN'L J. C. CALDWELL, PRES'T, TOGETHER WITH THE REPORT AND FINDING OF THE COURT (New York, 1865), 18-53, 56-61, Appendix, XIV, XXXV; Miller, PHOTOGRAPHIC HISTORY OF THE CIVIL WAR, 7:45, 145; Dow, REMINISCENCES, 719-20, 728; Bernhard Domschcke, ZWANZIG MONATE IN KRIEGSGEFANGENSCHAFT (Milwaukee, 1865), 55-56, 73, 78.

10Dow, REMINISCENCES, 729; Ole A. Buslett, DET FEMTENDE REGIMENT WISCONSIN FRIVILLAGE (Decorah, Iowa, /1895/), 240-41; Byers, DIXIE, 21; Domschcke, ZWANZIG MONATE, 63; Charles Robinson, STORY OF A PRIVATE, NARRATIVE OF EXPERIENCES IN REBEL PRISONS AND STOCKADES (Milwaukee, 1897), 37-38; Sanderson, MY RECORD IN REBELDOM, Appendix, XII, XXX, XXXIV.

11John Hussey to /Ethan A. Meredith7, November 7, 1863, Dow to Secretary of War, November 13, 1863, in O. R., Ser. 2, 6:483, 510-11; Dow to Abraham Lincoln, November 12, 1863, January 20, 1864, in the Robert Todd

Lincoln Collection, Library of Congress. The envelope found with Dow to Ethan A. Meredith, December 9 and 10, 1863, is endorsed, "The Secretary did not wish to see this--Does not think well of the writer." Van Dyk McBride, ed., "A Letter from Libby Prison" in THE STAMP SPECIALIST, BLACK BOOK (New York, 1945), 110; Dow, REMINISCENCES, 721.

[12]RICHMOND EXAMINER, October 30, November 3, 1863; UNITED STATES SANITARY COMMISSION BULLETIN, 1:48 (November 15, 1863), 1:77 (December 1, 1863); Dow, REMINISCENCES, 723-25; Sanderson, MY RECORD IN REBELDOM, 150, Appendix XLVI; Domschcke, ZWANZIG MONATE, 62, 239; S. A. Meredith to William Hoffman, November 3, 1863, John Hussey to E. A. Meredith, November 5, 1863, Dow to Robert Ould, November 8, 1863, Ould to Meredith, November 14, 1863, Report of the Committee of the Confederate Congress to Investigate the Condition of Prisoners of War, March 3, 1865, in O. R., Ser. 2, 6:459, 482, 522-23, 8:843.

[13]Sanderson, MY RECORD IN REBELDOM, 18-21, 23-53, 93, Appendix, XXIV, XXVII, XXXV - VII, XL. On the last three pages of Dow's diary for 1863-64, he noted offenses by Sanderson and other Union prisoners and the names of witnesses to Confederate atrocities.

[14]Benjamin F. Butler to William Hoffman, February 20, 1864, O. R., Ser. 2, 6:973-75; Dow to Frederick Dow, October 23, to wife, December 8, 1863, January 21, March 6, 1864; Dow Diary, January 30, February 16, 1864; Sanderson, MY RECORD IN REBELDOM, XV, XXVI, XXXV, XL. Dow recalled that he once threw his own shoes and stockings out the window to a barefooted captive Union enlisted man. Dow, REMINISCENCES, 720-21.

[15]Dow had secretly asked his relatives to tell correspondents of certain other prisoners to begin heating their letters from Libby. Ibid., 721-23; Dow to wife, November 11, 29, December 27, 1863, January 5, 21, 24, 1864, to Frederick Dow, December 21, 30, January 28, February 1, 1864.

[16]Dow, REMINISCENCES, 726-28; Samuel P. Bates, MARTIAL DEEDS OF PENNSYLVANIA (Philadelphia, 1876), 1059; Szabad, "Diary in Libby" in EVERY SATURDAY, 5:432 (April 4, 1868); Domschcke, ZWANZIG MONATE, 89-91; Dow Diary, February 17, 27, 1864.

[17]William B. Hesseltine, CIVIL WAR PRISONS, A STUDY IN WAR PSYCHOLOGY (Columbus, Ohio, 1930), 132; Cavada, LIBBY LIFE, 194-96; Dow Diary, March 1, 2, 5, 7, 8, 10, 1864; speech by Dow reprinted from the Portland PRESS in New York TRIBUNE, March 29, 1864; Dow and Eliakim P. Scammon to Edwin M. Stanton, March 3 and 5, 1864, in the Stanton Papers, Library of Congress.

[18]Dow to Frederick Dow, January 27, 28, February 1, to wife, February 26, March 17, 1864; Frederick Dow, "Reminiscences," ch. 11, pp. 1-2, a typed manuscript; Dow Diary, February 28, March 9, 1864, and notations in the back pages.

[19]Dow's fellow prisoners unfavorably contrasted his removal of his possessions with the conduct of his enemy, Lieutenant-Colonel James M. Sanderson. When exchanged, the latter left most of his goods for the remaining

Libbyans. Sanderson, MY RECORD IN REBELDOM, 156-57, Appendix, XV, XX, XXVI, XXXII, XXXV, XL; Szabad, "Diary in Libby" in EVERY SATUR-DAY, 5:432 (April 4, 1868); Dow Diary, March 14-17, 1864; speech by Dow reprinted from Portland PRESS in New York TRIBUNE, March 29, 1864; Dow to wife, March 17, 1864.

20Dow Diary, March 18-22, 1864; Dow, REMINISCENCES, 140-41; Dow to wife, March 17, 18, 1864; Sanderson, MY RECORD IN REBELDOM, Appendix, XL.

21Dow Diary, March 24, 25, 1864; Dow, REMINISCENCES, 734-36; PORT-LAND TRANSCRIPT, April 2, 1864; SPEECHES OF HON. JAMES H. LANE IN THE COOPER INSTITUTE, NEW YORK, AND OF GENERAL NEAL DOW IN THE NEW CITY HALL, PORTLAND, THURSDAY EVENING, MARCH 24, 1861 / sic.7, ON HIS RETURN FROM CAPTIVITY IN A REBEL PRISON (Washington, 1864).

22Sanderson, MY RECORD IN REBELDOM, 9-22, 49-52, 77-78, 97-139, Appendix I.

23PORTLAND TRANSCRIPT, March 26, April 30, 1864; Dow to wife, January 26, 1863; Dow Diary, December 15, 16, 1863, January 29, February 5, March 25-October 28 passim, 1864; Frederick Dow, "Reminiscences, " ch. 7, p. 6. Dow later stated, "My health for months was so poor that I scarcely expected to survive a year. " Dow, REMINISCENCES, 736.

24Dow Diary, September 11, October 16, November 5, 10, 13, 14, 18, 19, 26, 28, 1864.

25Dow to wife, April 15, 23, 30, 1865.

26Ibid., November 19, to Frank Dow, December 7, 1865; articles by Dow in the New York INDEPENDENT, February 22, March 29, 1866, July 23, 1868.

27Dow to William Pitt Fessenden, April 6, 1868, in Francis Fessenden, THE LIFE AND PUBLIC SERVICES OF WILLIAM PITT FESSENDEN, UNITED STATES SENATOR FROM MAINE, 1854-1864, SECRETARY OF THE TREAS-URY, 1864-1865, UNITED STATES SENATOR FROM MAINE, 1865-1869 (2 vols., Boston, 1907), 2:186-88; Portland PRESS, March 2, 1868; Dow to wife, October 24, 26, 28, 1868; Dow to Gerrit Smith, February 11, 22, 1868, in the Gerrit Smith Papers, Syracuse University; Dow to Charles Sumner, January 30, 1870, in the Sumner Papers, Harvard University; Dow Diary, November 12, 1876.

CHAPTER XIII

1D. Leigh Colvin, PROHIBITION IN THE UNITED STATES, A HISTORY OF THE PROHIBITION PARTY AND OF THE PROHIBITION MOVEMENT (New York, c. 1926), 52-61, 87, 96-106; Fifth National Temperance Convention, PROCEEDINGS; Neal Dow to Gerrit Smith, August 6, 1865, in Gerrit Smith Papers, Syracuse University; Dow to wife, July 30, 1865. Unless otherwise indicated, all manuscript items cited in this chapter are in the Dow Collection in the possession of Mrs. William C. Eaton of Portland.

[2]Neal Dow, THE REMINISCENCES OF NEAL DOW, RECOLLECTIONS OF EIGHTY YEARS (Portland, 1898), 89, 91-92; Dow to wife, December 4, 13, 1868, May 15, 1873; Frederick N. Dow, "Reminiscences," ch. 7, pp. 6-7, a typed manuscript; Dow's "Book of Rents."

[3]In 1870, Dow also made a pleasure trip to the Pacific coast. His voluminous correspondence with his wife and family covering the period 1865-82 and his diaries for 1865-67 and from 1873 to 1885, when he made his last extensive tours, are largely devoted to his travels and lecturing. For Dow's paid articles, see particularly Dow to wife, July 12, 1870; Dow Diary, May 31, 1877; and Dow to "Dear Sir," January 11, 1872, in Miscellaneous Papers, New York Public Library. For typical Dow articles, see NATIONAL TEMPERANCE ADVOCATE, 7:7 (January, 1872), 14:99-100 (July, 1879). For Dow's railroad passes, see Dow to wife, April 29, May 7, 9, July 19, 1870, and original passes pasted on the covers of the Dow Scrapbooks. All Dow Scrapbooks cited in this chapter are on deposit in the library of Drew University. For Dow's lecture fees, see the only extant packet of his incoming correspondence, with his endorsements thereon, and Dow Diary, June 3, 1877. For the method and content of Dow's speeches, see Dow Diary, July 2, 1876; packets of his lecture notes and clippings; CENTENNIAL TEMPERANCE VOLUME, A MEMORIAL OF THE INTERNATIONAL TEMPERANCE CONFERENCE HELD IN PHILADELPHIA, JUNE, 1876 (2 vols., New York, 1877), 1: 50-90; and Portland PRESS, August 10, 1876.

[4]Henry Carter, THE ENGLISH TEMPERANCE MOVEMENT, A STUDY IN OBJECTIVES, VOL. 1-THE FORMATIVE PERIOD, 1830-1899 (London, England, 1933?), 168-73; Dow, REMINISCENCES, 624-25; Dow to wife, September 24, 1865.

[5]Dow Diary, September 16, 21, 28-29, 1864, December 25-27, 31, 1865; Dow to wife, October 24, November 14, 30, December 11, 1865; editorial item and Dow to Thomas H. Barker in Manchester (England) ALLIANCE NEWS, January 6, 19, 1866, in Dow Scrapbook, 10:187, 185, respectively.

[6]Dow Diary, February 4, 8, April 27, May 3, 15-December 31, 1866, January 1-31, 1867; NATIONAL TEMPERANCE ADVOCATE, 1:142 (September, 1866); Dow's letters to his wife from February 3 through November 17, 1867; Bath (England) EXPRESS, May 4, 1867, in Dow Scrapbook, 12:6; Dow, REMINISCENCES, picture opposite 285, 597; Portland PRESS, November 28, 1867.

[7]Letters of Dow in Manchester (England) ALLIANCE NEWS, July 8, 1871, October 5, 15, 1872, in Dow Scrapbook, 12:162, 159, 160, respectively; Carter, ENGLISH TEMPERANCE MOVEMENT, 144-68.

[8]Dow to wife, April 6, 21, May 23, 30, ⌊June 17⌉, 20, 22, 25, July 1, 2, 10, 19, August 3, October 19, November 20, 1873, February 3, 18, May 4, July 15, 1874, February 21, 1875, to Cornelia Dow, May 4, 1873; Dow Diary, August 9, 1873-August 30, 1874; Carter, ENGLISH TEMPERANCE MOVEMENT, 183-95; Robert C. K. Ensor, ENGLAND, 1870-1914 (Oxford, England, c. 1936), 20-22, 34, 360-61.

[9]Dow Diary, September 1, 1874-June 3, 1875, December 10, 1876, March 20, 1878.

[10]Ibid., June 4-30, 1875; Portland PRESS, June 22, 1875; NATIONAL TEMPERANCE ADVOCATE, 10:116-19 (August, 1875); Carter, ENGLISH TEMPERANCE MOVEMENT, 183-218.

[11]NATIONAL TEMPERANCE ADVOCATE, 7:74-75 (May, 1872); Portland PRESS, 1872, clipping in Dow Scrapbook, 12:162d; Colvin, PROHIBITION IN THE UNITED STATES, 116-19.

[12]Dow Diary, September 2, 5, 1875, August 1-6, 8, 9, September 13, 14, 1876, July 31, August 2, 4, 22, 23, 25-31, 1877, and many subsequent references to camp meetings.

[13]On the very day of Dow's return from Great Britain, all of Portland's hotels closed their illegal bars, at least temporarily, in response to a notice from the sheriff. Dow to Cornelia Dow, May 31, 1874; PORTLAND ADVERTISER, June 3, 1875, in Dow Scrapbook, 13:106; Dow Diary, June 17, November 10, 15, 1875, January 31, February 19, April 18, 1876; article by Dow in NATIONAL TEMPERANCE ADVOCATE, 14:99-100 (July, 1879); Dow, THE MAINE LAW IN MAINE, HON. NEAL DOW ON MR. JOHN BRIGHT'S STATESMANSHIP, LOCAL OPTION IN THE SOUTHERN STATES IN AMERICA (Manchester, England, n. d.), 1-7; [Thomas McDougall, ed.], THE LIQUOR QUESTION, THE BEST LEGISLATIVE METHOD FOR THE SUPPRESSION OF THE EVILS OF THE TRAFFIC: TAXATION, PROHIBITION, LICENSE, DISCUSSION AS CARRIED ON IN THE COLUMNS OF THE CINCINNATI COMMERCIAL GAZETTE BY NEAL DOW, REV. J. M. WALDEN, D. D. AND THOMAS MCDOUGALL, ADDRESS AT URBANA, OPEN LETTER TO DR. LEONARD, &C., &C. (Cincinnati, 1887); Dow to "Dear Sir," September 7, 1887, in Iowa State Department of History and Archives; Washington Gladden to [William Henry Noble], April 13, 1883, in Noble Papers, Duke University. Photostats of the latter two documents are in the author's possession.

[14]Dow Diary, October 1, 22, 25, 1875, January 13, 19-21, December 1-2, 1876, January 19-25, February 11, March 1, 29, 1877, January 2, 21-26, 1878; Dow to editor of New York TRIBUNE and item from BOSTON HERALD reprinted in Portland EASTERN ARGUS, February 27, March 1, 1877; MAINE SESSION LAWS, 1877, pp. 160-61; letter of Dow in NATIONAL TEMPERANCE ADVOCATE, 13:28 (February, 1878).

[15]Dow to wife, August 13, 1871, July 15, 1874; Frederick N. Dow, "Reminiscences," ch. 9, pp. 10-19; Dow Diary, October 13, November 7, 8, 12, 1876, March 2, 1877; Dow to William Lloyd Garrison, March 19, April 24, November 10, 1877, November 25, 1878, in Rare Books Department of Boston Public Library. While promoting his son's candidacy for the Portland postmastership, Dow spoke of himself as "one who helped to lay the foundations of the Republican Party in this State, to which I have been loyal in act and thought from the first. . . ." Dow to Rutherford B. Hayes, December 12, 1879, in the Hayes Papers, Hayes Memorial Library. A typed copy is in the author's possession.

[16]Dow Diary, February 5, 9-12, 1880; Portland PRESS, February 12, 1880; MAINE SESSION LAWS, 1880, pp. 290-93; letter of Dow in NATIONAL TEMPERANCE ADVOCATE, 15:52 (April, 1880).

[17]Dow, REMINISCENCES, 142-45; Colvin, PROHIBITION IN THE UNITED STATES, 59-60, 82-116, 123-27; Dow Diary, May 25, June 17, July 12, 14, 1880.

[18]Ibid., July 19, 21-23, September 2, 3, 9, 10, 13, 14, 1880; Dow, REMINISCENCES, 147; Portland PRESS, July 23, 28, 31, August 20, 1880; Portland EASTERN ARGUS, September 3, 1880; MAINE REGISTER, 1881, p. 116; article by Dow in NATIONAL TEMPERANCE ADVOCATE, 15:165 (November, 1880).

[19]Dow, REMINISCENCES, 147-50; Dow Diary, June 5, 8, October 19, 28-November 3, 1880; PRESS, October 28, 30, November 3, 1880; Colvin, PROHIBITION IN THE UNITED STATES, 129-30; Edward McPherson, A HANDBOOK OF POLITICS FOR 1882 . . . (Washington, 1882), 186.

[20]Dow was personally signing complaints against Portland liquor-sellers. Dow Diary, November 29, December 5, 12, 1880, September 12, 1882, January 27, February 2, 3, October 20, 1883; PRESS, letters of "N. D." and editorial comments, January 27, February 2, 7, 1881, account of Prohibitionist meeting, June 26, 1882, March 2, 16, September 10, letter of Dow reprinted from BOSTON TRAVELLER in October 10, 1883; Dow, REMINISCENCES, 564-65; ARGUS, June 15, 23, 26, 1882, and letter of Dow in September 19, 1885; BOSTON GLOBE, August 26, 1886, in Dow Scrapbook, 20:418; Frederick N. Dow, "Reminiscences," ch. 9, pp. 19-23; Louis C. Hatch, MAINE, A HISTORY (3 vols., New York, 1919), 2:628-29; MAINE SESSION LAWS, 1883, pp. 204-05.

[21]Dow Diary, June 17, 24, 27, 1884; New York HERALD quoted in ARGUS, June 26, 1884; PRESS, June 26, 1884; NATIONAL TEMPERANCE ADVOCATE, 19:151 (September, 1884); Nathan F. Woodbury, THE REPUBLICAN PARTY AND ITS NOMINEES (BLAINE AND LOGAN), OPPOSED TO PROHIBITION AND IN FAVOR OF A CONTINUATION OF THE LIQUOR TRAFFIC, ENDORSED BY NEAL DOW, COMMENTS OF A PROHIBITIONIST ON THE INCONSISTENCIES OF NEAL DOW AND OTHER PROHIBITIONISTS WHO SUPPORT A LIQUOR CRIME PARTY (n. p., [1884]).

[22]Dow, REMINISCENCES, 150-51; Dow Diary, July 22-27, August 2-3, 11-19, 29, 31, September 1-9, 1884; article by Dow in NATIONAL TEMPERANCE ADVOCATE, 19:164-65 (October, 1884); PRESS, September 3, 6, 9, 13, 1884.

[23]Ibid., September 9, 30, 1884; Colvin, PROHIBITION IN THE UNITED STATES, 164-65; Dow Diary, September 12, 29, November 8, 1884; Frederick N. Dow, "Reminiscences," ch. 7, p. 16; article by Dow in NATIONAL TEMPERANCE ADVOCATE, 20:5 (January, 1885). Republican Governor Frederick Robie, whose re-election Dow had aided, recommended that no new prohibitory law be passed but the legislature enacted an act much milder than that favored by Dow. MAINE SESSION LAWS, 1885, pp. 307-12, 328-30.

[24]Letter of Dow to New York VOICE quoted in NATIONAL TEMPERANCE ADVOCATE, 20:62 (April, 1885); BOSTON GLOBE, March 1, 1885, letters of Dow in MANCHESTER (England) GUARDIAN, September 22, 1885, and PORTLAND HERALD, June 16, 1888, in Dow Scrapbook, 19:7, 22:40, 216; PRESS, March 2, 1885, February 12, 1886.

[25]Dow Diary, June 9, 15-17, August 5-6, September 3-7, 9-12, 1886; PRESS, June 17, August 5, September 14, 18, 1886; NATIONAL TEMPERANCE ADVOCATE, 21:166, 169, 170 (October, 1886) and article by Dow, 21:180 (November, 1886); McDougall, THE LIQUOR QUESTION, IV-V.

[26]Dow Diary, February 13, 14, 20, 23, March 4, 1888; PRESS, February 14, 15, 20-22, 25, March 2, 5-7, 1888; ARGUS, February 21, 22, 24, 27, March 5, 6, 1888; Portland PROHIBITIONIST, March 3, 1888, handbill, New York SUN, March 6, 1888, and letters of Dow in Belfast (Maine) CITY PRESS, March 13, 1888, and New York VOICE, March 29, 1888, in Dow Scrapbook, 21:107, 111, 119, 121, 142. In his old age, Dow became more friendly toward some of Portland's Irish. Before a local Irish group, he violently advocated Ireland's case against England. PRESS, January 17, 1882. He regarded Republican William Looney as a friend and once went to Mass with the Irish-American Portland politician. Dow Diary, April 13, 1884.

[27]PRESS, May 16, October 16, 1888; Dow Diary, May 27-June 3, July 16, 29, August 1, 12, 23, 28-31, September 4-8, 1888; clipping of Frances E. Willard, "Neal Dow at Home," from an unknown publication dated March 4, 1888, New York VOICE, June 7, 1888, and Dow, "The Result of the Presidential Election" in OUR DAY, December, 1888, in Dow Scrapbook, 22:174, 212, 365-66.

CHAPTER XIV

[1]Neal Dow, THE REMINISCENCES OF NEAL DOW, RECOLLECTIONS OF EIGHTY YEARS (Portland, 1898), 95.

[2]Mrs. Joseph Cook, "Neal Dow as Guest and Host" in OUR DAY, 13:515-18 (July-August, 1894); Neal Dow Diary, February 11, 1866, February 2, December 7, 1874, September 5, December 8, 19, 1888, February 5, March 20, 1889, May 14, December 7, 1890, September 14-October 6, 1891, January 10-February 4, March 20, August 17, November 23, 1892, September 7, 1893, March 20, 1896; Neal Dow to wife, January 10, 1875. Unless otherwise indicated, all manuscript items cited in this chapter are in the Dow Collection in the possession of Mrs. William C. Eaton of Portland. See also, Dow, REMINISCENCES, 28-29, 57-58; Frances E. Willard, "Neal Dow at Home," a clipping in the Neal Dow Scrapbook, 22:173, on deposit in the library of Drew University.

[3]Dow Diary, November 9, 1882-January 20, 1883.

[4]Frances E. Willard and Mary A. Livermore, eds., A WOMAN OF THE CENTURY, FOURTEEN HUNDRED-SEVENTY BIOGRAPHICAL SKETCHES

ACCOMPANIED BY PORTRAITS OF LEADING AMERICAN WOMEN IN ALL WALKS OF LIFE (Buffalo, New York, 1893), 257; Dow Diary, July 2, September 24, November 26, 28, 1888, October 7, 1889, July 3, 24-30, November 11, December 12, 1890, May 30-June 6, 1892, July 24, September 26, October 14, 29, 1893, June 26, 1894, January 15, 1895, July 3, October 29, 1896; Dow, REMINISCENCES, picture facing 292; notes of an interview by the author with Mrs. William C. Eaton.

[5]Dow Diary, June 25, 1880, November 24, 1882, August 28, 1884, September 14, 20, October 2, December 8, 1886; Dow's Ledger Number 5, pp. 66, 67, 76; Portland PRESS, September 20-23, 25, 27-30, October 1, 4, 1886; William A. Robinson, THOMAS B. REED, PARLIAMENTARIAN (New York, 1930), 160-61.

[6]Dow Diary, September 20-23, 1889, June 23-July 2, 1890, July 31-August 5, 1891, September 30-October 4, 1892, September 12-15, 1893, March 22-24, September 19-24, 1894, June 10-14, December 7-11, 1895; notes of an interview by the author with Mrs. William C. Eaton; Family Bible in the Dow Collection; A. N. Somers, HISTORY OF LANCASTER, NEW HAMPSHIRE (Concord, New Hampshire, 1899), 160.

[7]Dow Diary, October 1, 1890, February 4, November 26, 1891, November 30, 1893; Dow's Ledger Number 5, p. 79; Frederick N. Dow, "Reminiscences," ch. 7, pp. 16-20, ch. 9, pp. 32-33, ch. 10, pp. 13-19, a typed manuscript. In branding his son's newspaper as "an organ of Republican bosses of the straightest sect," Dow used the pseudonym "Yed." rather than his own name or initials. Clipping from PORTLAND HERALD, January 21, 1888, hand-initialed "N. D.," in Dow Scrapbook, 22:50, Drew University.

[8]Dow, REMINISCENCES, 151; comments by Dow in UNION SIGNAL, December 29, 1892, in Dow Scrapbook, 24:295, Drew University; letters by Dow in [FRANK LESLIE'S WEEKLY?], Portland PRESS, August 29, 1896, New York VOICE, July 16, 1896, in Neal Dow Scrapbook, 28:64, 82, in New York State Library; D. Leigh Colvin, PROHIBITION IN THE UNITED STATES, A HISTORY OF THE PROHIBITION PARTY AND OF THE PROHIBITION MOVEMENT (New York, c. 1926), 255-59. Dow did not fail to vote in the 1896 presidential election because of physical disability. He went riding on election day. Dow Diary, November 3, 8, 1896.

[9]Federal Writers' Project, PORTLAND CITY GUIDE (Portland, 1940), 41-47, 62; Dow's "Book of Rents"; Dow Diary, October 17, 1876, February 22, September 11, 1879, May 20, July 26, August 2, 1880, January 1, March 24, May 7, November 7, 1881, March 2, April 20, September 15, December 9, 1886, June 13, 1887, October 9, 1888, April 21, 1891, October 13, 1896; Dow's Ledger Number 5, pp. 41, 43, 45, 47, 49, 53, 69, 92; Neal Dow Pension File, Certificate 147693, Can 2765, Bundle 15, National Archives.

[10]Dow Diary, May 21, June 27, 1888, August 29, 30, September 8, 1890, July 23, 1891, May 23, July 11-15, December 20, 1893, July 27, 1895; notes of an interview of the author with Mrs. William C. Eaton.

[11]Willard, "Dow at Home," in Dow Scrapbook, 22:174, Drew University;

Dow Diary, May 2, 1888, May 5, 1890, February 26, March 9, 1891, February 24, April 11, 1892, February 5, 1895, July 5, 1896; lists of magazines and newspapers in the back of Dow's "Family Expense Book"; Dow, REMINISCENCES, 50; Alonzo A. Miner, "Neal Dow and His Life Work" in the NEW ENGLAND MAGAZINE, 10:410 (June, 1894).

[12]Dow Diary, December 10, 1876, November 22, 1878, August 8, 1880, November 2, 1885, March 14, 1886, April 15, November 4, 1888; notes of an interview of the author with Mrs. William C. Eaton; article by Dow in NATIONAL TEMPERANCE ADVOCATE, 16:7 (January, 1881); Dow, REMINISCENCES, 701, 749.

[13]Dow Diary, January 13, February 2, March 2, 5, 9, 31, April 23, 26, May 2, 19, 20, December 22, 1889, June 15, September 28, 1890, September 8, 1891, June 14, 1892, December 28, 1895, November 23, 1896; Dow, REMINISCENCES, 571; Portland SUNDAY TELEGRAM, April 28, 1889, in Dow Scrapbook, 22:A, Drew University; Dow to Dr. Funk, July 25, 1891, in the Eldridge Collection, Box 3, Huntington Library. A photostat is in the author's possession.

[14]Willard, "Dow at Home, " in Dow Scrapbook, 22:174, Drew University.

[15]Dow Diary, July 13, 1889, July 19, August 9, 1891, June 30, September 4, 1892, July 30, 1893, August 5, 1894, July 7, 1895, February 27, December 10, 1896; Portland PRESS, September 5, 14, 1892, July 8, 1895; letter by Dow in NATIONAL TEMPERANCE ADVOCATE, 26:119 (July, 1891); Portland EASTERN ARGUS, December 27, 1893, July 8, 1895, and BOSTON DAILY GLOBE, June 23, 1894, in Dow Scrapbook, 25:88, 27:87, 19:204, respectively, Drew University.

[16]Dow Diary, January 31, February 1, 13, 14, 1889, December 24, 1890, February 19, 20, 1891, January 26, 27, February 15, 21, March 1, 1893; BOSTON HERALD, June 21, 1891, in Dow Scrapbook, 24:27, Drew University; Portland PRESS, February 1, 2, 1889, February 20, 1891, January 27, 1893, January 19, 1895; MAINE SESSION LAWS, 1891, pp. 35, 144-48, 1893, pp. 373-74.

[17]NATIONAL TEMPERANCE ADVOCATE, 27:84 (June, 1892) and article by Dow in MAINE TEMPERANCE RECORD quoted in 27:140 (August, 1892); Portland PRESS, July 31, 1893; a series of articles by Dow in PORTLAND HERALD, in Dow Scrapbook, 25:48-51, Drew University.

[18]Dow Diary, July 16, 1894, January 7, 17, 22, 31, February 13, 20, March 7, April 24, 1895; Portland PRESS, January 18, 19, 21, February 21, March 22, 1895.

[19]So great was tightfisted Neal Dow's interest in the W. C. T. U. that he invested $1, 027. 67 in an ill-fated plan backed by Frances E. Willard for a great "Temperance Temple" in Chicago. Dow Diary, March 3, 1888, April 8, 1889, May 30, 1890, February 15, March 30-31, July 9, November 9-10, December 17, 1892, July 18, 22, 24, 1895; Cook, "Dow as Guest and Host" in OUR DAY, 13:315-18 (July-August, 1894); Dow, REMINISCENCES, 311; Mary Earhart, FRANCES WILLARD: FROM PRAYERS TO POLITICS (Chicago, c. 1944),

24, 374-82.

[20]Dow Diary, October 9, 18-25, 1888, November 4-15, 1889, June 8-16, August 8, October 7-13, 1890, June 20-24, November 12-14, 1891, September 19-23, 1892, May 30-June 7, 14, 22-23, August 31, October 15-16, 1894; Dow, REMINISCENCES, frontispiece.

[21]Frances Willard to Dow, October 4, 1893, and editorial and letter of "Alfred York" in ARGUS, December 27, 1893, [March, 1894?], in Dow Scrapbook, 25:112, 88, 254, respectively, Drew University; Dow Diary, September 25, 1893, January 1, February 1, 8, 21, 23, March 6, 9, 12, 16, 19-21, 1894; NATIONAL TEMPERANCE ADVOCATE, 29:26 (February, 1894); Portland PRESS, March 21, 1894; Dow, REMINISCENCES, 739-47; Mrs. William C. Eaton to author, March 12, 1957, in the author's possession.

[22]Dow, REMINISCENCES, 89; Dow Diary, February 4, 1866, November 21, 1889, May 15, 1894; Dow Scrapbooks in Drew University and the New York State Library.

[23]Dow, REMINISCENCES, preface and passim; Dow Diary, April 3, 1886, March 5, May 12, 16, 24, 25, 1887, October 23, 1889.

[24]Dow, REMINISCENCES, 747; Dow Diary, October 16, 1895, June 4, 1896, January 18, 19, 21, 25, 27, March 20, 1897; Portland PRESS, March 22, 1897; Frances Willard to Dow, November 4, 1896, in Dow Scrapbook, 27:271, Drew University; telegram of Willard to Dow, March 20, 1897, and other congratulations in Dow Scrapbook, 28:5, 13, New York State Library.

[25]Dow Diary, February 18, March 2, April 18, May 1, 22, June 26, 28, 29, July 21-23, 1897; Dow, REMINISCENCES, 747-48.

[26]Ibid., 748-56; photos from SATURDAY EVENING REVIEW, October 9, 1897, in Dow Scrapbook, 28:237, New York State Library.

[27]For a survey of newspaper opinion, see the clippings in Ibid., 28:174-271, New York State Library. Beginning in 1903, prohibitionists at Portland and elsewhere held annual celebrations of Dow's birthday. Those in 1929 of his 125th anniversary were especially widespread. Newspaper accounts are in Dow Scrapbook, 29:246-47, 272-75, Drew University.

ESSAY ON THE SOURCES

The bulk of the material for a biography of Neal Dow is in his native Portland. Retaining many buildings and other physical remains of its 19th century glory, the Maine city itself provides the backdrop for a study of one of its most prominent sons. At 714 Congress Street, the house built by Neal Dow still is occupied by his granddaughter, Mrs. William C. Eaton. Her courteous assistance made this biography possible. Though past eighty, she clearly recalled numerous illustrative incidents of her grandfather's later years. And she permitted the author free and full use of the old homestead's wealth of Dow memorabilia.

Neal Dow's letters and diaries are the principal source for his biography. During their more than fifty years of married life, his wife saved his letters to her and also some to their children. The correspondence is heaviest during the periods of his American Maine Law missions, his three trips to Great Britain and his Civil War military service. Dow frequently wrote extended letters with daily entries. He included personal and business matters but devoted particular attention to descriptions of distant places and to comments on his temperance work. In the early 1930's, Colonel Frederick N. Dow had typed copies made of his father's letters, bound them into two volumes of about a thousand pages each and destroyed all but a few of the originals. The frank contents of many of the copied letters make it probable, however, that they are complete transcripts. Only typographical errors in names and particularly in dates necessitate caution in the use of these extremely valuable papers.

In 1857, 1858 and 1860, Dow made very brief notations of his daily activities. But the first significant diary preserved in the Dow homestead deals principally with Dow's prison experiences. As a contemporary, unedited record of Libby life, it is quite unusual. The other diaries cover 1865-67 and 1873-97. They provide a day-to-day check on Dow's doings, descriptions of the places which he visited and other information. But they afford less insight into his personal life than do many of his letters. When on trips, he apparently intended his diary entries partly for the edification of his family. Many of Dow's remarks also indicate his wish to furnish data for future historians.

The account books remaining in Dow's mansion constitute the only source for most of his business activities. Highly important are two ledgers covering the time between 1830 and about 1848. In the back of the first are handwritten copies of twenty-three of Dow's business letters. For the same period, Dow also kept and preserved accounts of his personal and household spending. There are no financial records extant for Dow's middle years. From the late 1870's to his death, a ledger, a household account book and two rent books show many of his transactions. The Androscoggin and Kennebec Railroad's ANNUAL REPORTS, 1849-51, provide additional information on Dow's directorate of that company.

The Neal Dow homestead also houses much miscellaneous material on its builder and his family. Dow apparently saved his incoming letters but only a small packet from the late 1870's survived subsequent housecleanings. These letters indicate Dow's broad correspondence with the world's temperance men and give the only details of his lecture fees. The family collection also includes Dow's handwritten book of flute music, some of his lecture notes, pictures, original furniture and many other items. Frederick N. Dow's typewritten "Reminiscences" sheds light on Dow as a parent. Because Dow's son wrote when very old and without recourse to documents, his manuscript contains many small errors. But the "Reminiscences" offers much background material on old Portland and on later political developments.

After 1853, Dow carefully filled twenty-eight scrapbooks with newspaper clippings and a few letters relating to his career and to the prohibition movement. In the early 1930's, to make these more widely available, his son deposited them with a New York temperance foundation. The Reverend Robert Corradini of Madison, New Jersey, a former executive of the defunct foundation, has deposited twenty-one of these highly useful scrapbooks in the library of Drew University. Volume 28 is in the New York State Library. Six of the scrapbooks are missing.

Because of his voluminous correspondence, Dow's name appears in the manuscript holdings of many research libraries. The sixteen letters in Harvard's Charles Sumner Papers and the thirteen in Syracuse University's papers of Gerrit Smith are the largest groups. The Boston Public Library has nine of Dow's letters. Seven of them to William Lloyd Garrison deal mainly with Dow's view of the end of Reconstruction. In its Hannibal Hamlin Papers, the Maine Historical Society has several instructive letters on state politics. The Robert Todd Lincoln Collection and four others in the Library of Congress contain scattered Dow letters. There are from one to four Dow manuscripts in the collections of the American Antiquarian Society, the Chicago Historical Society, the Essex Institute, the Hayes Memorial Library, the Henry E. Huntington Library and Art Gallery, the Iowa State Department of History and Archives, the Historical Societies of Massachusetts, Minnesota and New York, the New York Public and State Libraries, Northwestern University, the Pennsylvania Historical Society, the University of Rochester, the Willard Memorial Library and the State Historical Society of Wisconsin.

THE REMINISCENCES OF NEAL DOW: RECOLLECTIONS OF EIGHTY YEARS (Portland, 1898) forms the most important single item in the printed record. Though Dow wrote his book late in life, he based it on his extensive personal papers and achieved a high degree of accuracy. After the fashion of the time, however, he edited considerably many of the published excerpts from letters and newspaper articles. He wrote as a convinced prohibitionist and often neglected incidents unfavorable to himself and to his cause. Before the posthumous publication of the REMINISCENCES, his son also excised at Dow's request most references to personal controversies. Nevertheless, Dow's work is the only significant source for his boyhood and youth. For the period to the close of the Civil War and for a few later incidents, the REMINISCENCES provides data on a multitude of personal acts, characteristics and opinions.

To supplement Dow's own discussion of his ancestry and family connections, a competently done work is Robert Piercy Dow, THE BOOK OF DOW: GENE-ALOGICAL MEMOIRS OF THE DESCENDANTS OF HENRY DOW 1637, THOM-AS DOW 1693 AND OTHERS OF THE NAME, IMMIGRANTS TO AMERICA DURING COLONIAL TIMES, ALSO THE ALLIED FAMILY OF NUDD (Rutland, Vermont, 1929). Daniel C. Colesworthy, SCHOOL IS OUT (Boston, 1876), a long narrative poem, and Cyrus Hamlin, MY LIFE AND TIMES (2nd ed., Boston, c. 1893) refer to Dow's youthful friends and describe early Portland. While undocumented, the Federal Writers' Project's excellent PORTLAND CITY GUIDE (Portland, 1940) contains much information essential to an understanding of Dow's city. The most important contemporary witness on Dow's role in several early controversies is John Neal. The latter's WANDERING RECOLLECTIONS OF A SOMEWHAT BUSY LIFE, AN AUTOBIOGRAPHY (Boston, 1869) demonstrates his own erratic personality and occasionally faulty memory. John Neal's highly interesting book drips with his poisonous bias against his cousin. Several references to the Portland Gymnasium, to which Dow belonged, are in John Neal's weekly Portland YANKEE.

Clifford S. Griffin, THEIR BROTHERS' KEEPERS: MORAL STEWARD-SHIP IN THE UNITED STATES, 1800-1865 (New Brunswick, New Jersey, c. 1960) supersedes earlier treatments of the era of reforms in which Neal Dow grew up. A well written work, it is especially helpful in throwing light upon the religious background of 19th century reform and in indicating the relationship of temperance to other movements. Covering part of the same ground, Charles I. Foster, AN ERRAND OF MERCY: THE EVANGELICAL UNITED FRONT, 1790-1837 (Chapel Hill, North Carolina, c. 1960) also gives attention to the interaction between British and American conservative reform groups. Bernard A. Weisberger, THEY GATHERED AT THE RIVER: THE STORY OF THE GREAT REVIVALISTS AND THEIR IMPACT UPON RELIGION IN AMER-ICA (Boston, c. 1958) has important insights into the connection between revivalism and reform and gives a good picture of Lyman Beecher whose published sermons were Dow's temperance primer.

By far the best secondary work on the pre-Maine Law temperance movement is John Allen Krout, THE ORIGINS OF PROHIBITION (New York, 1925). The reports and publications of the American Temperance Union and its subsidiaries are valuable primary sources. The New York Public Library in its James Black Collection has a very extensive holding of such 19th century anti-

alcohol literature. Charles Holden , CONSTITUTION OF THE MAINE CHAR-
ITABLE MECHANIC ASSOCIATION, INSTITUTED JANUARY 16, 1815, AND
INCORPORATED JUNE 14, 1815, WITH A HISTORICAL SKETCH (Portland,
1875) includes quotations from minutes referring to some of Dow's early tem-
perance work. Dow's own ORATION DELIVERED BEFORE THE MAINE
CHARITABLE MECHANIC ASSOCIATION AT THEIR TRIENNIAL CELEBRA-
TION, JULY 4, 1829 (Portland, 1829) is his first published speech and reveals
his views on temperance, education and social class.

Contemporary newspapers give the most detailed and continuous picture of
Dow's early temperance and political activities. Published throughout Dow's
adult life, the PORTLAND ADVERTISER represents the views of the Whigs
and later of the Republicans. Although at first as friendly to Dow and his
cause as the ADVERTISER, the Democratic Portland EASTERN ARGUS eventually becomes the voice of his bitterest enemies. The Portland CHRISTIAN
MIRROR, organ of Maine Congregationalism, often refers to Dow's earli-
est temperance efforts. After 1838, the Reverend Thomas Adams' Augusta
MAINE TEMPERANCE GAZETTE takes up the story. From 1841 to 1843,
Adams printed his weekly at Portland under the titles of the MAINE TEM-
PERANCE GAZETTE AND WASHINGTONIAN HERALD and the MAINE WASH-
INGTONIAN JOURNAL AND TEMPERANCE HERALD. From 1843 to about
1848, Dow's friend, George H. Shirley, edited the paper as the Portland
WASHINGTONIAN JOURNAL. THE TRUE WASHINGTONIAN AND MARTHA
WASHINGTON ADVOCATE, published at Portland in 1843 and 1844, illus-
trates the violent reaction of the moral suasionists to Dow's prohibitionism
and personal controversies.

For the period of the Maine Law crusade, the temperance press continues
to provide the bulk of the printed matter on Dow's doings. "Elder" Benjamin
D. Peck's Portland MAINE TEMPERANCE WATCHMAN reveals the abusive
tactics of its corrupt proprietor and his secret lodge. In 1854, Peck changed
his weekly's name to the MAINE TEMPERANCE JOURNAL and, between 1855
and 1858, to the MAINE TEMPERANCE JOURNAL AND INQUIRER. Until the
Civil War, in all its metamorphoses, this paper constitutes Dow's channel
to the public. From 1852 to 1855, the voice of Dow's most rabid opponents
is the Portland MAINE EXPOSITOR.

Louis Clinton Hatch, MAINE, A HISTORY (3 vols., New York, 1919) is
the best available secondary account of the Maine Law movement's political
background. Though limited in many respects, Hatch's book is based on extensive newspaper research. It is the only relatively modern, scholarly history of Dow's state. Francis Fessenden, LIFE AND PUBLIC SERVICES OF
WILLIAM PITT FESSENDEN: UNITED STATES SENATOR FROM MAINE,
1854-1864, SECRETARY OF THE TREASURY, 1864-1865, UNITED STATES
SENATOR FROM MAINE, 1865-1869 (2 vols., Boston, 1907) and Charles
Eugene Hamlin, THE LIFE AND TIMES OF HANNIBAL HAMLIN (Cambridge,
Massachusetts, 1899) are biographies of two of Dow's associates in smashing
the Maine Democracy. Philip Greely Clifford, NATHAN CLIFFORD, DEMO-

CRAT (1803-1881) (New York, 1922) tells of one of his enemies. All three books are in the filiopietistic tradition.

The most detailed account of the spread of the Maine Law to other states is Henry S. Clubb, THE MAINE LIQUOR LAW: ITS ORIGIN, HISTORY AND RESULTS INCLUDING A LIFE OF HON. NEAL DOW (New York, 1856). An "official" biography, Clubb's book depicts Dow as he wished to appear to the world. Frank L. Byrne, "Maine Law Versus Lager Beer: A Dilemma of Wisconsin's Young Republican Party" in the WISCONSIN MAGAZINE OF HISTORY, 42:115-20 (Winter, 1958-59) is representative of a number of articles, cited in the Notes, on the effects of prohibition upon various states. In his RECOLLECTIONS OF A LONG LIFE, AN AUTOBIOGRAPHY (New York, c. 1902), Theodore L. Cuyler reveals one type of Maine Law man and gives a flattering description of the Prophet of Prohibition. Other extreme examples of adulation by Dow's followers are John Marsh, THE NAPOLEON OF TEMPERANCE, SKETCHES OF THE LIFE AND CHARACTER OF THE HON. NEAL DOW, MAYOR OF PORTLAND AND AUTHOR OF THE MAINE LIQUOR LAW (New York, 1852) and a chapter of George W. Gungay, OFF-HAND TAKINGS OR CRAYON SKETCHES OF THE NOTICEABLE MEN OF OUR AGE (New York, c. 1854).

One of the few sources on the Portland Riot's mysterious anti-foreign background is the anonymous KNOW NOTHINGISM: ILLUSTRATED WITH "CUTS": THE PORTRAITS DRAWN FROM LIFE (Portland, 1855). A copy of this rare and unusual poem, which is one of the more bitter attacks on Dow, is in the Portland Public Library. John M. Gould's "Notes on a Ledger of a Portland Lodge of the Order of United Americans," in the Maine Historical Society, lists the names of many Know-Nothings. THE DEATH OF JOHN ROBBINS OF DEER ISLE WHO WAS SHOT IN THE STREETS OF PORTLAND BY ORDER OF NEAL DOW, MAYOR, JUNE 2D, 1855, A FULL REPORT OF THE TESTIMONY TAKEN BEFORE THE CORONER'S INQUEST, AS PUBLISHED IN THE "STATE OF MAINE" NEWSPAPER (Portland, 1855) is the anti-Dowites' indictment of their foe. The Dowite reply is the REPORT OF THE COMMITTEE APPOINTED BY THE BOARD OF ALDERMAN OF THE CITY OF PORTLAND TO INVESTIGATE THE CAUSES AND CONSEQUENCES OF THE RIOT ON THE EVENING OF JUNE 2, 1855 (Portland, 1855). Joseph Ashur Ware in his REVIEW OF THE TESTIMONY TAKEN BEFORE THE SECOND INQUEST ON THE BODY OF JOHN ROBBINS WHO WAS SHOT AT PORTLAND, JUNE 2D, 1855, TOGETHER WITH REMARKS ON THE REPORT OF THE INVESTIGATING COMMITTEE APPOINTED BY MAYOR DOW AND THE ALDERMEN, JUNE 9, 1855 (Portland, 1855) reaches conclusions unfriendly to Dow. A last-ditch justification of Dow's actions is [Charles Stewart Daveis7, "The Law of Riot: The Portland Riot" in THE MONTHLY LAW REPORTER, 8:361-86 (November, 1855).

For an understanding of Dow's three overseas missions, Henry Carter, THE ENGLISH TEMPERANCE MOVEMENT: A STUDY IN OBJECTIVES, THE BECKLY SOCIAL SERVICE LECTURE, 1932, VOL. 1 - THE FORMATIVE

PERIOD, 1830-1899 (London, /1933/) is essential. This book is one of the few pieces of fresh thinking on the effects of prohibitionism on teetotalism. Dow's own writings in the publications of the United Kingdom Alliance give his viewpoints on his cause in Great Britain and America. To present the prohibitionists' side of the "dead letter" controversy, Frederic R. Lees edited WHAT WAS IT? THE INNER-HISTORY OF THE TEMPERANCE LIBEL-CASE FROM THE MORAL-STAND-POINT (/Leeds, England7, 1860). The AUTOBIOGRAPHY AND PERSONAL RECOLLECTIONS OF JOHN B. GOUGH, WITH TWENTY-SIX YEARS EXPERIENCE AS A PUBLIC SPEAKER (Springfield, Massachusetts, 1870) attempts to justify the Washingtonian orator's criticism of Dow and his Maine Law. A convenient fund of background material on Dow's British associates is Peter T. Winskill, THE TEMPERANCE MOVEMENT AND ITS WORKERS, A RECORD OF SOCIAL, MORAL, RELIGIOUS AND POLITICAL PROGRESS (4 vols., London, 1892).

Aside from the contemporary newspapers, the only printed source on Dow's relation to the Maine Treasury scandal is the REPORT OF THE JOINT SELECT COMMITTEE ON THE DEFALCATION OF BENJ. D. PECK, LATE TREASURER OF THE STATE OF MAINE (Augusta, Maine, 1860). The REPORTS of the Maine Attorneys General from 1861 to 1873 carry through the story to the final settlement of the claims against Dow.

In the huge, undigested mass of THE WAR OF THE REBELLION: A COMPILATION OF THE OFFICIAL RECORDS OF THE UNION AND CONFEDERATE ARMIES (70 vols., Washington, 1880-1901) lies much of the data on Dow's Civil War Career. In addition, a considerable amount of useful unpublished correspondence is scattered through the War Department records in the National Archives. Hans L. Trefousse's much-needed BEN BUTLER: THE SOUTH CALLED HIM BEAST! (New York, c. 1957) and Fred Harvey Harrington's scholarly FIGHTING POLITICIAN, MAJOR GENERAL N. P. BANKS (Philadelphia, 1948) elucidate Dow's hostile superiors. For friendly accounts of Dow by men under his command, see Edwin B. Lufkin, HISTORY OF THE THIRTEENTH MAINE REGIMENT FROM ITS ORGANIZATION IN 1861 TO ITS MUSTER-OUT IN 1865 (Bridgton, Maine, 1898) and Charles McGregor, HISTORY OF THE FIFTEENTH REGIMENT, NEW HAMPSHIRE VOLUNTEERS, 1862-1863 (n. p., 1900). Gouverneur Morris, THE HISTORY OF A VOLUNTEER REGIMENT, BEING A SUCCINT ACCOUNT OF THE ORGANIZATION, SERVICES AND ADVENTURES OF THE SIXTH REGIMENT NEW YORK VOLUNTEER INFANTRY KNOWN AS WILSON ZOUAVES: WHERE THEY WENT--WHAT THEY DID--AND WHAT THEY SAW IN THE WAR OF THE REBELLION 1861-1865 (New York, 1891) tells of the prohibitionist officer's farcical relationship with these brawling subordinates.

William B. Hesseltine's dry but authoritative CIVIL WAR PRISONS: A STUDY IN WAR PSYCHOLOGY (Columbus, Ohio, 1930) and Frank L. Byrne, "Libby Prison: A Study in Emotions" in the JOURNAL OF SOUTHERN HISTORY, 24:430-44 (November, 1958) offer background and additional information on Dow's prison experiences. In his MY RECORD IN REBELDOM AS

ESSAY ON THE SOURCES

WRITTEN BY FRIEND AND FOE: COMPRISING THE OFFICIAL CHARGES AND EVIDENCE BEFORE THE MILITARY COMMISSION IN WASHINGTON, BRIG. GEN'L J. C. CALDWELL, PRES'T, TOGETHER WITH THE REPORT AND FINDING OF THE COURT (New York, 1865), James M. Sanderson defends his conduct in Libby Prison and bitterly assails Dow's. His book is a valuable coalmine of contemporary testimony designed to blacken Dow's name. Bernhard Domschcke, ZWANZIG MONATE IN KRIEGS-GEFANGENSCHAFT (Milwaukee, 1865) gives an account of the same incidents much more friendly to Dow. In addition, as indicated in the Notes, almost all the many writers on Libby refer to the "Temperance General."

The least inadequate general work on late 19th century temperance is D. Leigh Colvin, PROHIBITION IN THE UNITED STATES, A HISTORY OF THE PROHIBITION PARTY AND OF THE PROHIBITION MOVEMENT (New York, c. 1926). Written by a leading third party Prohibitionist, Colvin's book reflects a strong bias toward his general reform and his particular political method. The NATIONAL TEMPERANCE ADVOCATE, organ of the National Temperance Society and Publishing House, contains much information on the later stages of Dow's crusade. In post-Civil War Maine, the Republican Portland PRESS joins that city's earlier ADVERTISER and EASTERN ARGUS as fruitful sources for Dow's politico-temperance fights. Nathan F. Woodbury, a noted Maine third party Prohibitionist, is the author of several articles and pamphlets criticizing the inconsistent roles of Dow and other temperance Republicans.

The few unoriginal biographical articles written in Dow's later years cast little new light on the man himself. Among these are Thomas W. Organ, BIOGRAPHICAL SKETCH OF GENERAL NEAL DOW (/New York, 1880/), a presidential campaign tract, and Alonzo A. Miner, "Neal Dow and His Life Work" in the NEW ENGLAND MAGAZINE, 10:397-412 (June, 1894). Such books as the CENTENNIAL TEMPERANCE VOLUME, A MEMORIAL OF THE INTERNATIONAL TEMPERANCE CONFERENCE HELD IN PHILADELPHIA, JUNE, 1876 (2 vols., New York, 1877) contain examples of Dow's prohibitionist writing. Several letters in the Cyrus Woodman Papers of the State Historical Society of Wisconsin and one in the William Henry Noble Papers, Duke University, indicate the hatred felt toward Dow by the victims of his personal attacks. In her critical and well written FRANCES WILLARD: FROM PRAYERS TO POLITICS (Chicago, c. 1944), Mary Earhart tells of the woman whose publicity helped to transform the militant Dow's reputation. In Mrs. Joseph Cook's worshipful "Neal Dow as Guest and Host" in OUR DAY, 13:315-18 (July-August, 1894), the old man clearly emerges as his crusade's saintly symbol.

INDEX